# The Ideology of State Terror

# The Ideology of State Terror

## Economic Doctrine and Political Repression in Argentina and Peru

David Pion-Berlin

Lynne Rienner Publishers • Boulder & London

Published in the United States of America in 1989 by
Lynne Rienner Publishers, Inc.
1800 30th Street, Boulder, Colorado 80301

and in the United Kingdom by
Lynne Rienner Publishers, Inc.
3 Henrietta Street, Covent Garden, London WC2E 8LU



**Library of Congress Cataloging-in-Publication Data**
Pion-Berlin, David.
The ideology of state terror : economic doctrine and political repression in Argentina and Peru / by David Pion-Berlin.
p. cm.
Bibliography: p.
Includes index.
ISBN 1-55587-160-7 (alk. paper)
1. Political persecution—Argentina. 2. Political persecution—Peru. 3. Argentina—Economic policy. 4. Peru—Economic policy. 5. Trade-unions—Government policy—Argentina. 6. Trade-unions—Government policy—Peru. I. Title
JC599.A7P56 1989
323.4'9'0982—dc19 89-3469
CIP

**British Cataloguing in Publication Data**
A Cataloguing in Publication record for this book is available from the British Library.

Printed and bound in the United States of America

The paper used in this publication meets the requirements of the American National Standard for Permanence of Paper for Printed Library Materials Z39.48–1984.

*To*
*Lisa and Jeremy*

# Contents

## PART FOUR
## COMPARISONS AND CONCLUSIONS

# Tables and Figures

TABLES

## FIGURES

# Acknowledgments

This work had its beginnings at the Graduate School of International Studies at the University of Denver, which provided an especially conducive environment to reflect upon the linkages between politics and economics. My particular interest was in the determinants of state terror in Latin America. At GSIS, I was encouraged to explore the interface between economic ideologies and political behavior, to find some of the hidden (and not so hidden) political assumptions imbedded within economic doctrine that could provide motive(s) for governments to resort to terror and repression. This was unfamiliar terrain for me, and so I set out with some trepidation. The journey took me through some perilous twists and turns, over and occasionally into intellectual quicksand and a few mine fields. But it was challenging, and emerging relatively unscathed by it all, I am now gratified to have undertaken the project.

Along the way and through every phase of the project, I received strong intellectual stimulation and guidance from John McCamant. He was especially generous with his time and patient enough to put up with my incessant questions. I owe a special debt of gratitude to him. James Caporaso always offered me sound theoretical and methodological advice. William Loehr's command of economics made my tasks easier. I want to thank Julia Fisher for her typing. Dissertation funding from the National Science Foundation and post-doctoral research support from the Institute for the Study of World Politics made possible travel to several libraries within the United States, hiring a research assistant, and a field trip to Argentina. Finally, special thanks to my wife Lisa for her encouragement to complete the book.

*—David Pion-Berlin*

# PART ONE
# THE FUNCTION AND ORIGIN OF IDEAS

# 1
# Introduction

*The power of vested interests is vastly exaggerated compared with the gradual encroachment of ideas.*

—John M. Keynes

The precipitous rise and fall of authoritarian regimes in Latin America during the last two decades has captured the imagination of a generation of scholars, and we now have an impressive accumulation of research about the political, social, and economic dimensions of the birth, endurance, and demise of these dictatorships.[1] Curiously, less effort has been concentrated on the study of the state terror that sustained these regimes—it almost seems as if terror became so widespread and standardized that it was taken for granted. The purpose of this book is to elevate state terror to a topic deserving serious inquiry in its own right, and more specifically to reveal the motivations behind use.

Political repression has unfortunately become a customary tool of state craft in the twentieth century. As Amnesty International recently documented, 128 governments across six continents committed human rights violations in a single year.[2] These abuses ranged from brief detentions to torture and execution, and they occurred under the most politically diverse conditions. Nowhere has state terror assumed such regularity and taken on such proportions as it has in Latin America in recent decades. For years, human rights offices have been flooded with reports of the abduction and murder of members of the clergy, the mysterious disappearances of trade unionists, and the mass detention of students. The abuses have been widespread, and, with a kind of haunting Orwellian logic, the governments seem to strike arbitrarily, unpredictably, and nearly everywhere against alleged enemies of the state.[3]

Of course, acts of political repression are not always unprovoked. During the 1960s and the early 1970s, some governments were faced with formidable rural and urban guerrilla movements. Sparked by the victory of Castro's forces in Cuba and the daring exploits of men such as Che Guevara and Camilo Torres, rebels were determined to redress social inequities by overturning the political and economic order. Acts of armed aggression and unarmed violence (riots, mass demonstrations, politically motivated strikes) increased 30 percent from the 1950s to the 1960s.[4] This was a turbulent period, which gave vivid meaning to the phrase "violence begets violence."

The political repression that emerged by the mid-1970s in South America was not reactive in nature, however, and was undertaken at times without regard to levels of dissent.[5] The guerrilla forces that had posed a security problem in countries such as Argentina and Uruguay were firmly rebuked and reduced to committing random and futile acts of urban terror. Eventually, these groups disappeared altogether, but governmental coercion persisted with increased frequency and intensity even after the defeat of rebel forces. The worst forms of human rights abuses were not committed against violent persons, but rather against relatively compliant individuals, who, for the most part, had neither violated any laws nor participated in any clandestine activities, and had not shown any interest in radical causes. It is telling that nearly 70 percent of "the disappeared" in Argentina were abducted from the privacy of their homes or while peacefully assembled at work; only 25 percent were arrested on the street—where they were at least in a position to have been publicly dissenting.[6]

Defendants throughout the region were genuinely surprised by their detentions, having had no reason to suspect they would be placed under surveillance and treated as enemies of the state.[7] Specific charges were rarely brought against them. Instead, the authorities accused them broadly of conducting subversive or terrorist activities. These terms were arbitrarily defined, making a legal defense virtually impossible. In Brazil, those who allegedly committed subversive acts were seeking the "transformation of the existing order."[8] Argentina employed even less precision: military President General Jorge Videla labeled as subversive "anyone who opposes the Argentine way of life."[9]

For the most part, the authorities seemed unconcerned about the need to prove specific wrongdoing. State terror was carried out whether or not individuals had broken any laws or committed any offenses against the state. This policy of overkill resulted in the detention and trial by military tribunal of over 7,400 Brazilians between 1964 and 1979. In Argentina, it took the form of the "Dirty War," which claimed the lives of nearly 20,000. Chile experienced similar levels of state violence from 1973 to 1976. In Peru, levels of repression in the late 1970s were substantially lower, but directed nonetheless against groups that were relatively harmless.

At first glance, it appears that military governments were guilty of enormous miscalculations. In Argentina, for example, guerrilla and state security forces may have been evenly matched during 1974 and the first half of 1975, when 109 army and police officers were killed in battle compared to 137 leftists.[10] However, in October and again in December 1975, the armed forces thoroughly defeated the guerrillas in assaults against military arsenals. In the words of the army's commanding officer at the time, the failed guerrilla operation "demonstrated the absolute impotence of the terrorist organizations with respect to their presumed military power."[11] By 1976, the guerrillas had abandoned organized combat and could launch only scattered attacks. By 1977, the guerrillas reported 2,000 of their own killed—a crippling blow from which they never recovered.[12]

Yet at the same moment, the Argentine junta intensified its military campaign against this "enemy" with no military capacity. The number of victims of state violence rose in 1977, and while leveling off somewhat in 1978, still remained high. In April 1977, President Jorge R. Videla drew up a secret order to pursue "bands of delinquent subversives." In that same order, he admitted that 90 percent of the subversive organizations had already been destroyed.[13] At a time when it would have been logical to de-escalate, the military expanded its operations, intervening in industrial, educational, cultural, professional, and religious organizations with a full show of force. Military institutions are, after all, trained carefully to assess the strength of their adversaries. What reasons would they have for attacking a largely unarmed, defenseless population? That question has guided much of the research in this book.

We begin our inquiry with the idea that governments that regularly practice state terror do so because they feel threatened. Threat perception can best be understood as "an anticipation on the part of an observer, the decision maker, of impending harm—usually of a military, strategic or economic kind—to the state."[14] In the field of international relations, J. David Singer has argued that a state senses a grave, impending danger when estimates are that the offender is well equipped and highly motivated to cause harm.[15] Foreign policymakers assess the relative capabilities and intentions of their alleged adversaries, then formulate perceptions based on the combined impact of those capabilities and intentions. The idea is relevant to this study because scholars of political repression have acknowledged that threat perception normally intervenes between events and reaction. The use (or intended use) of coercion indicates that a government anticipates danger, and the higher the levels of force employed, the greater is the government's sense of threat.[16]

Scholars have debated the origins of threat perception; like many debates in social science, this one has not been settled. At one end of the debate we find Singer, who concludes that threat perception is grounded squarely in the objective assessment of evidence. Assuming for the moment this it true, we would expect rational policymakers to make a series of cautious estimates: first, to judge their opponents' capacity to inflict harm by examining whether resources could be mobilized to undermine, at a minimum, the regime's authority and at a maximum, to place in jeopardy the social and political order; second, to give some consideration to motives and intentions (e.g., Does the opposition have good reasons for rebelling? If so, does it actually plan to rebel?); third, to consider the nature of the act. Governments that perceive threats assume the worst—that opponents will choose aggression and, in general, destructive forms of behavior, or that even where peaceful and nonviolent forms of dissent are chosen, these will have as their ultimate purpose the subversion of the current order. Fourth, there is timing; governments must have some sense that danger is impending (threats that are far off in the future are less worrisome). And finally, there is direction; authorities normally assume that hostile and aggressive acts are aimed directly at them, or at least at some definable symbols of national economic, political, or military security that they are called upon to defend.

With this information in hand, the authorities could make some overall evaluation about hostile intent and decide what course of action to take. Following this logic, their decision to opt for terror (as opposed to numerous other forms of political control) will be predicated on some assessment of benefits and risks: does the government have a reasonable chance of overcoming its opponents, and can it do so in a manner that will minimize its own human, material, and political costs?[17] In short, military regimes would be conceived of as utility maximizers, who not only predicate their perceptions of impending danger on a rational appraisal of the evidence but weigh the benefits and risks associated with terror before choosing a course of action.

This approach seems pertinent at moments when governments encounter formidable and armed domestic opponents. Even the strongest military government would be unwise to engage in reckless (uncalculated) counterinsurgent activities in the face of skilled guerrilla or terrorist rebels. Perhaps, then, calculations such as those just described would account for the conduct of the Argentine military from 1974 to 1975, as they were besieged by guerrilla attacks. But the approach seems less appropriate to the study of unprovoked terror against a compliant Argentine population. If an opposition is unarmed and relatively defenseless, why should the regime bother with calculation of risk? With overwhelming resource advantages, the military is sure to prevail over its rivals. The costs of coercion—be they moral or political—should be extremely low, since comparatively speaking, military regimes are much less preoccupied with public image than are democratic regimes, and quicker to confer legitimacy upon themselves by virtue of their "historic mission" and assumption of state power. The uncertainties of coercion should be equally minimal, given the asymmetrical distribution of power between the men in uniform and their civilian foes. Yet scholarship indicates that, if anything, the military's sense of insecurity seems to grow over time and in proportion to its preoccupation with threat.[18] If the military senses its own vulnerability to an opposition that is unable to inflict harm, then some other account of threat perception is needed.

At the other end of the debate spectrum from Singer, is the thesis considered in this study: that the anticipation of impending harm is predicated upon subjective judgments. According to this thesis, while policymakers may take into consideration the resources and motives of others, they do so by piecing together scattered bits of information, which may be confusing, opaque, and contradictory. The meanings that humans assign to data will vary according to the interpretations they are predisposed to render. That is to say, we concur with scholars who have argued that threat perception may be less a reaction to and calculation of external events, and more a predisposition: it is an image of reality deduced from beliefs and formed prior to the assimilation of information—even at times irrespective of the objective environment.[19]

If true, this would have particular relevance for the study of unprovoked terror. The thesis suggests that governments sensing danger may in fact face none or at least misperceive its character. It also raises the possibility that the authorities may have legitimate fears, founded on their own disclosed or undisclosed predispositions; fears that make the resort to excessive levels of violence seem imperative *to them.* From their "angle of vision," the "enemy" is formidable and threatening; while to us it is hardly visible. For these reasons, any examination of cause should give serious consideration to the perspectives of human agents, and the concepts and doctrines underlying their perspectives. In exploring the motive for terror, this study will examine the economic perspectives of Latin American elites.

Most military elites cannot claim economic expertise, nor would we attribute such expertise to them. The competence of the armed forces lies in national defense and security: from their "angle of vision," no objectives are as paramount as the achievement of external and internal security, and no prospects as fearsome as the loss of that security. Security is, in the military mind, the yardstick by which all government performance is measured.

Although they lacked economic training, most Latin American officers (at least in the Southern Cone countries) had full confidence in their civilian economic advisers. Some became "true believers," and together with their technocratic advisers composed a hegemonic bloc in defense of particular economic programs. Moreover, Latin American military regimes have repeatedly acknowledged the pivotal role that economic development must play in the quest for security. (Brazilian officers, for example, remind us that their flag is inscribed with the motto "Ordem e Progreso" [Order and Progress], a slogan that more recently has come to stand for security and development. The Brazilian military takes the motto seriously, as do many other military institutions in the region.) Conversely, they recognize that economic stagnation or decline could very well undermine the political order. It is fair, then, to ask what concepts authoritarian elites use when they refer to economic well-being or misfortune. And how do these concepts shape their vision of a secure polity and their choice of policy instruments (including terror) to guarantee that security?

## ECONOMICS AS THE NEUTRAL DISCIPLINE

If a motive for terror is to be understood through economic theory, we must first overcome a fundamental misconception about economics in general.

Economics is often thought of as a neutral science: value-free and without political agendas or vendettas. We might agree, instinctively. After all, economists communicate to us in abstractions and predict future trends through the use of elaborate and often eloquent models—theirs is not the polemic language of politics. According to economists, their task is to explain the behavior of producers and consumers; the patterns of exchange of goods and services; and the nature of production cycles, employment, prices, and wages. These explanations are neutral because they are grounded in deliberate, scientific work. Thus, the policies and recommendations that emerge from those theories are themselves value-free—or so it is thought.

But the doctrine of economic neutrality cannot stand up under closer scrutiny. This "neutral science" was traditionally called political economy—not economics, and common sense tells us that if economics is the study of how society chooses to use scarce resources to produce and distribute commodities, then it is anything but neutral.[20] Allocative decisions—who gets what, when, and how—have always been at the center of political life. Whether made in zero-sum or nonzero-sum environments, such decisions will always benefit some more than others. Conflicts over power resources, income shares, and relative disparities of wealth are part and parcel of politics. Economic designs will, intentionally or unintentionally, have implications for how those conflicts get started and how they will be resolved.

Moreover, it is economics that informs those who govern the political world. Governments formulate and execute policies driven by economic theory. As consumers, regulators, employers, and sometimes producers, governments also directly influence the production and allocation of scarce resources in society. Thus, on the input and output sides, the "stuff" of economics has for decades been the trademark of governance itself.

Economics as value-free science has often been used as a device to disguise the contentious nature of allocative decisions. International lending agencies, for example, will go out of their way to insist that loan requests from developing countries are accepted or rejected only on the technical merits of a project. They tell us that borrowers prefer to go to them than to single-country donors, since they will make sound economic judgments with no partisan strings attached. Indeed, they inform us that their statutes prohibit them from doing otherwise.[21] But in a moment of candor, a former World Bank president said about his organization's loan decisions:

> We ask a lot of questions and attach a lot of conditions to our loans. I need hardly say that we would never get away with this if we did not bend every effort to render the language of economics as morally antiseptic as the language the weather forecaster uses in giving tomorrow's prediction.[22]

The language of economics may be antiseptic, but its remedies are not always soothing. For example, a government decision to devalue a currency can have profoundly negative consequences for certain groups: the prices of tradeable goods will rise relative to those that are not tradeable; oftentimes, export items such as sugar and wheat will go up in price, impacting low-income populations who must spend a large proportion of their weekly earnings on such goods. To offset the short-term inflationary impact of devaluation, some governments will restrict monetary emission, and government spending, and even suppress wages. These moves are recessionary and mutually reinforcing. They lower employment and reduce living standards for the lower classes even further.[23] This combination of policies, which hurts one class and not others, is itself predicated upon underlying economic concepts. We will argue that economic doctrines themselves are enormously evaluative and judgmental and that these characteristics can have serious political repercussions.

## THE ECONOMIC "MAP" OF TERROR

Once a doctrine is internalized, it may serve as a "map" of reality for policymakers who would rather rely on a few guiding principles than be forced continually to make new and numerous judgments in an uncertain environment.[24] Such a map sharpens some images of the political landscape while blurring others; it provides a cognitive framework that has structure, design, logic, and direction. It simplifies the world for policymakers so they can chart the difficult course of policymaking in a complex environment.

Of course at one level, all policymakers must rely on some form of cognitive map to make informed and timely decisions. But this reliance, when it is close-minded and rigid enough that objective conditions become obscured or irrelevant, is dangerous. Setting his sights on the achievement of cherished goals, the policymaker is not persuaded to consider contrary information or to react to pressures from interest groups.[25] Allowing his convictions to cloud his perception, he produces policies that are insensitive to changing realities and to the advantages of conceptual reformulations. When ideas are deeply held, and if those ideas are fundamentally discordant with objective events, the potential for seriously misguided policy is great.[26]

It is the central contention of this study that political repression in Latin America has often been an outgrowth of intellectual predispositions, and not a reaction to dissent. Ideas exert a force and do possess a life of their own. While always formulated within a social context, ideas also produce a self-contained reality for political subjects that does not always square with objective events. Ideas that are conceptually flawed, anachronistic, or simply incompatible with changing realities are sure to map the political terrain incorrectly. This generates serious misperceptions, because the more firmly perceptions are embedded in erroneous doctrines, the more glaringly discordant they become with the observable world. In light of strong conceptual biases and misperceptions, the commission of state violence against relatively compliant populations seems fathomable. Acts of state terror against nondissenting citizens are rational to the extent that they are "goal oriented acts from the point of view of their perpetrators."[27] Policymakers with strong ideological predispositions may logically take violence to be the most sensible instrument of policy for the achievement of desired ends.

This brings us back to the relationship between economic doctrines and state terror: not only do economic ideas generate their own maps of reality that define how the costs and benefits of productive and allocative decisions should be distributed within society; even more significantly, they render judgment on current and past economic affairs. In judging, they (explicitly or implicitly) attribute blame to those factors *and* to those people that are thought to have placed economic growth in jeopardy. Political elites have at their disposal various options to arrest economically harmful practices—indeed, they may propose economic reforms that can significantly weaken those who have allegedly wronged the economy. But these moves may not suffice. When economic performance becomes the sine qua non of legitimate governance, and where perceived threats to economic achievement are extreme, then state violence and terror may be used to eliminate undesirable members of society.

The intellectual foundations for the use of coercion can be found in the monetarist models applied in many Latin American countries.[28] A number of South American military and civilian regimes (and particularly those of the Southern Cone) have subscribed to a doctrinaire version of monetarist or free market economics that has by no means been universally adhered to elsewhere.[29] In a market they believe to be inherently stable, these monetarists shun even the most limited forms of government intervention and firmly reject the use of state funds to ameliorate the economic conditions of wage earners and the poor. They are obsessed with inflation and its causes. In theory, they should blame inflation on excessive expansion of the money supply (hence "monetarist"); but in practice, and particularly in Latin America and throughout the Third World, they wage war against fiscal irresponsibility as well. Control over the money supply, they assert, must often begin with budgetary curtailment.

This should be easier said than done. According to the monetarists, the state budget expands in proportion to the demands placed upon it by collective agents.[30] These agents (1) force the state to subsidize and protect highly unionized firms from international competition, (2) establish the public sector as a refuge for workers displaced by the market and, (3) politicize price, wage, and managerial decisions. Each new state program not only aids the wage earning sector and strengthens the trade union movement, but stands as a reminder for future governments that fiscal contraction cannot be achieved without severe political consequences. Leaders must weigh the costs of deficit reduction against the benefits of various compensatory measures.

For the monetarist ideologues, however, the choice is easy: the economic benefits of austerity clearly outweigh the political benefits of expenditure. A balanced budget and a carefully regulated money supply are the twin pillars of economic vitality. Once these goals are attained, benefits will trickle down to special interest groups such as labor. These economists do not verbalize the political ramifications of fiscal austerity, but monetarism clearly carries a hidden political agenda in its seemingly neutral attacks on excessive spending. Organized interest groups that press for immediate governmental assistance force the state into "misguided" spending patterns. To acquiesce to these groups is to accept future monetary instability, economic stagnation, recession, and, ultimately, systemic crisis. In the final analysis, elites must constrain these partisan demands and may do so by using force.[31] Unbalanced budgets and fiscal deficits may appear to be relatively mild irritants to some, but they assume overwhelming proportions when viewed through the lens of this free market doctrine. When monetary and fiscal frugality have become *central* themes for government, the activities of organized pressure groups become increasingly disturbing as they interfere increasingly with leading policy objectives.

## THE ROLE OF IDEAS

The political importance of economic bias is significant, but derivative of the more general and fundamental premise that ideas can have a significant impact on political life. If the conceptual bases of policy are relevant, they point the investigation toward an evaluation of the concepts themselves. In this case, one must explore the *content* of monetarist thinking in conjunction and interaction with sociopolitical *context* to uncover plausible motivations for the use of state coercion. In that respect, this book departs from previous studies of authoritarianism, which are exclusively contextual in nature. Those studies emphasize the impact of powerful classes and institutions on compliant political Third World actors.[32] They agree that the monetarist-styled stabilization programs of the International Monetary Fund (IMF) have been administered under politically repressive conditions.[33] They also recognize that the Fund's prescriptions for economic recovery are bitter pills for most Third World countries to swallow, and have met with social protest (often dubbed "IMF riots"). However, these studies emphasize that the governmental crackdown to quell these social disturbances results after powerful institutions and classes exert their wills on dependent Third World states, and are not a natural consequence of the chosen intellectual framework itself.

Debt-ridden and in need of foreign exchange, these countries have nowhere to turn but to those agencies of international capital that can provide financial relief. The price for this relief is the subjection of local economies to the onerous conditions of economic frugality and deprivation. The IMF, according to Frenkel and O'Donnell, "officiates as the technical secretariat of transnational finance," imposing conditions on debtor countries to guarantee repayment of loans to foreign financiers and to establish attractive investment havens for multinational firms.[34] The agency's "outlook and its growing influence correspond to the new and important role private finance capital has come to play in the peripheral economies."[35] At issue in these analyses is not the monetarist school of thought per se, but the classes and institutions that are presumed to be its principal sponsors and beneficiaries. The views of these capitalist agents are simply derived from and determined by their interests and the social-international positions they occupy.

In fact, most contextual studies of political repression resort to interest-like arguments.[36] Marxian analyses, for instance, contend that those who monopolize the means of coercion use force to preserve the position of those who control the means of production.[37] Although Marxism is primarily concerned with oppression—the perpetuation of the economic misery of one class by another—it is also concerned with repression, when the bourgeoisie can no longer keep workers in line and must call on the state to intercede on its behalf.[38] Dependency theory contends that the interests of advanced industrial (core) states are best served through authoritarian arrangements in the lesser developed (peripheral) countries. The expansion of capitalism in the core is achieved by the extraction of economic surplus from the periphery, leaving the periphery without the wherewithal for self-reliant growth. Elites in the core cannot enforce these unpopular relations by themselves; consequently, they rely on local elites who serve as junior partners, setting the political conditions for surplus extraction while materially benefiting themselves. The conditions they establish are coercive, since only force will quiet the revolt of popular classes (which are sure to challenge this unequal economic relationship).[39]

These same scholars normally discard ideas as topics of inquiry, because they presume that material interests will better serve the purposes of explication. Intellectual positions are often simply noted, and easily reduced to some expression of political power, social position or class preference. Ideologues, it is said, use jargon to mask the pursuit of economic or political gain for the select few—but these cunning disguises have no inherent value because their point of origin lies with underlying motives and, beneath those, with social position. The interest approach to politics draws the inquiry away from ideas and closer to those socioeconomic agents who allegedly condition or even create the ideas that serve them.

Were there a one-to-one correspondence between interests and outcomes, the study of ideas and the perceptions they shape would be superfluous. At best, ideas would enjoy an intermediate position between interests and outcomes, but they would exert no independent influence. Intellectuals—the bearers of ideas—would remain, in Gramsci's terms, mere handmaidens for classes seeking to consolidate their power. The theory portion of this chapter will provide a fuller account of the interest approach and will demonstrate why interests may fail to account adequately for political behavior, and how ideas help to fill the "explanation gap."

## REVIEW OF THE BOOK

Part One is devoted to a discussion of economic bias and its origins. In Chapter 2, we will compare and critique the *structuralist* and *monetarist* doctrines on economic stabilization and development. These are not the only available views on the subject, but they have been the most widely used and vigorously debated in Latin America over the last three decades. Although monetarists are sometimes referred to as "structuralists in a hurry" (since they advocate short-term remedies), one should not underestimate the clear differences between these two schools of thought: each carries different assumptions and arguments on the causes of and solutions for inflation, balance of payments deficits, and recession. Through a careful appraisal of their premises and assertions, it will be demonstrated that these two doctrines give rise not only to separate economic strategies but also to distinct political consequences. The theoretical motives for state terror against organized labor will be explored in accordance with the arguments and assumptions of each doctrine.

Chapter 3 traces the international origins of Third World monetarist policies to the International Monetary Fund. Mandated in 1944 to help chart a new course for international monetary management, the Fund provided a facility for extending credit to deficit-ridden countries. Its purpose was to promote world trade and national reconstruction. Its designated role was that of referee between creditors and debtors. By the late 1950s, however, it had become something of a policeman, requesting that weak, less developed countries (LDCs) comply with strict financial guidelines in exchange for credit. The Fund, as chartered, was not to become involved in domestic matters; however, it soon came to advise Third World ministers and heads of state. We will explain how the Fund's newfound influence over debtor nations had much to do with the development of monetary approaches to balance of payments adjustment within its research division. Equipped with impressive, easy to use quantitative models, IMF technicians were able to convince LDC officials of the merits of conforming to this brand of economics. Previous studies have correctly identified power and markets as two important sources of Fund influence but have largely overlooked the impact of ideas which will be emphasized here.

Argentina and Peru were among those countries of Latin America that, by the late 1950s, had accepted IMF-styled monetarist remedies for their ailing economies. Parts Two and Three are devoted to a study of economic ideas and the political repression of labor groups in these two countries. Argentina and Peru are very different societies in many respects. Argentina is a more economically developed system; an industrial society with a predominantly urban population. It is a land of European immigrants and customs, of fertile plains and cattle farms, and of workers who have organized into Latin America's most powerful trade union movement. Peru is poor in comparison. It remains a predominantly agrarian economy, though it has industrialized over time. Its heritage is that of the Incas and the Spanish, and its population remains racially mixed. It, too, has a labor movement, but one that has been more divided and not as well organized.

The contrasts between these two countries pose a challenge: could the same explanation for political repression hold true in both cases? Is there some connection between variations in preference for economic doctrines and political repression across systems? By its nature, the sample resists the successful search for uniformity, since it is reasonable that traits peculiar to each society would shape political and economic interactions in separate ways. If uniformity can be found, then the research findings would be enormously interesting and hold more general relevance.

Chapter 4 provides a historical account of state-labor relations in Argentina from the first administration of Juan Perón (1946–1951) to the military coup of 1976. It describes how Perón used the powers of the presidency and the federal budget to push the Argentine trade union movement to a position of political prominence. With Perón's ouster, the trade union movement, left to fend for itself, became more of an independent pressure group. Reform-minded governments were willing to meet labor requests for public sector employment, assistance, and subsidies because they perceived a political gain. Transitional governments were ambivalent, shifting between economic austerity and redistribution, which caused them to hesitate to use force against the trade unions. Finally, Perón's economically liberal critics would later accuse him of subsidizing working-class incomes at the expense of monetary and fiscal stability, and they would constrain trade union militancy with force. Thus, to some extent, the treatment of trade union dissent at the hands of the state varied with the economic strategies employed by each administration.

Chapter 5 is a case study of security ideology, economic liberalism, and military rule in Argentina from 1976 to 1983. The Argentine generals subscribed to two fundamental kinds of ideologies: the first, a national security doctrine, provided the authorization for unmitigated state violence and guided the creation of an elaborate security apparatus; the second, a free market ideology, provided a focus for the selection of victims. Pursuing the goals of competition, lower inflation, and fiscal balance, the government set out to deactivate those groups, such as the labor movement, whose interests were tied to a protective, interventionist, and expansionary state. We will assess the government's antistatist development model and its apprehensions about and interactions with the trade union sector, paying particular attention to public sector employees. That assessment will be followed by a critique of rival explanations for state terror.

Part Three looks at Peru. Chapter 6 discusses how shifts in economic preferences can give rise to incremental losses in political freedom. Manuel Prado was elected president in 1956, after eight years of dictatorship; his election unleashed tremendous pent-up pressures for social, political, and economic reform. The economy would not cooperate, and, under pressure from influential free market advocates, Prado reluctantly endorsed a liberal package for economic stabilization. This chapter investigates the tension between democratic rule and Prado's policies of orthodox austerity.

Chapter 7 is a study of military governance in Peru. We note how the Morales Bermúdez government, which came to power in August 1975, was forced to come to terms with a deepening economic crisis and was under considerable pressure to choose alternatives that would curry favor with the international lending agencies. The government reacted by grudgingly turning to liberal solutions, as had been done seventeen years before. There was little defense against the "monetarist pill" once it had been swallowed. The body politic had to succumb to the logic of orthodox management, as evidenced by the military's crackdown on mine workers, who stood in the way of improved export performance, and public sector teachers, who stood in the way of fiscal balance. In contrast with the Argentine case, terror was selective and uneven.

Part Four presents comparisons and conclusions. In Chapter 8, consideration is given to how contextual factors modify the influence of ideas. First, we note how the decline of previous reform-minded governments established the preconditions for more conservative political and economic policy. Second, we argue that though economic motives provided a strong impetus for terror, the higher levels of repression in the Argentine case could be attributed to the need of regimes to overcome a more formidable labor movement than that which existed in Peru. Oftentimes, the Peruvian government was able to rely on the divisive and self-injurious practices of the organized Left to dilute opposition to their economic practices.

The concluding chapter offers a defense of the thesis that ideas can matter as much as interests; demonstrating how one state leader in Argentina, embracing an unpopular economic model, was able to fend off powerful societal groups calling for policy reversals. The discussion then turns to the Chilean case to examine the remarkable autonomy of the regime's economic team, dubbed the "Chicago Boys," during their feud with the powerful economic clans. Both examples sustain the view that an international community of peers, bonded by an intellectual esprit de corps rather than material interests, can furnish an alternative base of support for political elites.

## INTEREST-DRIVEN APPROACHES IN SOCIAL SCIENCE

The interest-ideas debate is an old one, dating back to seventeenth- and eighteenth-century continental thought. Although seldom articulated in any explicit fashion, these concepts have continued to provide grounding for countless studies in the social sciences. The debate has not been resolved, but more often than not, interests have dominated the clash of viewpoints. It has become an article of faith that all social, economic, and political behavior can be ascribed to the pursuit of self-interest.[40] Interest-driven behavior is presumed to be reasonable, rational, and beneficial, not only for the individual, but, according to neoclassical economics, for the collective as well.

The articulation of interests has also been prescribed as one means by which to counter idealist propositions. Idealists, known for their preoccupation with abstraction, believed that the mental sphere of life was primary and the sensory world secondary. They held that any account of the world must start with the intellect, from which all else could then be deduced. The mental sphere is autonomous; it neither emerges from nor is reducible to the material world.

A key figure in the development of idealism was George Berkeley (1685–1753), who went so far as to deny that the material world had any independent existence. Objects came to life only through the mind's eye, which arranged sensory objects and imparted both shape and meaning to them. According to Berkeley, if it was impossible to conceive of something existing *un-thought-of*, then indeed such objects were illusory; there were no objects without thinking subjects.[41]

G. W. Friedrich Hegel (1770–1831) contended that rationality was both infallible and self-contained; it needed no empirical justification and could direct and determine itself according to its own procedures.[42] The mind, he argued, unfolded "from its first act of minimal awareness . . . through all the successive purifications . . . until it reached a form of awareness which was adequate to its content, i.e. the absolute."[43] Hegel's reification of the mental sphere was an exercise in metaphysics for which he was later criticized.

Hegel's most formidable critic was Karl Marx (1818–1883), who shared the idealists' curiosity about the relationship between the objective and subjective worlds but "stood them on their heads" by reversing the direction of influence: ideas were outcomes, not causes. Human consciousness was itself an outgrowth of social life. As Marx explains, "The production of ideas of conceptions of consciousness is at first directly interwoven with the material activity and the material intercourse of men, the language of real life."[44] This "material intercourse" of men took place within the system of production. Those classes that owned the means of production also controlled the instruments of communication with which to spread the ideology of capitalism. The dominant classes would protect and strengthen their interests not only with the force of the state but also with the force of ideas. According to Marx:

> The ideas of the ruling class are in every epoch the ruling ideas. . . . The class which has the means of material production at its disposal, has control at the same time over the means of mental production so that thereby, generally speaking, the ideas of those who lack the means of mental production are subject to it.[45]

Realism did not have its birth with Marx. Machiavelli, for instance, understood that the prince must advance his own power to the exclusion of others and at all costs.[46] In the thoughts of the sixteenth-century Huguenot statesman, the Duke of Rohan, "Princes order their people around and interest orders princes around."[47] Two centuries later, Adam Smith extended the application to society as a whole, arguing that the primary drive of every human being was self-interest:

> The natural effort of every individual to better his own condition, when suffered to exert itself with freedom and security, is so powerful a principle, that it is alone and without any assistance not only capable of carrying on the society to wealth and prosperity, but of surmounting a hundred impertinent obstructions with which the folly of human laws too often encumbers its operations. [48]

Those who pursued their interests were improving their advantage, or, in economic terms, maximizing their utilities through the accumulation of capital and other goods. Avarice was never a popular human trait, since it was thought to be ultimately destructive. However, once the concept of interest came into vogue, unabashed greed became a more acceptable, less harmful, and even virtuous form of behavior that could "tame" other less desirable passions.[49] Under the laws of the free market, if every individual were to pursue his own interests, society as a whole would benefit. Thus Smith's ideas were thought to have given a "new dignity to greed and a new sanctification to the predatory impulses."[50] Based on the assumption that the whole could benefit from individual accumulation, self-aggrandizement came to be seen as fundamentally rational and nondestructive.

Pursuit of interest referred not only to motive but also to design, typifying a kind of logical calculus necessary to achieve that ultimate accumulation of riches and power. Those who behaved instrumentally through the deliberate consideration of alternative means to an end were undoubtedly pursuing their interests, which were thought to provide the perfect guide for human conduct. Since no individual or collective could be deceived by interests, all could have confidence that conduct governed by the drive for acquisition would prove ultimately beneficial. The seventeenth-century political maxim became, appropriately enough, "Interest will not Lie." [51]

Because those who followed their interests were rational calculators, one could more easily anticipate the direction of human behavior.[52] Starting from a particular set of interests, one could predict with some degree of certainty an individual's course of action. Conversely, if outcomes were known, one could infer the motives that lay behind them. With powers of explanation and prediction, the concept and its application began to enjoy tremendous popularity in the social sciences. Individual and collective interests, national and state interests, and balance of interests are just some of the variations on the same theme still in vogue.

### The Problem with Interests

It is likely that the power of interest-driven analyses has been overstated. Even where interests influence human conduct, they hardly determine that conduct in any direct fashion, for a number of reasons. First, interests normally fail to establish clear parameters and guidelines for social and political action. They may, in Schumpeter's words, shape the "original vision" of policymakers, but they cannot specify the contents or determine the results.[53] This is often true because they are poorly defined to begin with and, for that reason, seldom provide precise rules for decisionmaking.[54] Interests are vaguely expressed: business elites must accumulate capital; the military must protect national security; politicians must maximize power and so must nations. Any one of these objectives can be satisfied through a diverse set of policy-relevant models. Failing to discriminate between them, interests can hardly predict outcomes.

For example, the interests of the industrial elite may be furthered either by a free market or by a state-interventionist model of capitalist development. The free market approach limits government's role in the economy. Subsidies, transfers, and other means by which the state tries to compensate individuals for market inequities are eliminated. Prices are set free, while minimum-wage laws are suspended. Social legislation aimed at helping workers collectively to organize against their corporate adversaries is terminated. Entrepreneurs can thus more easily exploit an atomized labor force and increase their profits.

An interventionist government could facilitate profit-making just as easily. When labor can gain economic advantages and legal rights within the normal channels of the system, it is more willing to negotiate and less predisposed to resort to disruptive tactics. Because labor has some stake in the system, it is more willing to play by the established rules of the game. Business has an adversary in organized labor, but the more institutionalized labor becomes, the more reliable an adversary it is. This reliability translates into predictability; business can more easily project labor costs in the future. Since government policies will look markedly different under state-led capitalist systems than under market-dominated ones, and because values as defined by class position cannot in this instance adequately discriminate between competing models of development, the burden of proof is thrown back on the models themselves.

Second, if interest articulation is akin to governmental input, then its transformation into output is anything but smooth.[55] Policymakers are translators: they must take the language of interests and reformulate it so that it emerges as policy. The translation is imperfect, however, and much is lost in the process. Problems may be poorly defined, setting off a series of misguided decisions that produce a final program incapable of satisfying its principal beneficiaries.[56] Poor definition can yield a greater number of plausible outcomes, making it less likely that an initial set of interests can offer any meaningful predictions.

More important, since interests are not specified to begin with, they can easily give rise to a myriad of possible interpretations. Even when elites understand an issue and have maximal amounts of information to work with, each will inevitably have a different perspective, which in turn shapes proposed solutions. Policymakers work from understandings about interests, not from interests themselves. The fit between understanding and interest is unlikely to be perfect. Ideas cannot "objectively" defend their correlative interests since they are not always created to do so. A decisionmaker's ideas are fashioned by intellectual tradition, academic training, historical precedent, or hands-on experience. These factors can work their influence on that decisionmaker in unexpected ways, producing unanticipated effects.

Put another way, the facts of political and economic life do not speak clearly for themselves. Special interests rarely impart particular knowledge in their own defense. One Marxist has admitted that state managers lack "special knowledge of what is necessary to make capitalism more rational; they grope toward effective action as best they can within existing political constraints and *with available economic theories*"[57] (emphasis mine). Such theories were designed by economists, not capitalists, and can no more insure a growing rate of profit for specific businesses than they can predict depressions with any degree of certainty. Not only are rulers *not* automatically guided toward appropriate action by virtue of their position of state power, they may also be misled entirely by the ideas to which they subscribe. In fact, governing elites could take actions that undermine the position of their own class allies.

For example, the IMF-styled austerity measures were originally devised for developing countries in order to insure free trade.[58] The Fund proposed fiscal, monetary, and income adjustments that were intended to forestall the use of trade controls. The *primary* objective of these measures was never to protect corporate profit, and thus it is not surprising to discover that trade balances have improved more consistently than business sales in countries with IMF programs. Clearly, the IMF model in principle was never incongruent with corporate goals, since it advocated nonintervention by governments, free markets, and stable prices. But neither was it specifically tailored to suit the needs of multinational firms. Curiously, officials who have been persuaded by the Fund model and yet were sympathetic to entrepreneurial motives have held onto these programs for long periods of time, despite the fact that quite often private enterprises have suffered severe losses as a consequence.[59]

Interest-driven theorists are not likely to admit that political elites can be so mistaken indefinitely. They insist that before too long, negative outcomes will lay bare the inadequacies of the doctrine to those who stand to lose the most. Pragmatic adjustments will more than likely be made in accordance with disarming economic data or changing political realities, since doing nothing would undermine the social bases of political support for these elites.

In fact, some theorists are convinced that these adjustments *must* be made to return the system to a kind of equilibrium, where political action serves the systemic function it was always intended to serve.[60] More than simply rational moves for particular elites, these changes represent systemic imperatives. For instance, if that larger system happens to be capitalism, then its agents are driven by pursuit of profit. It then follows that other related activities must somehow advance this objective for the system to endure and remain stable. Each actor has his role, every activity fulfills its purpose—and always has—or the system would not have survived so well for so long. Talcott Parsons explains:

> It [the system] must, that is, have a sufficient proportion of its component actors adequately motivated to act in accordance with the requirements of its role system, positively in the fulfillment of expectations, and negatively in abstention from too much disruptive, i.e. deviant, behavior.[61]

A functional inquiry of the causes of authoritarian rule begins with the observation of a correlation between corporate expansion and Third World terror. Profit remittances and market sales seem to be higher in Third World countries subjected to authoritarian forms of rule. Market-oriented systems relish the opportunity to do business in these regions, since even a small capital investment can yield a sizable return, large enough to subsidize corporate operations elsewhere. It is then claimed that profit rates of this level could not have been achieved without terror (e.g., under democratic-reformist rule) or that terror could have resulted without the profit motive. It is concluded that repression is a necessary condition for and a consequence of corporate success, and that terror is purposefully directed to achieve the economic results so described, serving a critical function not only for corporate expansion but for the capitalist system as a whole. This relationship is described by Noam Chomsky and Edward Herman:

> We have seen that there is a positive relationship between U.S. aid, investment climate and terror. A grim further fact is that the terror is not a fortuitous spin off but *has a functional relationship to investment climate* [emphasis mine]. Special tax privileges to foreign business and dependence on foreign investment for economic growth are not easy to achieve under a democratic order in this era of Third World nationalism.[62]

The functional view is the most overbearing form of interest-driven theory. It assumes that interests need not be explicitly articulated by sociopolitical agents since they are already implicitly and firmly embedded in a system. Political actors become trapped by their environment. Social, economic, and political structures are larger and more enduring than the political players. If the system is goal-oriented, then individual behavior is bound to follow suit or, at the very least, stay within clear parameters. These structures act like funnels, progressively narrowing the alternatives available to political elites. The stronger and more stable these structures become, the less freedom of choice they will afford to policymakers. Empirical variations occur from case to case, but are relatively insignificant compared to the more profound continuities fashioned by structural-historical forces.[63] Ergo, though particular decisions made by specific governments are important, these are almost always predictable given a set of prior conditions. Were this the case, it would obviate the need to examine specific policies and the ideas of the heads of state who made them.

Functionalism fails to acknowledge the fact that capital accumulation could thrive under nonauthoritarian forms of rule, or that terror could simply be an uninvited and unanticipated consequence of political and economic behavior. More importantly, it does not acknowledge that outcomes that are beneficial to interests need not be determined by them. Merilee Grindle demonstrates how the developmental ideology of the 1940s, which grew out of the import substitution strategies designed by the Economic Commission for Latin America (ECLA) and its founder, Raúl Prebisch, eventually strengthened the hand of the largest landowners in Latin America.[64] Developmentalists were convinced that rapid modernization of the agricultural sector was necessary and could be achieved only through mechanization, the rapid spread of technological innovation, and the capitalization of farms. Agrarian elites were in the best position to adopt these measures with the least "prodding" and were rewarded with easier access to credit, the benefits of agricultural research, and state-financed infrastructure. Developmentalism may have worked to the advantage of landed elites in the end, but its derivation preceded the unification of a strong rural capitalist class in Latin America and thus could not have been pressured into existence. Instead, Grindle concludes that state elites were principally influenced by the dominant intellectual model itself:

> Clearly the adoption of these perspectives on agricultural modernization was not isolated from the economic and political milieu in which they were put forth, nor were state elites either objective or isolated in the interpretations they adopted. The neoclassical and structuralist arguments were firmly rooted in the tradition of capitalist accumulation. . . . Nevertheless, it is important to acknowledge that the models themselves played a key role in shaping the content of the policies actually pursued and in the particular form of capitalist expansion that emerged in the period in question.[65]

## THE UTILITY OF IDEAS

Ideas can serve an independent purpose in a social science perspective; this is not to say that they are somehow immaculately conceived. Concepts are born in a social context, and in that respect, Karl Marx's revolt against eighteenth- and nineteenth-century idealism is to be applauded. However, Marx may have gone too far by assuming a new orthodoxy—historical materialism. He theorized that ideas are not only grounded in social reality but are also rigidly determined by that reality. What independent impact, if any, concepts have upon their subjects can never be known since they simply express underlying realities and never construct those realities.

Karl Mannheim escaped from vulgar materialism when he noted that social class is not the only form of social conditioning. Individuals, he argued, share a world view or *weltanschauung*, which cuts across the grain of interest groups, institutions, and classes. People are as easily united through outlook as they are through material relations and are unlikely to abandon their views simply because they change class position. Conversely, a single class is never so homogeneous as to impart a uniform belief system upon its members. According to Mannheim, since a multitude of world views may be embedded within a single class, it is nearly impossible to predict intellectual preferences from social context or to reduce ideas to class position.[66] Despite Mannheim's success at avoiding the trap of class reductionism, he remained a part of materialist tradition to the extent that he sought the meaning of concepts in social relations. He was convinced that an examination of the social origins of ideas would expose the biases and partiality of one's vision.[67] Since meaning could not be detached from existence, any assessment of ideas on their own terms was a fruitless exercise.

Mannheim, like materialists before him, presumed that ideas could not exert any independent influence. He was mistaken; while ideas are certainly affected by historical, economic, and sociocultural forces, "it is no contradiction to affirm simultaneously that ideas are conditioned and that ideas have a life of their own," (emphasis mine) as Robert Packenham has noted in the case of liberal-minded foreign aid programs.[68] Packenham analyzes aid programs that were designed to alleviate economic and political underdevelopment in the Third World but that proved to be ineffective. He acknowledges that the formulation of these plans was certainly affected by objective conditions (including economic abundance, social fluidity, and political decentralization) but concludes that the power of liberal doctrine, not material interests, kept these programs alive despite their infeasibility.[69]

Ideas offer perspectives—"angles of vision" that bring certain objects into sharp focus and blur others.[70] In research, perspective directs one's choice of conceptual categories, hypotheses, and methods to be employed; it renders some empirical work achievable but other work impossible.[71] Not surprisingly, two researchers with contrasting perspectives can articulate separate versions of the same event. Two classic examples are the explanations provided by Robert Dahl (1961) and William Domhoff (1978) for urban development in New Haven, Connecticut, between 1945 and 1957. Relying on a pluralist perspective, Dahl concluded that urban redevelopment policies were the result of conflicts and alliances between competitive interest groups. According to Dahl, no single interest group prevails at all times. The adept politician arranges compromises, provides rewards, and builds coalitions in an effort to assemble sufficient support for a policy among independent groups. However, Domhoff, using a power elite model, concluded that a single ruling class determined urban policy. This class was itself composed of an interlocking network of those interest groups and political figures that Dahl identified as independent.

As members of separate schools of thought, each scholar analyzed the same events but reached different conclusions, ignoring the evidence brought to bear by the other and remaining thoroughly insensitive to his opponent's arguments.[72] Undoubtedly, other members of these same intellectual communities, were they to undertake similar studies in the future, would reach parallel conclusions. Any school of thought furnishes a persuasive, singular frame of reference for its members that sets it apart not only from other schools of thought but also from other sociological configurations such as classes or interest groups.[73]

Like all groups, a school of thought has its own sociological identity. Groups exist when there are some significant rates of social interaction, engagement in common activities, conformity to norms and roles, definition of membership by individuals and those outside, and duration of the group itself.[74] Schools of thought possess most of these traits as well as others, including collaborations, citations, shared teaching experiences, and academic friendships. These elements are important to the survival of the community, since they facilitate interpersonal contact, mutual support, and recognition for its members. However, the core of any school, and the focus of this study, is its unique intellectual identity and contribution.

What holds true for scholars can easily hold true for political elites, who come to office with certain sets of ideas borrowed from one perspective or another. Knowing the school, we have a clue to the general predispositions of policymakers. For instance, we can identify whether they are more or less likely to favor market intervention over the free market, to favor welfare spending over fiscal austerity, or to use force before negotiation. These general positions are not reducible to emotional or cognitive states and do not vary dramatically according to the immediate pressures, problems, and evidence presented to the specific decisionmaker.[75] Although one or two steps removed from the individual decisionmaking process the identification of perspectives is equally important, because perspectives are sufficiently constraining to limit the range of options available to the policymaker at the time decisions must be made. For this reason, considerable mileage can be gained by examining the ideas rather than the individuals who hold them.

If ideas are persuasive, then it is perfectly reasonable for policymakers to persist with their preferred plans even in the face of disquieting information or political objections. Pure empiricism is impossible; facts cannot so easily be made to confirm one hypothesis while disproving another. Normally, the same event can justify opposing viewpoints.[76] Even where the evidence against a theory is overwhelming, "paradigm" abandonment, to use Kuhn's terminology, is uncommon. In fact, true believers are likely to reinterpret events to support theories rather than to abandon theories to the facts. The tendency to shape information so that it is coordinated with preexisting images is greatest where (1) that information is ambiguous and clearly open to varied interpretation, and (2) confidence in a doctrine is high.[77] Thus, the

Argentine economics minister, José A. Martínez de Hoz (1976–1981), could boldly assert that the recession was beneficial to the economy. Industrialists meanwhile were suffering huge profit losses and demanding policy change. From the vantage point of these producers, the facts of economic decline were self-evident. The minister took exception to their complaints, insisting that the recession was a sign of corrective pricing that would weed out less competitive firms. This was a peculiar evaluation, yet a logical one if the minister was to defend the monetarist doctrine to which he was so clearly committed.[78]

Familiarity often breeds retention. The longer a policymaker has been under the influence of a set of ideas and the stronger his commitment, the more difficult the rejection. Robert Jervis explains:

> Once a dominant percept . . . is established, there is a tendency to suppress inharmonious cues and to enhance harmonious cues. The most difficult mental act of all is to rearrange a familiar bundle of data, to look at it differently and escape from the prevailing doctrine.[79]

This is particularly so when ideas have generated policy successes. However, it is also possible when they have failed: a determined ruler may persist with more of the same, convinced that the plan has not been fully or adequately implemented in the past. He or she asserts that just a little more time is needed to "turn the corner," and that reconsideration to meet short-term and narrow-sighted political objectives will only diminish the chances for recovery. This is an important argument, made by the technocratic team of Argentine economists who were invited to serve the government after the military coup of 1976. They were persuaded that democratic regimes of the past had failed to provide the proper "environment" for policy implementation, free from interferences from politicians and interest groups. Now the strong authoritarian state offered them the policymaking context they dreamed of, and they could pursue monetarist programs with particular vigor, callously disregarding the complaints of numerous interest groups.

Whether policies succeed or fail, elites are pushed along by the force of intellectual inertia to pursue more of the same. The probability that they will opt for a change depends additionally on the availability of attractive alternatives. Ideas do not emerge from a vacuum; they must be presented to elites in an organized, visible, and convincing way. Policymakers are impressed by what can be called scholastic authority, which is the blending of intellectual achievement and institutional power. Those institutions that have accumulated the greatest number of assets—intellectual, financial, and communicative—are more likely to prevail in the competition for the successful transmission of concepts to heads of state.[80] In turn, their success acts as a reinvestment of capital by attracting contributions from supporters and lending them even greater power and prestige. This self-reinforcing mechanism insures that certain suppliers of knowledge will remain in greater demand than others, as will the ideas they produce. These ideas may not provide the conceptual alternative that is needed, but they will find an audience nonetheless. There is no completely free market place of ideas and thus no guarantee that out of failure will emerge the right plan.

By the same token, it does not follow that there is a complete monopoly of ideas. Policymakers have some freedom of choice and may discriminate between competing concepts, not merely on the basis of the authority of their sponsors but on the merit of the arguments, as they see it. They may be impressed with the internal logic of the model, its problem-solving capabilities, or its promise to deliver political payoffs. This suggests they may either stumble upon a more attractive alternative or persevere with whatever choice has been made.

## A NOTE ON METHOD

If ideas are important in their own right, they can be taken as the starting and not the end point of inquiry. In such a case, social science has as its raw material the concepts that individuals use to give meaning to their activities, not the activities themselves. Clifford Geertz notes:

> Social events do have causes but it just may be that the road to discovering what we assert in asserting lies less through postulating forces and measuring them than through noting expressions and inspecting them.[81]

These expressions may be found in written documents. The philosophical tradition of hermeneutics has grown up around the interpretation of texts.[82] Since Aristotle's *Peri Hermeneias*, which dealt with the logic of sentence structure, hermeneutics has assumed an important place in philosophy and theology. It flourished among the Protestant reformists, who took exception to the Catholic church's insistence that only it had the authority to interpret scriptures, suggesting instead that the texts were self-sufficient.[83] Scripture contained an internal coherence and continuity, they claimed, that could be discerned by any trained reader who "genuinely opens himself to the text by listening to it and allowing it to assert its viewpoint."[84] By freeing scriptural doctrines from the yoke of the church, these reformists enabled future generations to deal with texts as "living documents" capable of generating their own meaning.[85] Meaning does not vary, according to hermeneutics, though interpretations of that meaning do. The challenge for future readers of the text is to render the most plausible interpretation possible.

Of course, a fascination with textual material runs the danger of, in Geertz's words, "locking cultural analysis away from its proper object, the informal logic of actual life."[86] The danger is as follows: the reader finds a doctrine that he believes is significant and renders an interpretation of it; the interpreted text serves in his mind as an absolute reference point according to which all evidence can be evaluated; rather than study human behavior, he continually reverts to the doctrine itself, insisting that one need only appreciate intrinsic qualities of the text (its internal elegance, design, etc.) as one sees them. Convinced of the certainty of his insights, the analyst remains happily trapped within the "hermeneutic circle." Geertz explains the difficulty inherent in this approach:

> A further implication of this is that coherence cannot be the major test of validity for a cultural description. Cultural systems must have a minimal degree of coherence, else we would not call them systems. . . . But there is nothing so coherent as a paranoid's delusion or a swindler's story. The force of our interpretations cannot rest, as they are now so often made to do, on the tightness with which they hold together, or the assurance with which they are argued. Nothing has done more, I think, to discredit cultural analysis than the construction of impeccable depictions of formal order in whose actual existence nobody can quite believe.[87]

The disclosure of meaning must find a path that leads meaning away from the text toward some object outside it. It is through behavior that ideas find their articulation, and appraisal of concepts must at some point make sense of social action. Consequently, what began in hermeneutics as an interpretive exercise must, in the hands of the social scientist, become explanatory.

Interpretive and causal exercises are not incompatible. On the contrary, they form a complementary mode of inquiry.[88] Interpretivists use text to gain an empathetic appreciation of a subject's views. To understand fully social or political action, one has also to comprehend the significance that action has for the actors themselves. For Max Weber, the object of science is not behavior but meaningfully oriented behavior. Events have qualities and importance that are, in Weber's words, "conditioned by the orientation of our cognitive interest."[89] Subjects act according to their own cognitive and value preferences. It follows that the sum total of individual action—events—are themselves profoundly affected by these preferences. If interpretation did nothing more than supply a window into the mindset of political actors, it would offer a valuable first step toward a more lucid explanation of behavioral outcomes.

Interpretation by itself, however, cannot tell us whether ideas have consequence for the social or political world. Presumably, one would want to know that if all else were equal, the choice of one idea over another would make a real difference. If ideas are adequate to the task of explanation, then some assessment of empirical outcomes must be made.

This form of inquiry found one of its strongest applications in Weber's seminal work, *The Protestant Ethic and the Spirit of Capitalism*. Weber discovered a remarkable correlation between economic position and religious affiliation. An unusually large percentage of business elites in Western capitalist countries were Protestants; Weber postulated that Protestants were driven by an economic rationalism (not found among Catholics) that placed a premium on discipline, frugality, individualism, and profit-making. He also maintained that these personal qualities had their origins in the religious tenets and interpretations of the Calvinist doctrine of the sixteenth and seventeenth centuries. Calvinists maintained that only individual effort through a lifetime of good works would fulfill God's will and provide the possibility of final redemption: God helps those who help themselves.

Prominent interpreters of this doctrine extended these religious principles to economic matters. Each man was said to have his divine calling, and some were called upon to acquire wealth through hard work; others were to labor for menial wages. Material acquisition was legitimate so long as it led to savings and investment and was not an end in itself; frivolous and impulsive consumption was to be avoided. Thus, entrepreneurial skills could be squared with Protestant asceticism.[90] The bourgeois businessman could justify his social position and accept the inequitable distribution of income under capitalism because his "morally correct" pursuit of wealth fulfilled a special divine duty. More than a rationalization, the Protestant ethic was the driving force behind the development of "sober bourgeois capitalism."[91]

Weber was not an idealist. He was convinced that the founders of the Protestant doctrine were affected by the "totality of social conditions especially economic."[92] However, he was also sufficiently impressed with the power of ideas to initiate his analysis of the capitalist spirit with religious doctrine, and not with the complex of social forces that no doubt made an impact on the religious thinking of the time. In doing so, he treated ideas as independent causal agents, capable of generating explanations for future outcomes. We will do the same.

## NOTES

1. The works on this subject are too numerous to mention inclusively. Among the significant contributions are: Guillermo O'Donnell, *Modernization and Bureaucratic-Authoritarianism* (Berkeley: Institute for International Studies, 1979); David Collier, ed., *The New Authoritarianism in Latin America* (Princeton: Princeton University Press, 1979); James Malloy, ed., *Authoritarianism and Corporatism in Latin America* (Pittsburgh: University of Pittsburgh Press, 1977); Abraham Lowenthal and J. Samuel Fitch, *Armies and Politics in Latin America*, (New York: Holmes & Meier, 1986); Guillermo O'Donnell, Philippe C. Schmitter, and Laurence Whitehead, eds., *Transitions from Authoritarian Rule*, 4 Volumes (Baltimore: Johns Hopkins University Press, 1986).

2. Amnesty International, *Amnesty International Report 1986* (London: Amnesty International Publications, 1986).

3. The Argentine National Commission on the Disappeared observed: "All sectors fell into the net: trade union leaders fighting for better wages; youngsters in student unions; journalists who did not support the regime; psychologists and sociologists simply belonging to suspicious professions; young pacifists, nuns and priests who had taken the teachings of Christ to shanty areas; the friends of these people too, and the friends of friends, plus others whose names were

given out of motives of personal vengeance, or by the kidnapped under torture. (CONADEP 1986:4)

4. Ernest Duff and John McCamant, *Violence and Repression in Latin America: A Quantitative and Historical Analysis* (New York: Free Press, 1976), p. 51.

5. This form of political repression was prevalent in the 1970s, but it existed to a limited extent in earlier periods as well. Later chapters will provide an analysis.

6. Argentine National Commission on the Disappeared, *Nunca Más* (New York: Farrar, Straus & Giroux, 1986), p. 11.

7. Accounts of unsuspecting detainees are found in Archdiocese of São Paulo, *Torture in Brazil*, trans. Jaime Wright, ed. Joan Dassin (New York: Vintage Books, 1986), pp. xxvi–xxvii.

8. Ibid., p. 132.

9. John Simpson and John Bennett, *The Disappeared and the Mothers of the Plaza: The Story of the 11,000 Argentinians Who Vanished* (New York: St. Martin's Press, 1985), p. 76.

10. Richard Gillespie, *Soldiers of Perón: Argentina's Montoneros* (Oxford: Oxford University Press, 1982), p. 215.

11. Daniel Frontalini and María Cristina Caiati, *El Mito de la Guerra Sucia* (Buenos Aires: Centro de Estudios Legales y Sociales, 1984), p. 66.

12. Gillespie, *Soldiers of Perón*, p. 38.

13. The secret order is reprinted in *El Diario del Juicio* 28 (December 1985):529–532.

14. Raymond Cohen, *Threat Perception in International Crisis* (Madison: University of Wisconsin Press, 1979), p. 4.

15. J. David Singer, "Threat Perception and the Armament Tension Dilemma," *Journal of Conflict Resolution* 2 (1958):90–105.

16. Duff and McCamant, *Violence and Repression in Latin America*, p. 25.

17. Raymond Duvall and Michael Stohl, "Governance by Terror," in *The Politics of Terrorism*, 2d ed., ed. Michael Stohl (New York: Marcel Dekker, 1983), p. 179–219.

18. David Pion-Berlin, "The National Security Doctrine, Military Threat Perception and the 'Dirty War' in Argentina," *Comparative Political Studies* 21 (October 1988): 382–407.

19. See Klaus Knorr, *Historical Dimensions of National Security Problems* (Kansas City: University Press of Kansas, 1976), p. 84; Cohen, *Threat Perception in International Crisis*, pp. 6-13.

20. Paul A. Samuelson, *Economics*, 10th ed. (New York: McGraw-Hill, 1976), p. 3.

21. Richard Swedberg, "The Doctrine of Economic Neutrality of the IMF and the World Bank," *Journal of Peace Research* 23 (1986): 377.

22. Ibid., p. 388.

23. An excellent discussion of the social effects of this and other economic strategies can be found in John Sheehan, *Patterns of Development in Latin America: Poverty, Repression and Economic Strategy* (Princeton: Princeton University Press, 1987), pp. 110–120.

24. This terminology is borrowed from studies on the cognition of individual political elites. Cognitive maps, which are representations of the structure of assertions made by an individual, unveil the logic by which policymakers reach decisions. For example, see Robert Axelrod, ed., *Structure of Decision: The Cognitive Maps of Political Elites* (Princeton: Princeton

University Press, 1976). The model applied here, on the other hand, looks at the content of ideas that precede cognition. A similar approach was taken by one author to account for changes in U.S. monetary policy: see John Odell, *U.S. International Monetary Policy: Market, Power and Ideas as Sources of Change* (Princeton: Princeton University Press, 1982).

25. Ole Holsti's study of former U.S. Secretary of State John Foster Dulles confirms this view. See David Finlay, Ole Holsti, and Richard Fagen, *Enemies in Politics* (Chicago: Rand McNally, 1967), pp. 25–96.

26. Knorr, *Historical Dimensions*, p. 85.

27. Helen Fein, *Accounting for Genocide* (New York: Free Press, 1979), p. 8.

28. Albert O. Hirschman has speculated that the transition from import substitution strategies to more free market strategies contributed to the rise of dictatorial regimes. See Hirschman, "The Turn to Authoritarianism in Latin America and the Search for its Economic Determinants," in Collier, ed., *The New Authoritarianism.*

29. For a discussion of this doctrinaire version of monetarism, see Pilar Vergara, *Auge y Caida del Neoliberalismo en Chile*, Documento de Trabajo numero 216 (Santiago: FLACSO, 1984); Alejandro Foxley, *Latin American Experiments in Neoconservative Economics* (Berkeley: University of California Press, 1983).

30. This is a view not readily found in standard economics texts. However, from my conversations with former economic ministers of Argentina, and through a reading of ministerial speeches, it is abundantly clear that the free market–minded economists attribute excessive state expansion to interest group pressures and the irresponsibility of state managers.

31. In an interview with this author, a former secretary of commerce for the Argentine military regime and strong advocate of the monetarist program stated that popular pressures for higher wages, government jobs and services, credit liberalization, and tariff protection were "irrational." These were sectarian demands that would interfere with the macroeconomic designs of the administration. He added that fortunately the cabinet had the backing of a "strong" state to provide the necessary insulation for "rational" budget-minded policymaking. Alejandro Estrada, interview with author, Buenos Aires, July 1984.

32. This assessment has been made after a careful inventory of the literature on political repression and authoritarian rule in the Third World. The following is a representative sample of important studies that more or less rely on an interest approach to this subject: O'Donnell, *Modernization and Bureaucratic-Authoritarianism*; Edward S. Herman, *The Real Terror Network: Terrorism in Fact and Propaganda* (Boston: South End Press, 1982); Penny Lernoux, *Cry of the People* (Garden City: Doubleday, 1980), pp. 203–280; James Petras, *Class, State and Power in the Third World* (Montclair: Allanheld, Osmun, 1981), pp. 1–70.

33. For example, see Roberto Frenkel and Guillermo O'Donnell, "The 'Stabilization Programs' of the International Monetary Fund and Their Internal Impacts," in *Capitalism and the State in U.S.-Latin American Relations*, ed. Richard R. Fagen (Stanford: Stanford University Press, 1979); Thomas Scheetz, *Peru and the International Monetary Fund* (Pittsburgh: University of Pittsburgh, 1986); Cheryl Payer, *The Debt Trap: The IMF and the Third World* (New York: Monthly Review Press, 1975).

34. Frenkel and O'Donnell, "Stabilization Programs," p. 179.

35. Ibid.

36. Ibid.

37. See Karl Marx, "The Eighteenth Brumaire of Louis Bonaparte," in *The Marx-Engels Reader*, ed. Robert C. Tucker (New York: W. W. Norton, 1972).

38. See John McCamant, "Governance Without Blood: Social Science's Antiseptic View of Rule; or, The Neglect of Political Repression," in *The State as Terrorist: The Dynamics of Governmental Violence and Repression*, ed. Michael Stohl and George A. Lopez (Westport: Greenwood Press, 1984), p. 26.

39. Standard dependency works that make this general argument are: André Gunder Frank, "The Development of Underdevelopment," *Monthly Review* 18 (September 1966): 17–31; Susanne Bodenheimer, "Dependency and Imperialism: The Roots of Latin American Underdevelopment," in *Readings in U.S. Imperialism*, ed. K. T. Fann and Donald Hodges (Boston: Porter Sargent Publisher, 1971); Fernando H. Cardoso, "Associated Dependent Development," in *Authoritarian Brazil*, ed. Alfred Stepan (New Haven: Yale University Press, 1973), pp. 163–164; Kenneth P. Erickson and Patrick V. Peppe, "Dependent Capitalist Development, U.S. Foreign Policy, and Repression of the Working Class in Chile and Brazil," *Latin American Perspectives* 1 (Winter 1976):19–44.

40. See Mancur Olson, Jr., "The Logic of Collective Action," in Brian Barry and Russell Hardin, eds., *Rational Man and Irrational Society? An Introduction and Sourcebook* (Beverly Hills: Sage Publications, 1982), p. 43–44.

41. Paul Edwards, ed., *The Encyclopedia of Philosophy*, Vol. 4. (New York: MacMillan, 1967), pp. 111–113.

42. G. W. F. Hegel, *The Phenomenology of Mind*, trans. by J. B. Baillie (London: George Allen & Unwin, 1971), p. 32.

43. Quentin Lauer, *Hegel's Idea of Philosophy* (New York: Fordham University Press, 1971), p. 12.

44. Karl Marx, "The German Ideology," in Tucker, ed., *The Marx-Engels Reader*, p. 118.

45. Ibid., p. 136.

46. Niccolo Machiavelli, *The Prince and the Discourses* (New York: Modern Library, 1950), p. 66.

47. Albert O. Hirschman, *The Passions and the Interests: Political Arguments for Capitalism Before its Triumph* (Princeton: Princeton University Press, 1977), p. 34.

48. Adam Smith, *An Inquiry into the Nature and Causes of the Wealth of Nations*, ed. Edwin Cannan (New York: The Modern Library, 1965), p. liv.

49. Hirschman, *Passions and the Interests*, pp. 40–42.

50. See Max Lerner's introduction to Adam Smith's *Wealth of Nations*, p. ix.

51. J. A. W. Gunn, "Interest Will Not Lie: A Seventeenth Century Political Maxim," *Journal of the History of Ideas* 29 (December 1968):551.

52. Ibid., p. 557.

53. Schumpeter's idea can be found in Joseph A. Schumpeter, "Science and Ideology," *The American Economic Review* 39 (March 1949):351.

54. Hirschman, *Passions and the Interests*, p. 35.

55. The use of the term "interest articulation" as an input function can be found in Gabriel A. Almond and James S. Coleman, *The Politics of the Developing Areas* (Princeton: Princeton University Press, 1960), pp. 14–17.

56. The general point is shared by Merilee Grindle in *Politics and Policy Implementation in the Third World* (Princeton: Princeton University Press, 1980), pp. 10, 23. Also see the account by Stephen A. Quick (in the same

volume) of ideological policy in Zambia, where a rational set of policies designed to benefit the rural poor could not be implemented because goals were multiple, poorly conceptualized, and ambiguous. Within this brand of ideologically motivated statecraft, Quick states, "any activity can be (and was) justified in terms of some goal" (p. 57).

57. Fred Block, "The Ruling Class Does Not Rule: Notes on the Marxist Theory of the State," *Socialist Revolution* 7 (May–June 1977): 25–26.

58. See Chapter 3 for details on the purposes of the IMF.

59. An example of this phenomenon is provided in David Pion-Berlin, "The Defiant State: Chile in the Post-Coup Era," in *Armies and Politics in Latin America*, revised edition, ed. Abraham F. Lowenthal and J. Samuel Fitch (New York: Holmes and Meier Publishers, 1986), pp. 317–334.

60. This is a functional line of argument, best expressed by Talcott Parsons. See his *The Social System* (Glencoe: Free Press, 1951), pp. 26–36.

61. Ibid., p. 27.

62. See Noam Chomsky and Edward S. Herman, *The Washington Connection and Third World Fascism: The Political Economy of Human Rights*, Vol. 1. (Boston: South End Press, 1979), p. 54.

63. These arguments run through the discussions of underdevelopment and authoritarian rule found in dependency theory and bureaucratic-authoritarian theory. For the bureaucratic-authoritarian approach, see O'Donnell, *Modernization and Bureaucratic-Authoritarianism*, and, by the same author, "Reflections on the Patterns of Change in the Bureaucratic-Authoritarian State," *Latin American Research Review* 13 (1978), wherein O'Donnell states that "a certain socio-economic structure—a historical type of capitalism . . . tends to correspond closely to political formations and resultant policies" (p. 27).

64. Merilee Grindle, *State and Countryside: Development Policy and Agrarian Politics in Latin America* (Baltimore: Johns Hopkins University Press, 1986), pp. 47–78.

65. Ibid., p. 20.

66. See Karl Mannheim, *Essays on the Sociology of Knowledge*, ed. Paul Kecskemeti (London: Routledge & Kegan Paul, 1952), p. 186.

67. Karl Mannheim, *Ideology and Utopia* (New York: Harcourt, Brace and World, 1936), p. 171.

68. See Robert Packenham, *Liberal America and the Third World: Political Development Ideas in Foreign Aid and Social Science* (Princeton: Princeton University Press, 1973).

69. Ibid.

70. Perspective is defined in this way by Paul Desing, *Science and Ideology in the Policy Sciences* (New York: Aldine, 1982), pp. 11–12.

71. Ibid., p. 304.

72. Their arguments are summarized in Diesing, *Science and Ideology*, pp. 375–377.

73. An excellent application of this concept can be found in Diesing, *Science and Ideology*.

74. Robert K. Merton, *Social Theory and Social Structure*, revised and enlarged edition (New York: Free Press, 1957), pp. 310–326; also see Diesing, *Science and Ideology*, p. 9.

75. Odell, *U.S. International Monetary Policy*, pp. 62–63.

76. Jervis, *Perception and Misperception*, pp. 162–165.

77. Ibid., p. 195.

78. Statements on the economy made by the minister of economics can

be found in República Argentina: Ministerio de Economía, *Memoria 3/29/76–3/29/81*.

79. Jervis, *Perception and Misperception*, p. 188.

80. This same argument is made in the case of the Chicago School of economics. The predictions offered by this school attract wide attention in governing circles, so the authors claim, not because they are scientifically true but because they are issued by those who wield power and authority. See Charles Wilber and Jon Wisman, " 'The Chicago School': Positivism or Ideal Type?" *Journal of Economic Issues* 9 (December 1975):676.

81. Clifford Geertz, *Local Knowledge: Further Essays in Interpretive Anthropology* (New York: Basic Books, 1983), p. 34.

82. The following are some of the most important contributors to hermeneutics: Hans-Georg Gadamer, *Philosophical Hermeneutics*, trans. and ed. David E. Linge (Berkeley: University of California Press, 1976); W. Dilthey, *Selected Writings*, trans. and ed. H. P. Rickman (Cambridge: Cambridge University Press, 1976); Paul Ricouer, *The Conflict of Interpretations: Essays in Hermeneutics* (Evanston: Northwestern University Press, 1974); Kurt Mueller-Vollmer, ed., *The Hermeneutics Reader: Texts of the German Tradition from the Enlightenment to the Present* (Oxford: Basil Blackwell, 1986).

83. Mueller-Vollmer, *Hermeneutics Reader*, p. 2.

84. Gadamer, *Philosophical Hermeneutics*, pp. xx–xxi.

85. Ibid.

86. Geertz, *Interpretation of Cultures*, p. 17.

87. Ibid., pp. 17–18.

88. This point is made by Max Weber, *The Methodology of the Social Sciences*, trans. and ed. Edward A. Shils and Henry A. Finch (Glencoe: Free Press of Glencoe, 1949), p. 59.

89. Ibid., p. 64.

90. Ibid., p. 172.

91. Ibid., p. 26.

92. Ibid., p. 183.

# 2

# Structuralism, Monetarism, and Political Repression: An Interpretation

## STRUCTURALISM VS. MONETARISM: CONTENDING THEORIES ON ECONOMIC STABILIZATION

For over two decades, monetarists and structuralists have clashed in countless debates concerning the ills of Latin American economies, seldom reaching consensus on vital issues. Structuralist critiques dominated in the mid-1950s and early 1960s, while monetarism prevailed during the 1970s and early 1980s. The domination of monetarism had less to do with the viability of the model per se than with political forces ushering in regimes partial to monetarist thinking. Once embraced by ruling elites, ideas seem to carry more force than they do simply circulating within the universities or private think tanks. We must also remember that Latin America had been plagued in the 1970s by severe economic crises. Given the need for swift adjustments, monetarism often appeared more appropriate, since it offered prescriptions in the short term while structuralists seemed to be stuck on long-term payoffs. However, the recent failures of orthodox stabilization measures derived from monetarist principles have placed the viability of such approaches in doubt.

At an ideological level, these doctrines are similar: they both defend the free enterprise system; neither model subscribes to worker-controlled or centrally planned economies. But at an operative level, they differ: the structuralists seek greater state involvement in the economy, the monetarists less; the structuralists look at the role of power in the international and national system and its effects on the allocation and distribution of goods, while the monetarists ignore power. Both structuralists and monetarists are deeply concerned with impediments to economic growth. Both recognize the dangers of galloping inflation and loss of foreign reserves, but they disagree on their causes. The structuralists contend that supply rigidities force prices up and retard productive investment. The monetarists agree that supply rigidities are inflationary and growth-prohibitive but attribute these bottlenecks to government-induced price distortions. Both approaches concur on outcomes, but each takes a different starting point.

The purpose here is not to ascertain the truth of the monetarist or structuralist position. Economists have argued about the pros and cons of each view for some time, providing an adequate body of literature on the debate.[1] Our objective rather is to deduce *political consequences* from the fact that each school of thought is convinced that its view is correct. How will governments' behavior toward labor groups be influenced by adherence to either model?

## Structuralism

*Foundations.* Policymakers in Latin America have often been guided by structuralist economics.[2] Structuralism was born out of the work of the ECLA, established as a regional organ of the United Nations in 1948. With its seat in Santiago, Chile, ECLA influenced many of Latin America's intellectuals and statesmen. Raúl Prebisch was the chief architect behind ECLA's philosophy, and it is his original theoretical work that laid the groundwork for the structuralist approach.

Structuralism is actually more a compilation of similar approaches than a uniform theory. Nonetheless, there are some fundamental continuities to this brand of economics. Generally, Prebisch's thesis took issue with neoclassical theories of trade benefits, and in particular the Heckscher-Olin theory, which has been the twentieth century's free trade manifesto.[3] This theory argues that once two countries begin trading goods for which they have comparative advantage, the general welfare of both will improve equally. Prebisch agreed trade would result in greater gains overall but objected to the idea that benefits were equally distributed.

Prebisch's empirical study of trade between Great Britain and primary producing countries revealed that the average price of primary goods relative to manufactured goods had declined over time. This worsened the terms of trade for poor rural states while improving it for wealthy industrialized states. The steady deterioration in prices for primary producers lead to welfare losses for them and welfare gains for the wealthier states. Since Prebisch believed that rural societies would inevitably suffer trade disadvantages because of the nature of their production systems, he urged them to switch from food exports to import substitution industrialization. To shift output from the farm to the factory, governments would have to provide the appropriate incentives in the form of technology, finance capital, and state-led investment: the market could not reallocate resources on its own. In short, market intervention at home was a legitimate response to the inequities of uneven development internationally.

Inflation is of central concern to the structuralist critique. The structuralists attribute inflation to three primary causes: foreign-exchange deficits, supply constraints, and deficit spending.[4] The first derives from trade. Where export earnings in primary producing states cannot pay for imports, the foreign exchange gap will prompt governments to devalue the currency. This move will stimulate international demand, place pressure on domestic supplies, and hence raise prices for tradeable items.

Domestic shortages have internal origins as well. Food production shortfalls are common to LDCs, where large landowners are reluctant to improve yields by investing in technology. Food supplies can never keep pace with a growing urban population, and prices will inevitably rise. Ideally, inflation can be avoided where food demand is met through imports, *if* the terms of trade problem does not reduce the country's import capacity.

The structuralists contend that there is an additive effect between domestic supply rigidities and international trade constraints.[5]

Structuralists are convinced that in the long term, inflationary problems can only be overcome through expanded output and productivity. This in turn requires investment—which the Latin American entrepreneurial class is often unwilling to undertake. In the interim, stagnant industries fail to provide jobs for a growing working class, putting the onus of employment on the public sector. Government must undertake entrepreneurial tasks as well. As in the cases of Mexico and Brazil,[6] the state is often compelled to invest in upstream endeavors, selling output to private business at below cost. This encourages downstream industrial development, aids growth of related industries, and relieves underlying supply rigidities. Ideally, such expenditures would be covered by higher tax revenues. However, this is seldom the case, given the concentration of wealth in Latin American societies and the difficulties of enforcing progressive tax measures on the propertied classes. Understandably, therefore, governments must draw deficits to undertake the growth-promoting activities the private sector ignores. Deficit spending, the third source of inflation, is, ironically, endorsed by the structuralist position in order to ward off greater inflation later on.

*Supply and demand for inflation.* Inflationary deficit spending may be inevitable, according to the structuralist approach, given the deficiencies in private sector levels of savings and investment. If so, is deficit spending ever justifiable—or in fact desirable?

To begin with, structuralists often make a distinction between primary and secondary causes of inflation. Food bottlenecks and trade disadvantages are "original inflationary sins," while government deficit spending is a "propagating mechanism."[7] Thus, the structuralists condemn nonproductive landowners more than government spenders in assigning blame for economic misfortune. Moreover, government expenditure is in part a legitimate response to labor's wage and employment demands, which are "defensive measures" taken to protect labor groups against the ravages of structurally rooted price increases.

The erosion of purchasing power is particularly acute for lower income groups. Preexisting inflation acts as a tax on the economically disadvantaged, who lack inflationary hedges such as property. Wage earners need relatively larger sums of money to acquire the same bundle of goods as property owners; those owners of capital meanwhile protect their income from inflationary erosion through interest-bearing assets. The result is a transfer of income from lower to higher income groups. Where wages cannot keep pace with inflation, governments may defend working-class living standards through providing subsidies, transfers, and services.

Of course as the demands for state deficit spending rise, the costs of fulfilling those demands also rise, given the limits of revenue expansion. Any economist would be wary about government deficit spending, regardless of the plight of wage-earning groups; but, as Robert Gordon has persuasively demonstrated, cost/benefit ratios are not simple economic formulas. Governments also have solid political reasons for supplying inflation.[8] Where constituencies with political clout press for government spending, leaders must weigh the advantages of a balanced budget against the disadvantages of popular resistance. The need to insure political support is as much a value as is the need to manage the fiscal affairs of the state. What is unique about Gordon's formulation is that it conceives of inflation as a *valued* commodity.

In economic terms, the total cost of spending is minimized when the marginal cost of increasing inflation is equal to the marginal cost of increasing taxes. In political terms, the cost is minimized when politically optimal spending is properly weighed against fiscally optimal spending.[9] Gordon's idea suggests that greater amounts of deficit spending will be tolerated where governments attach greater value to the need to accommodate political constituents (or appease adversaries). In sum, cost/benefit calculations will shift as the model for interpreting economic and political problems changes. From the vantage point of the structuralist doctrine, balancing budgets carries less importance than satisfying socially legitimate spending demands.

When it comes to fiscal expenditure, structuralists have utilitarian and normative concerns. The utilitarian perspective is that the benefits gained by spending (wider political support) will outweigh the costs (higher deficits); that strategy makes goal achievement more likely than do alternative strategies. The normative standard is based on the degree to which these social demands are perceived by structuralists to be legitimate and, therefore, worthy of support. Of course, notions of legitimacy normally refer to favorable judgments cast *by society upon authorities*. The judgments are personal (charisma), procedural (democratic vs. authoritarian), or substantive (concrete performance) in nature. Legitimization may also be more diffuse, in that governments may accrue support from either their association with legitimate systems or important prior events (e.g., revolutions). In short, authorities gain legitimacy according to who they are, what they represent, what they do, and how they do it.

We argue that similar judgments are made *by authorities about societal groups*. These perceptions are in turn colored in at least two fundamental ways by the nature of the structuralist model. The first begins with the assumption that the market system—if left to its own devices—will produce an inequitable division of goods and income. Since these inequities are deeply rooted in the historical organization of international and national economies, it is reasonable to expect the "victims" of such a system to fight back to regain the losses they have suffered. Consequently, their appeals for government assistance are just because they represent attempts to redistribute resources that were inappropriately distributed by the market in the first place.

The second and related way refers to the distinction between original and propagating mechanisms for inflation. Labor sectors are to some extent responsible for inflation, since their demands for compensation are inflationary, as the structuralists admit. But because labor groups did not precipitate the problem in the first place, they are attributed less blame. Because their behavior is defensive in nature—an attempt to forestall further losses that arise from higher prices—their claims on the resources of the system are valid. The perception that labor demands are valid is an important link in understanding the structuralists' attitude toward coercion.

*Structuralism and repression.* Regimes partial to structural critiques are more apt to justify labor demands, given the presumption that such demands are defensive in nature and only secondary contributors to inflation. Still, could not demands of this nature complicate life for governments with finite resources and talents? The "problem-solving" capabilities of the authorities may decline, while requests for wage and employment compensation rise. The result would be a demand–performance gap that drives political opposition and destabilizes the regime. In this situation, and irrespective of economic ideology, popular sectors will be excluded and deactivated coercively.[10] In other words, repression is triggered once a critical gap is reached between political agitation and resource depletion.

A mobilized popular sector may well upset the balance between available resources and those required. The degree to which this becomes threatening is primarily a subjective—not objective—evaluation. The perception of a viable threat is lowered once claims are validated. Regimes partial to structuralism may still perceive conflicts of interest between themselves and popular sectors. The reforms they propose may not be far-reaching enough to satisfy more ideological and radical proponents of change. By the same token, they are less likely to perceive irreconcilable conflicts between themselves and the social groups seeking compensation than are those with nothing but disdain for such groups. Moreover, once they recognize the seriousness of structural impediments to development, they may want to deepen the reforms already under way. In that case, they would solidify their support among lower-income groups to provide themselves with a mandate for more ambitious undertakings. As the fiscal cost of spending rises, the political gains will rise even more rapidly. Hence, the regime will be more reluctant to resort to coercive tactics.

## Monetarism

*Foundations*. The theoretical elaborations of monetarism are normally associated with Milton Friedman, its chief disciple, and the University of Chicago. Friedman and other notable members of the Chicago School, including Harry Johnson, Arnold Harberger, and Robert Mundell, have been credited with developing models to account for spending patterns, price increases, and international goods and currency flows utilizing monetary variables.[11]

The more policy-oriented approach to monetarist thought took shape in the 1950s in the IMF's research department. As a result of contact with developing countries, and in an effort to design trade-promoting policies, the Fund investigators worked on models to adjust balance of payments, utilizing both monetarist and Keynesian principles. The Fund can be credited with making the first theoretical advances in a monetary approach to balance of payments, predating academia's contributions by some fifteen years.

These two centers of monetarist thinking have, in the last twenty-five years, come together to shape what are known as Third World orthodox stabilization programs. Economic stabilization has been defined by Andrew Crockett as "an improvement in the balance between supply and demand in an economy, aimed at moderating inflationary pressures and strengthening the balance of payments."[12] The orthodox strand qualifies the definition by locating the source of price and payment imbalances in the excessive growth of the money supply. Nonorthodox variations, such as the structuralist stabilization critique, also concern themselves with inflation and balance of payments disequilibrium but emphasize nonmonetary factors.

The monetarist position, as advocated by Friedman, narrowly focuses on regulating the growth rate of the money supply.[13] The monetarist label is somewhat misleading in the Third World context since its proponents are eclectic: in addition to calling for restrictive monetary policies, they have also endorsed strong fiscal measures and, in some cases, income measures as well. A typical IMF–monetarist proposal might include ceilings on bank credit, sharp cuts in budget deficits (particularly on the current account), removal of price controls and subsidies for publicly supported enterprises, devaluation of the currency, and limits on wage increases.[14] The emphasis, however, is on fiscal and monetary control.

The IMF–monetarist doctrine is set apart from its structuralist counterpart on general philosophical grounds as well as on more specific policy grounds. The monetarists are modern-day economic liberals with a belief in the dictum: governments that govern less govern better. Monetarists fervently advocate a free market and a laissez-faire state where the economy "reduces the range of issues that must be decided through political means."[15] The capitalist market, they maintain, is inherently stable, both domestically and internationally.

Whereas structuralists such as Prebisch urge governments in the Third World to intervene in order to shift comparative advantages from agriculture to manufacturing, the monetarists tell government to keep out and let the market reallocate resources in an "unbiased" fashion. The structuralists see inadequacies in the entrepreneurial class which is unwilling to save and invest productively; consequently, they urge the state to take on certain economic initiatives of its own. The monetarists counter that the productive capabilities of the free enterprise system are inherent, and that capitalists need only be freed from politically imposed constraints to be sufficiently motivated. Once capitalists receive proper price signals, resources will be efficiently reallocated to the most productive sectors, and overall output will increase. Governments may facilitate but not manage economic recovery, according to the monetarists. Consequently, the monetarists assign policymakers a *minimal* role in the task of promoting economic growth, income, employment, and external balance.

Structuralists locate inflationary pressures on the supply side; criticizing nonproductive capitalists for failing to expand output to meet the demands of a burgeoning urban population. In a reversal of structuralist logic, the monetarists claim structural bottlenecks are effects, not causes. The state robs the entrepreneur of profit-maximizing incentives when it intervenes to control prices and exchange rates. Landowners lose confidence in the economy, letting land lie fallow for tax purposes rather than increasing yields; industrialists invest in real estate rather than factories; exports are withheld, lowering the nation's imports of vital capital goods and thus preventing adequate growth.

Monetarists worry more about demand than supply. Inflationary spirals result from excess consumption of goods and services, which in turn is triggered by monetary expansion. Inflation, in Friedman's words, "is always and everywhere a monetary phenomenon, produced in the first instance by an unduly rapid growth in the quantity of money."[16] When the supply of money suddenly rises, individuals try to discard extra cash through spending, which raises nominal incomes and, of course, prices. In short, too much money chases too few goods. Friedman advises governments to maintain a relatively slow and stable growth in the money supply, consonant with the underlying natural rate of real growth in the economy.[17]

Monetarists are ultimately more preoccupied with the *origins* of inflation than its *levels*. They are sympathetic to "open" inflation, the result of price markups to correct the effects of previous control policies. However, inflation is not tolerated as a consequence of monetary mismanagement. In Latin America, monetary measures can seldom be taken independently of fiscal measures. No matter how sympathetic to monetarist doctrine, central bank officials cannot regulate credit emission without government cooperation. Governments are tempted to draw funds from the bank since they cannot raise revenues through the sale of treasury bonds or other financial intermediaries as easily as can be done in advanced industrial states. There is a closer correspondence between variations in the current and capital expenditure accounts of federal governments and the supply of credit in Latin America. Control of the federal deficit is as critical a component of the IMF–monetarist attack on inflation and balance of payments deficits as is the control of the money supply.

*Fiscal management and politics.* Governments often resort to deficit financing to counteract cyclical downturns in the economy. Greater spending, during recessionary times will, according to the Keynesian multiplier effect, trigger even greater consumption of goods and help to restore economic growth. But Friedman and other monetarists insist that governments have an easier time turning on the spending spigot then they have turning it off. Moreover, policymakers are poor predictors, inaccurately gauging the appropriate spending levels needed to restore sound growth. In their clumsy attempt to stabilize the economy, they may indeed destabilize it. Friedman says: "Far from being a balance wheel offsetting other forces making for fluctuations, the federal budget has if anything been itself a major source of disturbance and instability."[18]

Federal officials lack the knowledge effectively to adjust fiscal and monetary levers to stabilize an economy. As a result, Friedman advises government to adopt procedures that will lead to "reasonable stability in its flow of expenditures."[19] He continues:

> What we need is not a skillful monetary driver of the economic vehicle continuously turning the steering wheel to adjust to the unexpected irregularities of the route, but some means of keeping the monetary passenger who is in the back seat from occasionally leaning over and giving the steering wheel a jerk that threatens to send the car off the road.[20]

Of course as Gordon has demonstrated, federal expenditure is as much a political decision as it is an economic one. Governments must be sensitive to the pressing needs of mobilized constituents. This is particularly so during stagflationary periods, when nominal wage gains are eroded, employment opportunities are fewer, and the organized public clamors for some form of compensation from the state. In Latin America, the scene is familiar: organized wage-earning groups press the state to set minimum wage guidelines; to widen subsidies on a host of basic consumer goods; to provide more social services below cost; and to employ those thrown out of the private sector. State bureaucracies and payrolls often swell in response to an ever-expanding and increasingly frustrated wage-earning sector. Unfortunately, tax revenues will not keep pace with needed expenditures, and leaders must then weigh the political benefits of compensation against the economic costs of deficit spending.

The choice is not an easy one, but monetarist literature does not explicitly recognize the quandary facing the authorities. Policymakers are either praised for taking "rational" fiscal and monetary measures, or they are scorned for making "irrational" economic judgments. Rational actors are those who conform to theories that understand the inherently stable nature of the free enterprise system; governments act reasonably when they bring fiscal and monetary measures into harmony with the ebb and flow of the market. Irrational actors acquiesce to group pressures and then try to steer the economic vehicle with short-term, "knee-jerk" spending maneuvers. For the monetarists the choice is simple: the economic benefits of austerity clearly outweigh the political benefits of expenditure—strap the policymaking passenger down and level out fiscal expenditure and monetary emission. A balanced budget and a carefully regulated money supply are the keys to economic growth and stability. Besides, the monetarists claim, a strong capitalist economy will eventually achieve redistributive ends by allowing benefits to "trickle down" to special interest groups such as labor.

*Monetarism and repression.* Monetarist economists do not verbalize the political ramifications of fiscal austerity, but monetarism clearly carries a hidden political agenda in its seemingly neutral attacks on excessive spending. A government that insists on stabilizing and minimizing its economic functions in the face of continuously shifting and unpredictable demands of organized pressure groups must also be prepared to insulate itself from these pressures. Ultimately, the elites must constrain these partisan demands and might do so by force.

Governments are often unable to act like rational economic agents when confronted with labor pressures. Labor behaves unreasonably and in a self-defeating manner by attempting to force government to secure employment levels in the short run, which, the liberals argue, will lead to accelerated inflation and lower levels of employment in the long run.[21] In the interim, labor "irrationality" provokes economic instability and must not be tolerated.

The structuralists balance the costs and benefits of fiscal austerity with socially legitimate deficit spending. They reason that demands for spending are valid appeals for compensation against the inequities brought on by historically rooted inflation; consequently, the use of popular political influence is a legitimate means to redress these misfortunes. Monetarists reach alternate conclusions: freeing prices and restoring equilibrium in the balance of payments are paramount. Only market forces can insure long-term stable growth in the economy; only rational behavior—which minimizes the scope and intensity of economic "steering"—can allow the free enterprise system to function in an uninhibited fashion. The costs of supplying inflation clearly outweigh the benefits. Where politically generated demands force misguided and ultimately dangerous state policies, and political authorities are prevented from acting rationally or in the best interest of the system as a whole, then something must be done to constrain those demands and to free government from the burdens imposed on it. This provides a strong motivation to use coercion against organized labor.

According to Milton Friedman, the market is not simply the most efficient mechanism for allocating resources; it is the foundation for societal freedom.[22] It provides an arena in which dissenters and minorities can sell their ideas without fear of retaliation from tyrannical majorities. Attempts to limit individual freedoms will fail, since there will always be buyers willing to pay a price for unpopular ideas (e.g., Hollywood continued to hire writers and directors in the 1950s even after they were blacklisted, as Friedman points out).

To tolerate labor pressure means to accept the resultant threats to price and payments equilibrium, and eventually to the free market system itself. Since, according to the monetarists, the market is the basis for overall freedom in society, labor demands are clearly illegitimate: they endanger the very normative standards upon which society rests. Paradoxically, once that position is accepted, a government can claim that its resort to coercion is in defense of freedom. By closing off channels of popular political influence, policymakers may again perform "rationally." As the money supply comes under greater control, and fiscal behavior is stabilized, the twin hurdles to economic growth and development—inflation and balance of payments deficits—are overcome. The utility of coercive acts is also maximized, as monetarist-oriented regimes solidify their tenure by promoting economic efficiency and growth.

The foregoing discussion has provided a set of pathways from economic arguments to political outcomes. A word of caution is in order: these are not inevitable pathways, but they are likely ones. There is, in other words, a greater probability that monetarist-minded regimes would resort to political repression than would those guided by structuralist critiques. And yet, the political context within which these economic plans are drawn may modify the choice of policy in various ways. There is no simple one-to-one correspondence between economic bias and political preference, as subsequent chapters will make evident.

## NOTES

1. For a representative sample of economic writing on the subject see: Dudley Seers, "A Theory of Inflation and Growth in Underdeveloped Economies Based on the Experience of Latin America," *Oxford Economic Papers* 16 (1962): 173–195; Robert Campos, "Two Views on Inflation in Latin America," in *Latin American Issues*, ed. Albert O. Hirschman (New York: Twentieth Century Fund, 1961); Werner Baer, "The Inflation Controversy in Latin America: A Survey," *Latin American Research Review* 2 (Spring 1967): 3–25; Susan M. Wachter, *Latin American Inflation: The Structuralist-Monetarist Debate* (Lexington: Lexington Books, 1976).

2. For a basic structuralist text, see United Nations Commission for Latin America, *Development Problems in Latin America* (New York: United Nations, 1970); also see Osvaldo Sunkel, "Inflation in Chile: An Unorthodox Approach," *International Economic Papers* 10 (London, 1960): 107–131, and various issues of the CEPAL review.

3. Richard E. Caves and Ronald W. Jones, *World Trade and Payments: An Introduction* (Boston: Little, Brown, 1973).

4. For a structuralist approach to inflation, see Rosemary Thorp, "Inflation and the Financing of Economic Development," in *Financing Development in Latin America*, ed. Keith Griffin (London: Macmillan Press, 1971).

5. Wachter, *Latin American Inflation*, pp. 9–15.

6. Thorp, in Griffin, ed., *Financing Development*, pp. 107–210.

7. Sunkel, "Inflation in Chile," p. 111.

8. Robert Gordon, "The Demand for and Supply of Inflation," *Journal of Law and Economics* 18 (1975): 807–835; and for a related argument, see John H. Goldthorpe, "The Current Inflation: Towards a Sociological Account," in *The Political Economy of Inflation*, ed. Fred Hirsch and John H. Goldthorpe (Cambridge: Harvard University Press, 1979), pp. 186–214.

9. Gordon, "Demand for and Supply of Inflation," pp. 811, 825–827, 830–833.

10. Guillermo O'Donnell, *Modernization and Bureaucratic-Authoritarianism: Studies in South American Politics* (Berkeley: Institute of International Studies, 1979) p. 91.

11. Milton Friedman, *Dollars and Deficits: Inflation, Monetary Policy and the Balance of Payments* (Englewood Cliffs: Prentice Hall, 1968).

12. Andrew D. Crockett, "Stabilization Policies in Developing Countries: Some Policy Considerations," *IMF Papers* 28 (March 1981): 54.

13. Milton Friedman, "The Role of Monetary Policy," *The American Economic Review* 58 (March 1968): 14–17.

14. Free market advocates operate according to efficiency criteria. In that vein, wage rates will be adjusted to reflect the value added of the products workers could produce elsewhere. Since these opportunity costs are lower in countries with high unemployment, the application of efficiency criteria will suppress the wage rate. For more on this see John Sheahan, "Market-oriented Economic Policies and Political Repression in Latin America," *Economic Development and Cultural Change* 28 (January 1980): 274–275.

15. Milton Friedman, *Capitalism and Freedom* (Chicago: University of Chicago Press, 1962).

16. Friedman, *Dollars and Deficits*, p. 18.

17. Friedman, "Role of Monetary Policy."

18. Friedman, *Capitalism and Freedom*, p. 77.

19. Ibid.

20. Ibid.

21. Paul Samuelson, *Economics* (New York: McGraw-Hill, 1976), pp. 831–835.

22. Friedman, *Capitalism and Freedom.*

# 3
# The International Monetary Fund

Ideas know no national boundaries. They are easily disseminated throughout the international system—particularly with respect to North-South flows, where the cultural hegemony of the advanced states encourages the best and the brightest of the Third World to emigrate to the finest universities of the First World. The knowledge they gain is likely to be more suited to the needs of those core states but is nonetheless transported and superimposed upon divergent systems within the periphery. These ideas may be entirely inappropriate to the conditions of an impoverished Third World country—nonetheless, they often gain acceptance by ruling elites.

The international supply of knowledge has also been historically uneven and limited. A few knowledge-producing centers have gained recognition by virtue of their oligopolistic control over resources and intellect. An LDC hard pressed for solutions to critical problems will often take cues from the "authorities." In the absence of attractive "home-grown" options, policymakers will look to external sources for guidance. In this sense, the international origins of ideas become an important object of study; one particular multilateral financial institution that has been a significant source of ideas for these countries—the International Monetary Fund—is examined in this chapter. The IMF's influence upon Latin American economic policy has been considerable. Much is currently known about the relationship between the Fund and debt-ridden borrowers of Latin America; our understanding of the origins of Fund influence is less extensive. During the debt crisis of the 1970s, Peru and Argentina were subject to tremendous pressures to conform to the Fund's formula for economic recovery. They frantically tried to keep pace with annual interest payments on private bank loans, while struggling to satisfy domestic constituencies. But this dilemma is not new to either country; by the late 1950s Peruvian and Argentine elites were struggling to balance similarly competing claims, under the duress of economic crisis. Each country was trying to satisfy tough IMF conditions and grapple with politically delicate circumstances. Why had the Fund become so influential with domestic policymakers? And what were the factors that persuaded the heads of state to adopt the Fund's brand of economics?

## CONSENSUS AND CONFLICT IN DEFINING A PURPOSE

By the advent of World War II, there was generally widespread agreement that a new multilateral monetary framework was needed to replace the anarchical arrangements that had brought on the great depressions of the 1930s. The gold standard had worked relatively well where countries played by the rules of the game: deficit countries would sell off the precious commodity, an act that, according to the quantity theory of money, would lower prices as well. Lower prices would encourage exports and reduce imports. Surplus traders would import gold, raising internal prices and fostering increased imports; in principle, equilibrium between trading partners would thereby be obtained. However, problems arose when governments intervened in this otherwise automatic adjustment process to counter price effects. The United States and France experienced trade surpluses in the late 1920s yet tightened credit to keep prices from rising. Gold continued to flow into these countries until shortages elsewhere led to a run on gold in London. Britain was forced to abandon gold convertibility, and the system collapsed.

During the depression, countries resorted to devaluations to correct deficits, rather than subject themselves to contractive measures, which would have reduced employment levels even further. Unfortunately, other nations retaliated in an international system already fraught with uncertainty and mistrust. These competitive devaluations led to trade restrictions that only aggravated the depression.

It was with this historical context in mind that financial and political leaders met at Bretton Woods in 1944 to chart a new course for international monetary management. There they established the IMF to provide a facility for extending credit to countries experiencing temporary shortfalls in export revenue. The Fund was primarily intended to give members the confidence to make adjustments in their balance of payments without jeopardizing internal growth or world trade.[1] Secondarily, it would enhance cooperation among member states through a permanent institution designed to promote expanded world trade, exchange stability, and shortened periods of disequilibrium.[2] John Maynard Keynes's original blueprint for the Fund envisioned an international clearing union that would cushion borrowers against the potentially disruptive effects of balance of trade deficits. This would insure that they could borrow liberally against their quota and thus ride out temporary external imbalances. Debtors would owe foreign exchange to the union, not to any one country; nations in surplus would be rewarded by accumulating credit, which would be reusable by debtor nations, rather than being withdrawn from circulation as was often the case with gold.[3]

Both Keynes and his U.S. counterpart, Harry White, agreed that exchange controls and devaluations should be avoided. New members were obliged to maintain their currencies within a par value range to be established by international agreement. Members would consult with the Fund should they desire to diverge from par, but divergence was strongly discouraged. Prohibitions against controls or devaluations raised the question as to how deficit-ridden countries would attain external balance. Classical theory suggested that countries in this situation pursue contractive policies, but this was precisely what Keynes was trying to avoid. It was for purposes of overcoming this contradiction that Keynes and others argued that the new agency should extend credit more liberally to deficit states, which would have the effect of forestalling exchange restrictions or devaluations while permitting domestic expansion.

The IMF charter held that the organization was not responsible for counselling members on appropriate domestic policies as preconditions for drawings. As long as they accepted the basic purposes of the Fund, they could borrow freely within the limits imposed by their respective quotas. The Fund's objectives made specific reference only to the need for exchange stability, decontrol, and avoidance of competitive devaluations. Nations had to accept the ground rules for the new international economic order; but these were limiting only with regard to *external*—not *internal*—adjustments.

The articles of agreement specify the Fund's purpose:

> To give confidence to members by making the Fund's resources available to them under adequate safeguards, thus providing them with opportunity to correct maladjustments in their balance of payments without resorting to measures destructive of *national* or international prosperity [emphasis mine].[4]

Article IV, section 5f, says that changes in par values "cannot be objected to because of domestic, social or political policies of the member proposing the change."[5] The benefit of automatic drawing was, according to Keynes, to give rebuilding nations the confidence that credit was available, thus increasing confidence in the new multilateral system as a whole. IMF conditionality or surveillance would only deter nations from participating and foster a return to bilateralism and economic instability. It followed that Keynes was also concerned with maintaining the impartiality of the multilateral institution. For a group of politically and economically diverse nations to part with valuable foreign exchange meant that the organization's directors would have to put aside narrow interests for the sake of the international good. Therefore, there was basic agreement not only about the rules governing international lending and liquidity, but also about the norms and principles governing the Bretton Woods system as well: *free trade and domestic expansion were compatible and legitimate goals*.[6]

During the reconstruction period of the late 1940s and early 1950s, this made perfect sense. Inflationary pressures were negligible, and with countries operating well below productive capacity, mild price increases were welcome signs of economic recovery and growth. Yet, even in the midst of this recovery, certain parties within the Fund began to resurrect classical arguments about the need for domestic contraction to counterbalance trade deficits. These parties minimized the external origins of balance of payments disequilibrium, instead dwelling on domestic factors.[7] They agreed to the norms of free trade, but now a disagreement surfaced concerning the principle of state-led growth: domestic expansion was a right reserved for the advanced states; however, demand management was to be an obligation for less developed countries. If this were to become official policy, it would challenge the liberal credit philosophy envisioned by Keynes: LDC preferences for state-led growth and social reform would be held hostage to balance of payments adjustment. It also called into question the legitimate role of the Fund: where would the IMF's attempt to facilitate national prosperity end, and its attempt to influence national policymakers begin? At first, these internal debates, which surfaced in the early 1950s, did not alter the Fund's relations with LDC members. One scholar, commenting about the Fund during that time, stated: "In any clash between the external and internal economic interests of members it would be the former which would go by default, leaving the Fund to advise, cajole or threaten, not very convincingly."[8]

But by 1958, the IMF's influence had risen dramatically, and few developing countries could ignore its demands. A host of Latin American states, including Argentina and Peru, had succumbed to orthodox stabilization programs at the prodding of the Fund. The IMF staff was intimately involved in formulating detailed policies and targets for member states, holding out the prospects of enormous foreign exchange aid in return for compliance. How and why had the Fund's power over domestic policymaking within LDCs grown so much? And why did demand management become the standard by which creditworthy members were judged?

## STATE AND CLASS POWER

One potential explanation for the IMF's rising influence lies in the role of a dominant state power. It can be argued that as the supreme political, military and economic power of its time, the United States utilized its post–World War II position to orient the Fund's policies and philosophies so as to further its own interests. There are two analytically distinct approaches within this general theory.

### State Power

The state power perspective[9] treats the state as an autonomous actor, whose goals transcend those of any particular interest group or class. As a result, the state develops a set of coherent strategies to maximize *national*, not class, interests. A global system of such actors shapes the form and content of international organizations for self-serving ends, so that multilateral institutions are dependent entities that operate to serve independent states.

A dominant power could use the IMF to promote free trade practices.[10] States with highly productive and competitive economies are at an advantage in the world market: products can be manufactured more efficiently and sold in greater volume, thereby increasing export revenues (assuming price elasticity). Strong domestic industries can operate without tariffs, thereby improving a nation's balance of trade. Product diversity will shield economies from price fluctuations in any one commodity.

Free trade may increase benefits to the world as a whole, but it may distribute them unequally, with benefits normally flowing to states with greater market power. While unequal market power is a contradiction in terms within the neoclassical framework, it makes sense within a political economy framework: a state can utilize trade to increase its economic strength,[11] procuring reliable trading partners through colonial or neocolonial domination. These client states become dependent on the powerful actor for supplies of vital goods, thereby precluding retaliatory measures through protectionism. The superordinate state insures itself a steady flow of low prices, raw materials, and access to Third World markets for its finished goods. It can shift its demand for a single commodity between competing, yet dependent, weak states, and consequently lower the trading price of that commodity; its own monopoly on important finished or intermediary goods precludes its trading partners from exerting similar pressures in return. Hence, the stronger power will profit from terms of trade and reliability of supplies.

### Class Power

In a class-analysis approach,[12] state power is utilized not for national but for class-based interests; the state is either a relatively autonomous or nonautonomous actor. In general, the state's behavior reflects the changing priorities of domestic actors, and it functions as an intervening variable between corporate agents and international institutions. A strong state would manipulate these institutions to promote policies beneficial to domestic entrepreneurs. For instance, the IMF's encouragement of free convertibility of currencies would facilitate profit remittance to corporations doing business abroad.

Class-based analyses of IMF policies emphasize the important relation between the Fund's anti-inflationary austerity programs and corporate investment.[13] The assumption is that anti-inflationary strategies in developing countries benefit multinational investors. They believe that lower inflation facilitates long-term planning by increasing confidence in returns to capital investment; local credit restraint favors foreign conglomerates that have ample sources of external funds; restricted wages of course help increase profits. On the other hand, tight monetary and fiscal policies reduce incomes and thus contract markets for corporate goods, the same difficulty presented in the state power argument. This time, shrinking demand within LDCs will reduce imports from the advanced countries and hurt their balance of trade. Nevertheless, recessionary measures are logical corollaries to free trade preferences. Overvalued currencies only tempt nations to control imports as exports sales decline. Since overvaluation is often induced by rising prices, the state power thesis would approve of austerity measures for deficit-prone trading partners.

## The IMF and the United States

If the IMF has been an expression of state and class power, could the Fund have *enhanced* such power as well? The empirical test would be to discover congruence between IMF policy outcomes on one hand and trade and investment gains on the other. Naturally, it is conceivable that U.S. power increased during the 1950s independently of the Fund; that gains to traders or investors doing business with Fund members could have materialized without the Fund playing a causal role. This leads us to ask: to what extent did U.S. power manifest itself and develop *within* the institution? Is there evidence that U.S. leverage over other members helped transform the institution into a tool of state or corporate power? If that were true, we should see some relation between the dramatic rise in IMF influence in 1957–1958 and the variations in strong state power within the Fund.

At the close of the Savannah Conference of 1946, few denied that the United States had emerged as a dominant force. Shortly after the conference, Keynes lamented the fact that Washington had used steamrolling tactics to imprint its preferences on the institution's future activities.[14] Not only had the United States emerged unscathed from World War II, but its currency had become the most sought after in the world, reflecting an underlying economy that was growing by leaps and bounds. Its capital was chosen as the site for the IMF headquarters. The geographic proximity of the Fund to the center of state power had more than symbolic significance: it reflected the strength of the U.S. vote within the organization. By virtue of its enormous quota based on national income, gold and dollar balances, and contributions to world trade, the United States commanded a 30 percent voting share by 1950.

The United States used the dollar to its advantage: by withholding credit from the Fund and attempting to obstruct its operations, its representative tried to maneuver other directors toward its position. One of Washington's main objectives was to promote greater conditionality in lending, and by 1955, the IMF had fully accepted the concept of conditional borrowing as embodied in the standby loan. Standby agreements provided borrowers with advance lines of credit for a full year, so countries could actually count future funds as part of their overall reserves. Should their economies improve in that time, the credit would not have to be released. Each member's quota was accessed through credit tranches. Drawings within the first tranche were nearly automatic; but the 1955 ruling made drawing beyond the first tranche progressively more difficult. The ruling stated that "the larger the drawing in relation to a member's quota, the stronger is the justification required of the member;"[15] by 1958, the policies for higher tranche drawings were finalized:

> Requests for transactions beyond these limits require substantial justification. They are likely to be favorably received when the drawings or standbys are intended to support a sound program aimed at establishing or maintaining the enduring stability of the member's currency at a realistic rate of exchange.[16]

"Sound program" was a reference to appropriate *domestic* measures, which would prevent currencies diverging from their market values.

The legal changes that were made a permanent feature of the organization did not manifest themselves in practical leverage over LDC members until 1957. Hence, while U.S. power was increasing within the institution, the IMF remained in a distinctly moribund state during the first half of the 1950s. Its influence was limited in the main by its inability to secure drawing arrangements with its members. Between 1952 and 1956, only four countries used standby arrangements for a total of U.S. $325 million in loans.[17] Even for those who did reach terms, the Fund's impact on internal policy was negligible.

Provisions on domestic policy preferences were not precise. The first formal set of terms was laid out in a 1954 agreement with Peru. This included a commitment by the Central Bank to "conduct its exchange operations within a range which would promote equilibrium in the balance of payments" and to consult the Fund should it wish to alter that range.[18] The Fund stated only *general* preferences for credit restraint and deflationary fiscal measures, and these ideas were seldom worked into the body of the actual agreements. In fact, until 1957, most standby agreements were oral. Without specificity written into contracts, countries could still pursue a wide range of domestic policies without fear of retribution from the Fund.

To summarize: by the late 1940s, the United States had indisputably become the major power within the IMF, by virtue of its large voting share and ownership over the dollar, in demand internationally. It successfully coerced other members to support increased conditionality. Washington's influence helped create a more interventionist Fund, one willing to challenge borrowers' domestic priorities and to threaten credit blockades should desired changes not materialize. To that extent, the power thesis seems to be a useful, and, perhaps necessary, ingredient in an adequate accounting of Fund influences in the developing world. But the power analysis fails to tie up all the loose ends. U.S. hegemony had been well established by the late 1940s, yet the United States gained little leverage over LDCs in the early and mid-1950s through the use of the IMF. Power cannot explain why the IMF's influence over domestic policymakers in Third World (particularly Latin American) states had become so impressive by 1957–1958, with no apparent rise in U.S. dominance at that time, either within the Fund or without. Actually, U.S. economic power suffered a large decline in 1958, as the country found itself in the throes of a severe recession. Unemployment, which had averaged 4.2 percent over the previous three years, rose to 6.8 percent, the highest figure since 1941. Gross national product (GNP), after years of steady growth, declined in real terms by 2.2 percent in 1958.

What about the consequences of IMF–induced austerity measures? If these measures benefited U.S. national and corporate interests in the end, then (plausibly) the years of patient and persuasive pressure by the strong state had finally paid off. In that case, the power/interests analyses would apply. An examination of trade data indicates that after a period of increased exports from the United States to Latin America between 1953 and 1957, export sales declined by over 22 percent from 1958 to 1962.[19] Even when divided between finished goods and intermediate capital goods, similar patterns are revealed. One might have expected U.S. capital goods products to show great improvement at a time when Latin American states depended on foreign inputs and when multiple exchange rates often discriminated against luxury goods in favor of capital.

U.S. exports to Latin American states that underwent stabilization programs from 1958 to 1962 show either absolute declines or rates of increase that were, on average, less than those experienced in the four years prior to standby arrangements (1954 to 1957), as shown in Table 3.1. For each year between 1958 and 1960, Chile bought more goods from the United States, but the rate of increase was less than during 1954–1957. Brazil showed real declines in U.S. imports from 1958 to 1960; Colombia showed a temporary increase from 1958 to 1960, and a decline from 1961 to 1962. Only Peru registered a demand for imports that exceeded the 1954–1957 levels. Finally, the U.S. share of each country's (except Argentinas) total imports declined steadily after 1958, and the U.S. portion of Latin America's imports in general declined steadily from 22.9 percent in 1958 to 14.8 percent in 1962.[20]

Conceivably, U.S. exports fared poorly because austerity programs were providing conditions attractive enough to convince investors to establish subsidiaries abroad and to forego exportation. Figures on net capital outflows from the United States to Latin America and reinvested subsidiary earnings show no significant changes from 1952 to 1962. The same can be said for flows to the stabilization nations in particular, with the exception of Argentina which did show sizable increases from 1959 on (see Table 3.2).

The data cannot confirm either a state power or class power analysis. The U.S. economy grew consistently stronger after the 1958 recession, and U.S. products and businesses found markets in Europe and elsewhere. But this was not the case in the Latin American states that had agreed to standby arrangements with the Fund.

## MARKET FORCES

Conceivably, laws of supply and demand forced deficit states into tighter relations with the Fund. If trade balances had deteriorated, generating deficits on the current account and a loss of international reserves, an LDC could have become dependent on foreign lenders. This would occur when the loss of reserves made capital importation so prohibitive as to deter domestic investment. Inflationary financing of domestic programs and subsidization of industry would become less desirable for balance of payments reasons. In this

**Table 3.1 Imports from the United States by Latin American States with Stabilization Programs (annual index of imports with 1952 = 100)**

| Year | Argentina | Chile | Peru | Brazil | Colombia | Bolivia |
|---|---|---|---|---|---|---|
| 1952 | 100.0 | 100.0 | 100.0 | 100.0 | 100.0 | 100.0 |
| 1953 | 62.5 | 92.7 | 98.1 | 43.6 | 121.1 | 58.1 |
| 1954 | 67.1 | 73.3 | 80.2 | 63.9 | 151.3 | 65.1 |
| 1955 | 71.3 | 84.3 | 92.6 | 36.8 | 150.5 | 72.1 |
| 1956 | 106.5 | 84.3 | 110.5 | 42.4 | 145.5 | 88.4 |
| 1957 | 142.1 | 119.4 | 117.3 | 65.4 | 103.6 | 100.0 |
| 1958 | 94.0 | 111.5 | 96.9 | 57.6 | 84.6 | 86.0 |
| 1959 | 88.4 | 114.7 | 81.5 | 55.1 | 89.2 | 65.1 |
| 1960 | 151.4 | 125.1 | 101.2 | 52.9 | 106.1 | 72.1 |
| 1961 | 177.3 | 123.6 | 127.2 | 61.4 | 105.0 | 69.8 |
| 1962 | 184.3 | 103.1 | 131.5 | 54.6 | 101.4 | — |

*Sources*: United Nations Statistical Office, *Statistical Yearbook*, 1962, pp. 428–429; 1963, pp. 450–451. United Nations, *U.N. Yearbook of International Trade Statistics*, 1954, pp. 41, 74, 81, 123, 134, 430; 1958, pp. 61, 90, 96, 145, 153, 424; 1962, pp. 56, 81, 91, 150, 160, 553.

**Table 3.2 U.S. Direct Investment in Latin American Countries with Stabilization Programs (net capital outflow in millions of U.S. dollars)**

| Year | Argentina | Chile | Peru | Brazil | Colombia |
|---|---|---|---|---|---|
| 1952 | 8 | 37 | 13 | 125 | 20 |
| 1953 | 4 | 26 | 39 | 35 | 1 |
| 1954 | (3)[a] | (28) | (13) | 8 | 33 |
| 1955 | 9 | 1 | 7 | 30 | 16 |
| 1956 | 10 | 34 | 40 | 45 | 24 |
| 1957 | 15 | 24 | 47 | 48 | 9 |
| 1958 | 8 | 25 | 29 | 26 | (2) |
| 1959 | 50 | 35 | 18 | 34 | 11 |
| 1960 | 70 | 2 | 7 | 83 | 15 |
| 1961 | 104 | (15) | 14 | 7 | (7) |
| 1962 | 96 | 13 | 14 | 14 | 21 |

*Source*: U.S. Department of Commerce, *Survey of Current Business* 34 (November 1954), p. 9; 35 (August 1955), p. 19; 37 (August 1957), p. 24; 39 (August 1959), p. 30; 41 (August 1961), p. 22; 42 (August 1962), p. 22; 43 (August 1963), p. 18; 44 (August 1964), p. 10.

[a]Figures in parentheses reflect capital flows plus transfers between primary and secondary foreign affiliates.

position, LDCs would look for noninflationary foreign aid to help cover deficits and to protect ongoing programs. Bilateral aid was scarce in the 1950s, as was credit from private banks. The IMF's near monopoly on credit and its ability to pry loose alternative sources gave it considerable leverage over members. Consequently, as demand for credit increased, the IMF could logically exact a heavier price for the privilege of borrowing. In this circumstance, one could expect to see harsher conditionality and greater oversight.

Many Latin American regimes of the early 1950s utilized export revenues to fuel economic expansion and subsidize social welfare programs. When the Korean war ended and demand for raw materials subsided, these regimes drew on accumulated reserves to sustain their programs. Foreign exchange reserves were soon depleted, but not the commitment to fulfill popular demands through inflationary financing (since tax structures were inadequate). To lessen the regressive impact of rising prices on wage earners, populist governments resorted to price controls, subsidies, and periodic wage adjustments. When internal inflationary pressures upset the balance of payments, many Latin American states turned to trade controls, or more often to multiple exchange rates. Frequently, these measures were not enough to narrow the foreign exchange gap. When inflationary growth schemes finally caused political problems for these governments, the attraction of non-inflationary borrowing became self-evident.

From 1954 to 1959, market forces undeniably worked against the primary producing nations of Latin America. During this time, the net value of Latin American exports declined by 20.1 percent, while the value of imports declined by only 1.2 percent, resulting in an uneven but persistent decline in Latin America's terms of trade, from an indexed value of 133.8 in 1954 to 109.5 in 1959 (Table 3.3).[21] Meanwhile, the IMF experienced a tremendous surge in drawings during 1956–1957. Borrowing during this time equaled $1.478 billion, greater than all preceding drawings in the nine and one-half years of Fund operations. Concurrently, $1.2 billion in standby loans was approved, compared to $325 million in the previous three years. Nineteen standbys were inaugurated or renewed with fourteen countries from 1956 to 1957, as opposed to nine standbys with four countries from 1952 to 1955.[22] To handle the larger requests for balance of payments financing, the Fund's executive directors approved a 50 percent increase in quotas for all members in December 1958.[23]

The association between trade difficulties and IMF activity is compelling but somewhat misleading. A closer examination of the terms of trade figures for the stabilization countries weakens the market approach. First, the loss of export revenues in 1958 was part of a pattern that had begun in 1954. Second, though many countries experienced their steepest drop in relative prices in 1958, these figures were not known until after standby loans were signed, and fiscal and monetary programs were designed. Reserve losses are of

**Table 3.3 Terms of Trade for Latin American Countries with Stabilization Programs (base year 1958 = 100)[a]**

| Year | Total Latin America | Argentina | Chile | Peru | Brazil | Colombia | Bolivia |
|---|---|---|---|---|---|---|---|
| 1954 | 133.8 | n.a. | n.a. | n.a. | 127 | 153 | 102 |
| 1955 | 126 | 109 | 128 | 121 | 99 | 124 | 100 |
| 1956 | 124.9 | 100 | 141 | 126 | 99 | 114 | 104 |
| 1957 | 129.2 | 102 | 113 | 122 | 104 | 122 | 104 |
| 1958 | 119.7 | 100 | 100 | 100 | 100 | 100 | 100 |
| 1959 | 109.5 | 111 | 107 | 96 | 84 | 93 | 106 |
| 1960 | 107.3 | 118 | 123 | 89 | 85 | 96 | 106 |
| 1961 | 104.7 | 108 | 122 | 86 | 84 | 91 | 114 |
| 1962 | 99.1 | 92 | 118 | 87 | 78 | n.a. | n.a. |

*Sources*: United Nations, Economic Commission on Latin America, *Boletin Estadístico de América Latina* 1 (March 1964):122. *Statistical Abstract of Latin America* 20 (1981):410.
[a]For the total Latin America column, 1970 = 100.

course cumulative, and by 1958, these Latin American states were feeling the pinch of several years of decline. The market analysis alone is insufficient because it cannot account for the timing of Fund influence over domestic programs, which became considerable in 1957 and 1958. It also fails to identify the characteristics of this new relationship between international financial elites and domestic policymakers. Certainly, states were lured to the Fund by virtue of their trade disadvantages. But once there, what would be demanded of them? The power analysis explains the institutional evolution of conditionality and interventionism; market analysis explains, in part, the greater lending activity of the Fund. Both help to define the form of IMF–LDC relations, but not its contents; neither adequately predicts the watershed years of IMF influence.

For these reasons, we turn to a discussion about the role of ideas in international institutions. Specifically, we shall consider the development of balance of payments theories during the post–World War II era in hopes of uncovering some important connections between economic concepts and the exact nature of the relations between the Fund and its LDC clients.

## ECONOMIC THEORY AND CONDITIONALITY

In 1957, the operative clauses within standby arrangements were changed in two fundamental ways: first, the receipt of standby loans was tied to fiscal and monetary objectives; second, the objectives (which were often binding) were quantified in the form of specific ceilings and targets. For instance, a standby loan with Paraguay in July 1957 included the following two clauses:

> If at any time before January 1, 1958, the credit ceiling as described in ——— is exceeded, Paraguay will not draw further amounts under this standby arrangement before consulting the Fund and obtaining its consent.
>
> If, at any time before January 1, 1958, the government of Paraguay exceeds the maximum commitment level for ordinary budget expenditures or the maximum level for the implementation of the four year public works program as described in the annexed report, Paraguay will not draw further amounts under this standby arrangement before consulting the Fund and obtaining its consent.[24]

After this loan, stipulation of precise policy goals spread quickly. By 1959, most standby credit agreements included similar language. Some executive directors within the Fund were clearly troubled by the Paraguayan loan, believing that should a precedent be set, the Fund would most assuredly cross the line from a multinational manager of liquidity to an international policeman. Indeed a precedent was set, which to this day imprints itself on IMF policies.

In 1958, Argentina, Peru, Chile, Bolivia, Brazil, Colombia, and Paraguay obtained standby loans, all characterized by strict conditionality.[25] Never before had so many countries receiving so much credit been subjected to such obligatory measures. To understand these facts, we must back up and briefly trace the development of theory and its relation to research activity within the IMF.

Macroeconomics in the post–World War II years was clearly dominated by John Maynard Keynes's theories on income and employment. Attention was given to internal economies, but theories on external equilibrium were also affected by Keynes's work. Prior to Keynes, the classical price-specie flow theory offered the most acceptable explanation for balance of payments adjustment.[26] The classical model assigned to money a central role in the overall adjustment process. Keynesian theory reduced money's role in external balance; Keynes argued that wages and prices had a tendency to be rigid in the downward direction. Hence, changes in the money supply could affect output and employment as well as, or instead of, prices. If that were the case, then strong positive correlations between money supply and price would be weakened. The Keynesian approach attached more significance to interest rates, investment decisions, income, and consumption patterns. For instance, the income–expenditure approach said that a contraction of credit combined with higher interest rates would produce increased capital inflows and lower imports in the following manner: the higher rates would lure in foreign funds and choke off investment and, through the multiplier effect, reduce incomes. Since imports were, in the Keynesian framework, directly associated with income levels, they, too, would decline.[27]

The income-expenditure approach worked with the assumption of fixed or pegged exchange rates; the elasticity approach began with a depreciating currency. Once a currency is devalued, the nation's products appear to be less expensive to foreign purchasers. *If* demand is sufficiently price-sensitive (elastic), then a devaluation would help the trade balance once goods became cheaper on world markets. Likewise, elasticity of imports must be sufficient such that higher prices would discourage purchases enough to restore trade balances.[28]

In 1952, Sidney Alexander, working within the IMF research division, demonstrated that changes in output and consumption were just as important in determining the impact of a devaluation on the balance of payments as were price and elasticity changes.[29] He began with a new assumption: the balance of trade would be equal to the difference between output and absorption. Output meant new economic activity generated by export revenues. Absorption equaled consumption plus investment and was linked to increases in income. Where output exceeded absorption, balance of trade would be in surplus; where absorption exceeded output, deficits would arise.

Naturally, output and absorption would offset each other were a devaluation to trigger a chain reaction of industrial growth, income, consumption, importation, and deficits. The impact would depend on the marginal propensity to consume. Alexander thought that where absorption was less than unity, foreign trade balances would improve after devaluation. He also reasoned that devaluations would contribute to trade surplus more effectively when an economy was at less than full employment. Otherwise, trading prices would lead only to higher domestic prices, stimulating import purchases.

Alexander's model contained an element of uncertainty that troubled Fund economists. If, for instance, output could not keep pace with added consumption, excess absorption would nullify the price effect of a devaluation. There was also a great reluctance to put faith in exchange rate flexibility, given the preferences of the Bretton Woods system for par values. The absorption approach would work only if there were no competitive devaluations between trading partners. In the late 1940s and early 1950s that possibility was still of great concern to financial planners; hence the discussion within the Fund moved from exchange rate to internal adjustment models. If the real problem was to prevent absorption from surpassing output, why not concentrate on limiting demand through monetary and fiscal measures?

Part of this search for new theory within the IMF was induced by policy considerations.[30] The Keynesian approach may have made sense theoretically, but it posed certain problems for financial policymakers. For one, information requirements were considerable; data was needed on investment decisions, multipliers, consumption propensities, and national income accounts. Measurement posed an even greater problem, according to the IMF. Investment responses to interest rates were difficult to predict; national income accounts, necessary to ascertain the income absorption effect, were inaccurate and not readily available to many LDCs in the 1950s (and are still unreliable today, according to one Fund official). On the other hand, central banks had fairly accurate and extensive monetary data, raising the possibility of resurrecting the money supply variable, assuming that some definite relations could be discerned between it and the balance of payments.

The need to provide a theoretically coherent yet manageable system for balance of payments adjustment propelled Fund research into monetary models. These efforts became quite extensive in the mid-1950s. J. J. Polak, an economist working for the Fund, published an article in the 1957 IMF staff papers—"Monetary Analysis of Income Formation and Payments Problems."[31] He acknowledged already existing theoretical work that linked anti-inflationary policy to balance of payments stability. What was lacking, in his view, was a quantitative basis for associating a given increase in credit with a given deficit. How, in other words, might one predict trade imbalances given changes in money supply?

In line with classical theory, Polak made two assumptions: that velocity of money was constant; and that excess cash balances are spent, not held. He retained Keynes's relations between income levels and marginal propensities to import but added a new dimension: money supply and income were positively correlated. Polak based his assumption on empirical observations of data from many countries over a five-year period. Polak used bank credit rather than money supply as an exogenous variable in his equation. He made this substitution because of the difficulty in controlling for money in an open economy affected by capital flows. For practical policy reasons, bank credit could be more easily manipulated.

Polak's model showed how and to what extent excessive expansion of central bank credit would lead to balance of payments deficits, given a corresponding increase in income. Income expansion would foster spending which would outstrip domestic output, thus spilling over into imports. Like Alexander's income-absorption approach, Polak's model warned of the dangers to the balance of payments if output and expenditure remained unbalanced. Unlike Alexander, who relied on the expansionary effects of a devaluation, Polak favored domestic contraction.

As far as the Fund was concerned, the model had tremendous policy relevance. Its reliance on monetary data systematically recorded by central banks greatly reduced the information requirements of previous models and made it highly usable; its parsimonious treatment of variables contributed to its simplicity; its mathematical precision adapted it to predictive purposes. As Polak indicated at the beginning of his article, he hoped to provide answers to previously unanswered questions:

> What would be the effect of a credit expansion of 10 million pesos in country A? The money supply in country B has increased by $x$ percent during the last year; is this or is it not, too much from the point of view of the balance of payments or from that of international balance?[32]

Given stable political conditions, governments could control credit and budgets knowing that such actions would have decisive impacts on the balance of payments. Based on calculations derived from the model, IMF technicians could work out precise policy targets and ceilings with client states. In short, the Polak model lent specificity to standby conditionality, helping to "put teeth" into agreements that hitherto could not effectively demand compliance. It raised monetary and fiscal adjustment practices to a preeminence they had never enjoyed.

Certainly Fund leadership had previously espoused austerity measures, but the Fund had, for some time, lacked the theoretical and technical capabilities to turn its preferences into tangible policy proposals. It took a good six or seven years to develop the techniques required to present a believable set of guidelines to member states, according to Polak.

Once perfected, these techniques became, according to the Fund, "revelations" to government officials in Latin American states grappling with complex adjustment problems.[33] The model, and subsequent revisions of it, proved to be invaluable to IMF missions as well, giving staff people "something to work with" that they had never had before.[34] IMF missions became much more active in 1958, partly as a result of their newfound confidence in the theories that had been bandied about for some time and were only then coming into their own.

In the early 1950s, developing states worldwide rarely approached the Fund for aid. When they did, it was with enormous trepidation and uncertainty—uncertainty over what the Fund would say and fear that future loans might be cut off. But by 1957–1958, borrowers were freely negotiating with the Fund as the development of quantitative models offered a more productive basis for discussion. IMF representatives could speak the language of credit ceilings and deficit targets, rather than offering vaguely worded proclamations of policy dissatisfaction. Meanwhile, LDC ministers and officials could be more easily drawn into the logic and simplicity of these formulas. The possibility of correcting external balances by using equations was appealing, if not seductive.

At the 1957 annual meeting of the IMF and World Bank, the U.S. governor, W. Randolph Burgess, commented on the organizations' greater ability to meet currency demands over the past year. He felt that this was primarily a function of the fact that the Fund had developed "a body of principles to guide it and the members both in devising of policies in the use of its resources."[35] He went on to emphasize that the IMF's missions had taken on great importance for the first time, resulting in many programs of financial stabilization. The key ingredient, in his view, was the derivation of a coherent manageable approach to the balance of payments problem, consistent with principles of fiscal and monetary restraint. Clearly, the timing of these statements coincided with the formulation of the quantitative models within the Fund's research division. This correspondence points up the relevance of ideas in accounting for the Fund's influence.

By 1958, the IMF's *Annual Reports and Summary Proceeding* reflected an uncompromising adherence to cardinal principles of demand management, fiscal austerity, and free market predominance. The Fund was willing to push these ideas on deficit-ridden countries to a degree not evident prior to the formation of the Polak model.[36] The IMF was presumably aware that such pressure tactics would have harsh social consequences: a loss of jobs, given reduced government spending and credit restrictions to the private sector; a lowering of income standards with the removal of price controls and subsidies; and, most assuredly, an increase in absolute poverty for those at the bottom of the income ladder who had depended on government support. The poor would now be fully exposed to the ravages of a market-oriented economy.

The IMF's readiness to opt for deflationary rather than expansionary measures, at a time when Latin American governments were struggling just to keep pace with the demands of a growing population, implied an acceptance of social unrest as a likely outcome, and, as has been pointed out in Chapter 2, a willingness to use force to counter these disturbances.

Many Latin American elites who resorted to repression had experienced an erosion of domestic support for austerity measures. With their popularity declining at home, these officials legitimized themselves through their association with like-minded economists and financial experts from abroad. The sense of shared knowledge, of being part of a novel theoretical approach to a difficult problem, created a bridge between domestic and international financial experts. In the future, their paths would cross in banking circles, at international meetings, or in consultation with one another. The consolidation of this transnational professional "community" provided tremendous psychological rewards for elites who were politically isolated, as will be discussed in greater detail in Part Four.

It is certain that the stabilization strategy, as perceived by some Latin American leaders, was a healthy dose of realism—perhaps the optimal strategy at that. These were administrations that came to power with less commitment to social justice than to economic efficiency. Orthodox programs were touted by the Fund as necessary prescriptions to cure "diseased economies" plagued with controls, subsidies, loose credit, and overpaid workers. The deflationary plan, coupled with a strong bias against state interference in market forces, was precisely the kind of strategy that in any event might have been favored by these particular governments; the Fund simply reinforced existing predilections with the strength of sophisticated modeling. Thus, elites who were in principle partial to these ideas had the advantage over adversaries and fence sitters who lacked clear theoretical guidelines.

It is reasonably evident that the development of quantitative monetary models for balance of payments adjustment provided the IMF with newfound leverage over LDC elites. These elites were *convinced* by Fund representatives, armed with new concepts and techniques, that one approach was preferable to another. The Fund had successfully employed knowledge as a policy lever.[37] How did the ultimate choice of ideas influence relations between the government and organized labor? To answer this question, we turn to a study of Argentina and Peru. Our investigation begins with a historical review of economic thinking and state-labor relations in Argentina, followed by a series of case studies of economic doctrine and political repression.

## NOTES

1. Keith J. Horsefield, *The International Monetary Fund 1945–1965: Twenty Years of International Monetary Cooperation* (Washington, D.C.: IMF, 1969), vol. 1: *Chronicle*, vol. 2: *Analysis*, vol. 3: *Documents*.

2. Horsefield, *IMF, 1945–1965*, vol. 3, p. 188.

3. Horsefield, *IMF, 1945–1965*, vol. 3, pp. 3–36.

4. Ibid., p. 188.

5. Ibid., p. 190.

6. John Ruggie, "International Regimes, Transactions and Change: Embedded Liberalism in the Postwar Economic Order," *International Organization* 36 (Spring 1982): 379–415.

7. See various issues of IMF *Summary Proceedings*, 1948–1956.

8. W. W. Scammell, *International Monetary Policy: Bretton Woods and After* (New York: John Wiley & Sons, 1975).

9. This view corresponds to the realist paradigm in international politics. It treats the state as a unified and autonomous actor, which can pursue national goals in the international system, often in opposition to private domestic groups. For representative works, see: Hans Morgenthau, *Politics Among Nations: The Struggle for Power and Peace* (New York: Alfred Knopf, 1967); Kenneth Waltz, *Man, the State and War: A Theoretical Analysis* (New York: Columbia University Press, 1959); Robert Gilpin, *U.S. Power and the Multinational Corporation* (New York: Basic Books, 1975); Stephen D. Krasner, *Defending the National Interest: Raw Materials, U.S. Investments and U.S. Foreign Policy* (Princeton: Princeton University Press, 1978).

10. The relationship between a hegemonic power and competitive world trade is explored in Stephen D. Krasner, "State Power and the Structure of International Trade," *World Politics* (April 1976):317–347.

11. Albert O. Hirschman, *National Power and Structure of Foreign Trade* (Berkeley: University of California Press, 1945).

12. For classic studies using this approach, see: Harry Magdoff, *The Age of Imperialism* (New York: Monthly Review Press, 1969); Paul A. Baran and Paul M. Sweezy, *Monopoly Capital: An Essay on the American Economic and Social Order* (New York: Monthly Review Press, 1966).

13. Cheryl Payer, *The Debt Trap: The IMF and the Third World* (New York: Monthly Review Press, 1975).

14. Richard Gardner, *Sterling Dollar Diplomacy: The Origins and the Prospects of Our International Economic Order* (New York: McGraw Hill, 1969).

15. Horsefield, *IMF, 1945–1965*, vol. 2, p. 404.

16. Ibid., p. 404.

17. Ibid., pp. 490–491.

18. Ibid., p. 373.

19. United Nations, *Statistical Yearbook*, 1962, 1963, pp. 436, 458.

20. Ibid., 1954, pp. 41, 123; 1958, pp. 61, 145; 1962, pp. 56, 150, 428–429, 436, 450–451; 1963, p. 458. *International Trade Statistic Yearbook*, pp. 81, 91, 96, 134, 153, 160, 424, 430, 553.

21. *Statistical Abstract of Latin America* 20 (1979): 410.

22. Horsefield, *IMF 1945–1965*, vol. 2, pp. 460–463, 490–491.

23. Ibid., p. 358.

24. Ibid., p. 484. Exact ceilings were specified in the written agreement between Paraguay and the IMF, although they were not published.

25. By 1958, the Fund required that monetary and fiscal goals be spelled out in a letter of intent. The letter would be signed by the member country and included in the standby arrangement. This gave the Fund criteria with which to judge whether a borrower was complying with loan conditions.

26. Horsefield, *IMF, 1945–1965*, vol. 1, pp. 432–433.

27. Ingo Walter, *International Economics*, (New York: Ronald Press, 1975), pp. 368–379.

28. The change in relative prices of international goods through depreciation would have an impact on balance of payments deficits. But according to the Marshall-Lerner condition, one would need to know the elasticities of demand for each of the trading partners to know if such price changes would result in balance of payments equilibrium. For more on the Marshall-Lerner condition, see Walter, *International Economics*, pp. 384–394.

29. Sidney S. Alexander, "Effects of a Devaluation on a Trade Balance," *IMF Staff Papers* 2 (April 1952): 263–278.

30. International Monetary Fund, *The Monetary Approach to the Balance of Payments* (Washington, D.C.: IMF, 1979), pp. 6–8.

31. J. J. Polak, "Monetary Analysis of Income Formation and Payments Problems," *IMF Staff Papers* 6 (November 1957):1–50.

32. Ibid., p. 1.

33. Telephone interview with J. J. Polak, May 20, 1983.

34. Ibid.

35. International Monetary Fund, *IMF Summary Proceedings of the Twelfth Annual Meeting of the Board of Governors*, September 1957, p. 57.

36. Despite persistent attempts by LDC members to get the Fund's leadership to recognize the external origins of much of their problems, Per Jacobsson, the chairman of the Executive Board of the IMF in 1958 tended to minimize such arguments, saying:

> The Fund in its work is necessarily aware of the difficulties of primary producers. Their difficulties are of course, not all due to adverse price movements; their domestic policies have not infrequently been inadequate to eliminate inflationary financing, even in years when export earnings were good and there was thus the possibility of building up reserves.

Then, in an allusion to the Fund's recent leverage over recalcitrant borrowers, he added:

> On the other hand, it is only fair to say that in the last two years

> there have been signs of a more *realistic* attitude on the part of most of these countries; with a growing distaste for inflation, and a strong desire to avoid the reimposition of controls, the authorities have been able to pursue sounder fiscal, credit, and exchange policies [emphasis mine].

Quoted in *IMF Summary Proceedings*, September 1958, p. 35.

37. Of course, some governments were never persuaded by the model but conformed to IMF rules *solely* out of economic self-interest. The terms of trade had deteriorated during the 1950s and Latin American governments had little confidence that world market conditions would improve substantially enough in the short run to sustain recovery. Under pressure to replenish international reserves, and desiring to keep the lid on domestic prices, these governments searched for foreign sources of credit, which were few. They ultimately had to depend to a considerable degree on the IMF. This dependence forced governments that were not particularly fond of the Polak model to reluctantly agree to its provisions nonetheless.

# PART TWO
# ARGENTINA

## 4

# Argentine State-Labor Relations and Economic Policies: A Brief Historical Review

Union power in Argentina is a product of state policy. Juan Perón, through ambitious regulatory and fiscal activities, lifted the Argentine trade union movement from fragmentation and weakness to unity and strength.[1] Prior to Perón's appointment as head of the Department of Labor and Social Security in 1943, the labor movement had been damaged by thirteen years of military rule and ideological disputes among socialists, communists, and syndicalists. In the ensuing twelve years of Peronist leadership, the movement consolidated behind a single political bloc, the membership of the General Confederation of Labor (CGT) expanded fifteen times to cover 80 percent of the organized work force,[2] the real wages of its affiliates rose 37 percent, and wage-earners' share of national income increased from 38.7 percent in 1946 to 45.9 percent in 1950—the largest redistribution of income in the history of the republic.[3]

These advances were made possible by a federal budget that had become a potent instrument in Perón's hands. The president pursued an expansionary program of consumption, subsidization, and investment that provided jobs, raised income levels, and lowered the cost of living for the working class. Through regulatory decrees, he facilitated the emergence of new unions and the enlargement of old ones, quickly building trade union support for and defense of each new budgetary allotment. In this manner, an important link was established between the fiscal state and the trade union movement, which was to influence the decisions of future administrations. Any contraction of the public sector had negative repercussions for those groups that were dependent on state expenditures, and whose interests would be adversely affected. While these groups were many, the organized labor movement became the most formidable agent of political and social change and would thus pose the gravest threat to governments contemplating fiscal adjustments. Democratic and military governments alike have responded with varied forcefulness to the state-labor nexus that Perón created.[4]

## PERÓN'S FISCAL MEASURES AND UNION POWER

Perón expanded the regulatory, administrative, and fiscal dimensions of the state, then marshaled these forces to encourage unionization and the improvement of the socioeconomic status of a newly integrated workforce. So thoroughly had the state penetrated the socioeconomic sphere by the end of Perón's rule that it is difficult to assess the trade union movement on its own terms. What the movement would have become without Perón's assistance is anyone's guess, though most assuredly the pace of development would not have been as fast.

Indeed, a consensual form of dependency evolved whereby the labor movement came to rely less on its own devices and more on the good graces of state ministries, courts, and Perón himself. Perón was its guardian, stepping in when needed to insure that redistributive justice was served. Irreconcilable differences between labor and management were frequently resolved by the president, who would simply impose a settlement by decree, in one stroke raising the wage level for employees industry-wide. Conflicts over severance pay and back salaries numbered in the thousands annually and were arbitrated in favor of workers by labor courts sympathetic to the Peronist cause. Perón rounded out his program with minimum-wage laws, enforcement of employment security measures, compensation for industrial accidents, and a new constitution guaranteeing that work and improved working conditions were a right, not a privilege.[5] These new regulations, as Samuel Baily notes "guaranteed the workers a meaningful identity as part of society,"[6] giving protection under law to those who had been second-class citizens.

Perón encouraged this dependency, hoping that the working class would link its fortunes with the state and not with independent political power brokers. He desired a monolithic movement—not a democratic one—and was quick to disarm his opponents. He became the first head of state to extend the practice of intervention from the political to the social realm. Nineteenth-century Argentine law allowed the federal government to seize provincial seats of power in defense of "national welfare." Tailoring this for his own purposes, Perón took control of the CGT's executive council and used this handpicked organ to replace democratically elected union officials with more compliant labor bosses. In addition, unauthorized strikes were repressed, and legal recognition was withdrawn from "uncooperative" syndicates.

Although Perón established a penchant for official meddling in labor affairs, he always held out the carrot of economic reward. As no other figure before him, he unleashed the fiscal energies of the state to the advantage of the working class. Perón could pursue expansionary policies owing to a fortuitous set of economic conditions. In the immediate post–World War II era, Argentine products were in great demand abroad, and the country enjoyed healthy trade surpluses (which totaled U.S. $439 and U.S. $580 million in 1945 and 1946) and favorable terms of trade.[7] Perón forced farmers to sell their produce to the government at low prices and then resold the commodities abroad at market value. The difference became a surplus that was siphoned off into state coffers.

These funds made possible the enormous expansion of the state apparatus. An array of agencies and subagencies cropped up overnight to administer the state's labor programs. The Secretariat for Labor and Welfare (later upgraded to the ministerial level) became a giant bureaucracy with eight directorates and twenty subagencies under its jurisdiction. By 1948, it employed a staff of over 6,000, and its budget grew by 176 percent between 1946 and 1948.[8] Within the secretariat, the social welfare division that administered retirement, pension, and leisure benefits to workers, and the social assistance division that provided subsidies, social services, and educational benefits for labor grew impressively. Salaries for social welfare employees were raised 630 percent between 1946 and 1948 and 1,100 percent for workers in the social assistance sector.[9] Total administrative expenditures in the central government accelerated from 1.2 billion pesos in 1946 to 9.9 billion pesos in 1948, a 778 percent increase. The government's particular commitment to labor is highlighted by the fact that outlays to the Ministry of Labor during this time were on average twice that of the total for the next three largest government agencies combined.

Parallel with this internal expansion of the state came the growth of public consumption expenditures, subsidies, and investments. Governmental current expenditures increased by 28 percent between 1946 and 1948.[10] Much of this was spent to employ a public sector labor force, whose numbers increased by 25 percent between 1945 and 1948, while their salaries grew in real terms by 35 percent. Between 1949 and 1955, the public sector had become the fastest growing employer in Argentina, outpacing agriculture and industry.[11] Midway through Perón's first term, subsidies on basic consumer goods such as meats, oil, milk, sugar, bread, and other commodities totaled nearly $1 billion dollars, and between 1950 and 1955 averaged over 4 billion. By Perón's final year in office, subsidies accounted for over one-quarter of the total current expenditures of the government.[12] Public sector employment and subsidies were redistributive devices. State jobs raised the total wage share of the national income, and subsidies lowered the price of commodities purchased primarily by lower classes.

Under Perón, the state emerged as an important investor as well as consumer. Post–World War II levels of public sector investment were double those of the prewar period. One-third of all capital formation in Argentina between 1946 and 1948 occurred in the public sector, and this share grew to 71 percent between 1950 and 1955.[13] These figures are somewhat misleading, however, since by and large the state's contribution did not augment the productive potential of the economy. The bulk of these funds went into nonproductive spheres such as construction (which accounted for about half of all public investment). This was not at all troublesome to the Peronist leadership, because the principle objectives of the program were social, not economic. Construction more than met the tremendous current and anticipated demand for housing from the influx of labor migrants—117,000 annually between 1943 and 1947.[14] This project was extremely important in Buenos Aires, where housing conditions were notoriously poor even by Latin American standards. Additionally, it provided a labor-intensive form of employment that not only satisfied but in fact ran ahead of the demand for urban jobs (labor shortages did not disappear until 1950).

Perón's state grew by acquisition as well as investment. The government spent a staggering U.S. $1 billion to retire the public external debt and to purchase foreign-owned railroads, ports, telephones, and energy and transportation service companies.[15] The important feature of these acquisitions was the state's indifference to their economic cost or feasibility. A long-awaited agreement, signed on February 13, 1947, turned over the British-owned rail system (constituting 66 percent of Argentina's rail network, including 16,000 miles of track and related real estate). After a month of negotiation, the price of the rail system settled upon by both sides was 1 billion pesos. However, Miguel Miranda, Perón's economic "czar," president of the newly nationalized Central Bank, and chief negotiator for Argentina, voluntarily offered to pay Great Britain 2 billion gold pesos "for reasons of sentiment."[16] Miranda knew full well he was buying a rail system in disrepair, and he later estimated that subsequent breakdowns of the system had cost 547 million pesos a year. Nonetheless, one Peronist journal admitted that

> the recovery of the railways by the state cannot be considered a business transaction. . . . It was no more a business transaction . . . than was the battle of Ayacucho, or the campaign for our national independence. . . . Liberty has no price.[17]

The nationalization of railroads had obvious symbolic importance for a people anxious to emancipate themselves from foreign economic control, and even Perón's staunchest political opponents were wildly enthusiastic about the agreement.

More than an act of independence, the acquisition typified the state's readiness to spend lavishly and to bear the costs so that employment and income objectives could be met. Once nationalized, firms acted like magnets, drawing in more laborers than were needed and resulting in a huge, unproductive, and overpaid work force. Millions of dollars worth of diesel locomotives and freight cars were purchased from the United States even as the rail system continued to operate at a loss. In fact, in its first five years, the system lost income reported to equal one-half the purchase price. These losses were absorbed by the government, whose transfers to all deficit-ridden, state-owned public enterprises totaled 20 percent of expenditures in the public sector by 1955.[18] Transfers such as these pleased the union chiefs, who could win recruits with the assurance of more jobs. They also pleased Perón who could, with every peso transferred, purchase another vote of confidence for himself.

Each state-funded operation laid the economic groundwork to strengthen the trade union movement. The railroad union (Unión Ferroviaria), which claimed 90,000 affiliates in 1941 and 150,000 in 1951, had more than doubled its membership by the time of Perón's ouster in 1955, thus becoming the largest union in Argentina and one of the two most powerful. The union was fiercely independent and did not always see eye to eye with Perón. However, recognizing the enormous employment and wage benefits that could accrue to its members once the railways were in state hands, the union staged important public rallies in support of nationalization. Founded in 1943, the construction workers' union (Unión Obrera de la Construcción) had 30,000 members in Perón's first year in office. By the time he left office, his public works program had helped to triple the union's ranks.[19] Similar gains were made by scores of other federations who benefited directly or indirectly from state spending.

These trends also had financial significance for the unions. Perón's Professional Association Law rendered the payment of membership dues obligatory. The law proved to be an economic windfall for a movement whose numbers had grown fifteen times during Perón's tenure as president, and whose structure had become increasingly centralized. Contributions made by workers at local unions throughout the nation were channeled into the bank accounts of federation headquarters in Buenos Aires.[20] These accounts made possible the hiring of full-time union organizers, the extension of patronage, support for industry-wide strikes, and political propaganda—all of which strengthened the hand of Peronist unions. Although socially and politically acquiescent under Perón's rule, Argentine trade unions had, by 1955, acquired the resources needed to fight as independent pressure groups in defense of their own interests, should that be necessary. Ironically, while the dependency relation kept the unions at bay as long as Perón held power, it also cultivated a powerful latent social force whose structural and financial assets later proved to be formidable weapons.

Perón's fiscal policies established a structural reliance that would be hard to dismantle. Governments desiring to "trim the bureaucratic fat" off the state apparatus could not simply release the redundant labor force without generating redundancy somewhere else, since the rate at which public sector jobs had been created from 1940 to 1954 actually outpaced the GNP growth.[21] Businesses were not likely to hire former state employees in excess of what they needed, particularly since these workers were usually less skilled than those in the private sector. Administrations were pressured to achieve economic growth rates that were sufficient to absorb the labor pool. Should they fail, they would face a Hobson's choice: either drastically scale down their bureaucratic rationalization schemes or pay the political price of higher unemployment.

The expansion of the state under Perón stood as a benchmark for future administrations. Those elites who leaned toward fiscal austerity would point to Perón's failure to establish a stable foundation for economic growth as evidence that such models were futile. Perón fall in 1955 gave new life to a free market doctrine that had been badly discredited by the Great Depression.[22]

The liberals' historical faith in Argentina's comparative advantage in grain exports was shattered as the market for primary products bottomed out during the 1930s. Agricultural production slumped and could no longer underwrite the nation's economy—even under competitive conditions. It was actually the military government of 1930 that first enlarged the state's role in the economy to compensate for the inadequacies of market forces during the depression years. The generals launched a partially successful import substitution strategy that freed the nation to some extent from its dependence on an unstable world market.

The liberal view was reawakened not by the shortcomings of the military's program but by those of Perón's. Economic liberalism of the 1950s shifted its focus from comparative advantage to fiscal and monetary equilibrium. In retreat from their previously disparaged position, the Argentine free marketeers traced economic disequilibrium more to the inflationary effects of deficit spending and excess demand than to the loss of international competitiveness. The inflationary spirals and declining growth rates of 1948 to 1952 bolstered their contention that exorbitant state spending habits were to blame for Argentina's economic malaise. Interestingly, Perón's stabilization plan of 1952—which included a wage freeze, selective price controls, and restrictive monetary and fiscal policy, and which produced a surplus on the trade account as well as the sharpest annual drop in inflation in Argentine history to date (from 38.7 percent in 1952 to 4.0 in 1953)—was not enough to restore the reputation of his populist program among his economic critics.[23]

It was not the end result of the program that mattered to Perón's successors so much as his retention of the basic political-economic model throughout. Hidden behind the apparent success of the stabilization plan were food subsidies (which by 1955 comprised 30 percent of all government current expenditures), selective price controls (which had merely kept the lid on latent inflationary pressures), and public sector expenditures (which after a year inched their way up again).[24] These blunders, so the liberals argued, were symptomatic of a thoroughly misguided strategy that emphasized current expenditures and market intervention to the detriment of productive capital investment in a competitive environment. Hence, while the government continued to consume lavishly, it did nothing to build a productive economic base. Not surprisingly, the federal deficit became a more visible target for the austerity-minded advisers of the 1950s and early 1960s.

Reducing the state's budget would be easier said than done. Perón had achieved short-term stabilization by establishing a strong line of moral credit with the working class. As its benefactor during his first term in office, he reminded workers of the real gains that had been achieved for them under his administration. When it came time to ask that they save more and spend less—even as real wages were declining—he found he could draw easily on that line of credit. The working class was compliant, remembering full well that wages in 1953 were still 35 percent higher than in 1943, the year Perón became head of the Labor Department.[25]

Future non-Peronist administrations would not be so fortunate; they were confronted by a rigid and self-reinforcing system of state-labor relations. Perón had built an edifice of trade union solidarity around each new public sector program or regulation he decreed. This construction stood as a reminder for governments to come that fiscal and monetary levers could not be manipulated without severe social and political consequences. Any tampering with hard-earned state privileges would meet with swift resistance in the form of walkouts, confrontations, and general insubordination. Peronist fiscal policy had, in short, created a set of powerful vested interests that made reversal of policy exceedingly difficult. It would take a regime equally committed to a free market philosophy—and prepared to use high levels of coercion—to bring down or at least weaken the edifice. The military establishment that overthrew Perón in September 1955 in the name of the "liberating revolution" would not be the one to implement that change.

## MILITARY RULE AND ECONOMIC TRANSITION

The military government that came to power in 1955 was confronted with two major problems: how to restore stability and growth to the economy, and how to maintain political order in the face of a hostile and formidable opposition. Juan Perón had left a balance of payments deficit, a shortage of foreign exchange, a sluggish economy, and one even greater burden: an organized labor force 5 million strong and loyal to Peronism.

The new regime's initial strategy was cautious. They wanted a trade union movement that would not antagonize the landed elite, the church, or the armed forces. At the same time, they wanted to avoid the kind of repression that could unleash uncontrolled resistance from the workers' movement. Toward that end, General Eduardo Lonardi replaced CGT leaders who had been most closely associated with the previous regime with ones who had been less active. The state intervened at the individual union level, promising to restore normalcy once politically acceptable officers were elected. The CGT approved of these moves and pressed Lonardi to take stronger measures to insure that trade union rights would be protected. The CGT's attempt to draw closer to Lonardi proved to be fatal. It alienated Lonardi from the military hard-liners who feared a Peronist resurgence.[26] As a result, General Pedro E. Aramburu replaced Lonardi on November 13, 1955.

Aramburu quickly intervened in the CGT, outlawed all strikes, and prevented political parties from operating. His interventionist strategy was different from that used by Perón. For example, the military men appointed were unfamiliar with union practices, insensitive to labor concerns, and bent on imposing a mode of discipline that was functional for the armed forces but not for the unions. These interveners were outsiders, and their presence served as a reminder of better times and of the need for workers to struggle to regain their freedoms.

Aramburu's strategy was twofold: coercively to rid the trade union movement of Peronist influence; and to reintegrate the rank and file into state-sanctioned syndicates. This exclusionary form of corporatist control[27] was aimed at retaining an organized labor force compliant with the economic objectives set out by the state. Decree law 9270, passed in May 1956, broke with the Peronist Professional Association Law of 1945 by permitting more than one representative union per sector. The object was to expose Peronist-dominated unions to competition from "independents." Naturally, the coercive disruption of Peronist-affiliated unions gave the "independents" an edge in the "competitive" struggle. This led to divisions within the movement, particularly between Peronists, on one hand, and Democrats, Socialists, and Communists, on the other. The Peronists became known as the *grupo 62*, the Democrats and independents as the *grupo 32*. The schism was formalized at a CGT congress called by the military in 1957. The armed forces set up the meeting in hopes that the independent delegates they had sponsored would prevail, cracking the Peronist hold on union power once and for all. When many of these delegates voted with the Peronists for the removal of restrictive legislation, the military adjourned the congress.

In the end, the trade union movement, though divided, remained dominated by the Peronists, and the military refused to escalate its use of force to levels necessary to remove them. Why did the generals not carry out a ferocious campaign to rid the labor movement of Peronism? One explanation can be found in the government's transitional economic strategy.

The military sought the counsel of Raúl Prebisch and the ECLA. Prebisch proposed an economic strategy that would abandon the heavy hand of state intervention (as practiced under the preceding government) and shift instead toward greater market reliance. Prebisch argued that Argentine goods had become too susceptible to the fluctuations of the international market. It was time to reduce dependence on foreign exchange earnings as the catalyst for growth; the alternative was import substitution. The plan was to generate dynamic sectors that could manufacture products hitherto imported. Such a program would require greater public savings and correspondingly reduced current expenditures. The government was urged to eliminate subsidies, free prices, and devalue the peso. The state was also asked to invest in technology to enhance agricultural productivity. Once farming became more efficient, labor would be free to migrate toward an expanding industrial sector. Improved yields would raise agricultural profits, placing more disposable income in the hands of farmers who could then purchase industrial goods.[28]

The ECLA team's overriding purpose was to remove supply bottlenecks to meet demand, rather than to trim demand to meet supply. The economists also knew that an inflationary spiral could reduce investment incentives, so they tried to keep wages in line with productivity, while asking business to exhibit voluntary price restraint. Not surprisingly, the burden of development shifted slightly toward the labor sector as the wage share of national income declined under Aramburu's rule. On the other hand, the economic strategists wanted to avoid the worst features of the free market strategy, which would impose intolerable sacrifices on the working class. For this reason, subsidies were retained on essential food items, and tax reforms were undertaken to buffer the effect of exchange devaluation on lower-income groups.

Clearly, certain aspects of the plan were contradictory, leaving the military in an ambiguous position. If public savings were to be increased by reducing expenditures, income levels of those dependent on state support would surely fall. If those same sectors were protected through subsidies, the measures would reduce risk-taking ventures in the private sector and create latent inflationary pressures that budget-cutting endeavors were designed to forestall. Actually, the whole program hinged on the successful growth of industrial productivity to satisfy demand and to avoid inflationary spirals, which were likely once wage controls were lifted. It was a transitional plan, since it moved toward free market criteria without entirely abandoning the interventionist functions of the state.[29] Correspondingly, the military's political strategy aimed to create a more compliant labor force, yet without unduly punishing the workers.

A major devaluation was enacted in 1955, but only minor ones thereafter. The internal terms of trade improved for landowners, but not enough to restore their confidence in the state's commitment to the export sector. Uncertain of future prices, producers held back; as a result, the country experienced trade deficits and a loss of foreign exchange.[30] Meanwhile, the business sector raised prices beyond state-negotiated levels agreed, and the labor movement demanded compensation. Wage hikes were granted in February 1956, and renegotiation of contracts thereafter boosted labor earnings an additional 30–40 percent. Real hourly industrial wages actually improved during the Aramburu years, from 42.5 pesos per hour in 1955 to 45.9 in 1957.[31].

Mounting deficits and a depletion of reserves induced the government to seek credit from external sources. It received a modicum of support from international creditors (having affiliated with the Paris Club in 1956) that temporarily relieved its reserve shortfall. These sums were insufficient, and the IMF was unwilling to commit larger amounts until the authorities agreed to implement a strict, orthodox anti-inflation plan; such a plan was never part of the scenario[32] because it would have required high levels of coercion to restrain labor sectors. Instead, the military attempted to ameliorate the regressive features of the economic plan through subsidies, wage adjustments, and tax reforms.

Still, labor was by no means satisfied. Strike activity grew enormously in 1956, with 845,000 participants and over 5 million working days lost, compared to 1955 when strikes involved only 11,990 participants and the loss of 144,120 working days.[33] Aramburu's government announced legal restrictions on strikes and rallies, invoking a state of siege in September 1956, but for the most part did not physically disrupt these protests. Since the state would not enforce its decrees, labor perceived that the costs of defiance were low enough to continue protesting.[34] In fact, the state's moderate application of coercion only persuaded unionists that further confrontation would work to their advantage, and they were right. Labor actions pressed Aramburu to abandon the wage freeze. Consequently, 281 labor contracts were signed in 1956 and 1957, and organizational restrictions were eased considerably.[35] By April 1957, fifty-nine out of 119 CGT-affiliated unions had been normalized, signaling the defeat of the military's policy of intervention. The labor movement emerged triumphant, with its confederation intact, its leadership's prestige enhanced for having withstood the state's assaults on trade union freedom, and the Peronist influence very much alive. The armed forces had succeeded only in temporarily reopening an ideological divide within the movement, which the Peronists quickly sealed.

The military's top brass was less fortunate. The glaring shortcomings of economic and labor management produced fissures within the military, with factions warring over the appropriate role of the armed forces in politics. In May 1958, officers returned to the barracks, leaving the civilian government of Arturo Frondizi to grapple with the problems they had been unable to resolve.

## THE FRONDIZI APPROACH: FROM DEVELOPMENTALISM TO LIBERALISM

Arturo Frondizi, the candidate of the UCRI Party (Unión Cívica Radical Intransigente—Intransigent Radical Civic Union, formed after a Radical Party split in 1957), won the presidency in an election that had proscribed Peronist participation. In a deal with Perón, Frondizi gained labor's vote in exchange for promises to rescind the antilabor laws issued under the military. Frondizi's strategy was intended to achieve more than the creation of a winning electoral coalition; he hoped that political liberalization and economic nationalism would solidify a more permanent base of support for his administration.[36]

Law 14455, passed in 1958, returned Argentina to a system of one representative union per industry, thus restoring the Peronist principle established in the late 1940s. A general amnesty released labor detainees and allowed exiles to return. Many important unions disrupted by Aramburu were granted autonomy, and the ban on political activity was lifted.

Like his predecessor, Frondizi invoked the structuralist critique, albeit of a different variety. Under the guidance of his ECLA-trained team of economists and his chief economic adviser, Rogelio Frigerio, Frondizi opted for a more ambitious import substitution strategy.[37] Taking the Prebisch thesis seriously, he argued that Argentina's position in the international division of labor harmed development and thus had to be changed. Progress could never be achieved through exportation of primary goods. The nation's terms of trade had deteriorated and would only continue to deteriorate, limiting the supplies of foreign exchange needed to purchase capital goods. The government's plan was to bolster the country's internal supply of capital by attracting foreign investment and credit.[38] Frondizi laid the groundwork by improving the nation's petroleum, steel, and chemical industries. The production of machinery and equipment, including motors, automobiles, and electrical goods, grew by 255 percent from 1955 to 1965.[39]

The president also fulfilled his campaign promise to restore labor's purchasing power with a 60 percent wage hike granted shortly after his inauguration. The combined strategy of stimulating demand while building infrastructure and *heavy* industry set Frondizi's program apart from those of both Perón and Aramburu.

Labor initially seemed pleased, but the peace between the president and his Peronist rivals was short-lived. Long-term investment projects could not offset the short-term loss of export revenues and the depletion of foreign exchange resulting from previous policies. By the fall of 1958, Argentina could not pay for vital capital imports. The country was in desperate need of foreign credit. An IMF team, visiting in July 1958, laid down strict conditions for the release of international funds: wages must be frozen; government deficits cut; money supply restricted; price and exchange controls lifted; and the peso devalued.

In November 1958, Frondizi agreed to these basic terms, rupturing his pact with the Peronists. He also alienated his support within the General Economic Confederation (CGE), an important association of small businesses that objected to the IMF's credit restrictions. However, Frondizi's switch garnered support from the larger industrialists and landowners, who figured to prosper from stabilization. On December 29, the largest single aid program ever devised for a Latin American nation was formulated. Argentina would receive U.S. $329 million in funds from multinational government and private sources.[40] Frondizi formally launched his orthodox plan that evening.

Political repression, which had been low during the first eight months of the Radical Party rule, suddenly rose dramatically in the fall of 1958 as delicate negotiations between the government and the IMF neared completion. According to one report, the government thought that its use of force to end a railroad strike in November would enhance its chances of gaining Fund credit.[41] Apparently it was right. Reneging on his promise to restore individual and collective liberties, Frondizi declared a state of siege in November 1958, prohibited labor strikes and public rallies, and arrested 700 Peronist and Communist political and labor leaders.[42]

Frondizi's reversals jolted a labor movement that had expected to profit from the Peronist–Radical Party electoral alliance. Feeling betrayed, the unions resorted to the strike weapon in 1959 as never before. Over 1.4 million workers participated in forty-five major work stoppages, resulting in a loss of 10 million worker-days of production.[43] These well-coordinated actions were designed to disrupt the economy and place the political blame on Frondizi for having failed to prevent them. They were also labor's answer to a December 1958 decree that had placed collective bargaining under the close supervision of the armed forces. Unable to negotiate freely, workers suffered a 25 percent cut in pay in 1959. That year, state and labor were locked in a dialectic of confrontation: each governmental act elicited another round of paralyzing work stoppages that in turn encouraged more punitive measures. For example, a plan to privatize a meat packing plant in January 1959 touched off a forty-eight-hour general strike joined by 75 percent of the work force, shutting down the capital's public transportation system. The government countered by raiding the homes of Peronist leaders, closing Communist Party headquarters, and installing military officers in top positions in the petroleum, communications, and transportation workers' unions.[44] Additional interventions in April triggered yet another round of work stoppages.

Frondizi had succeeded in lowering the wage bill, but at a significant cost: production losses resulted in an 8 percent decline in the gross domestic product (GDP) for that year. To preempt further trade union rebellion, the president formalized his coercive campaign against labor with *Plan Conintes* (*comoción interno del estado*—internal commotion of the state), which went well beyond the simple suspension of individual liberties permitted under the constitution's state of siege provision; it assembled a complex apparatus of repression. Declaring Argentina to be in a state of internal war, the president placed much of the nation under military jurisdiction and divided this area into "zones of operation."[45] Within those zones, the armed forces assumed executive and judicial powers, enabling them to arrest and detain suspects and to prosecute civilians in military courts.

The government insisted this was nothing more than an antiterrorist decree. The armed forces claimed it had uncovered an elaborate terrorist network replete with stockpiles of weapons and incendiary devices. The network was a significant threat to national security, so they stated, and justified taking exceptional measures. For the most part, reports of terrorism were wildly exaggerated and served as a smoke screen behind which to launch an attack against normal Peronist and trade union activity. Not only were a disproportionate number of the detainees CGT leaders with Peronist affiliations, but terrorists were defined loosely by the law to include all those who "incited public fear or posed threats to the political and economic order"—a catchall for legal collective activities.[46]

The government had intentionally overreacted to create a climate of fear, which it hoped would quickly quell the Peronist-labor disturbances.

Frondizi's greatest enemy was time. The president had to seize the initiative before unrestrained trade union resistance brought the military into the political arena once again. *Plan Conintes* was a form of concession to Commander-in-Chief General Carlos S. Toranzo Montero and other hard-liners who were anxious to rid themselves of the "Peronist menace." The plan was also an admission that new economic priorities had considerably narrowed the president's political options. With a turn toward austerity measures, the redistributive arm of developmentalism had been severed, and Frondizi could not depend on market forces to revitalize the economy quickly enough to salvage a tenable coalition of Radicals and Peronistas; he abandoned the coalition in order to save his stabilization program.

In his December 1958 speech outlining the proposed stabilization program, Frondizi sounded a note of alarm over the tremendous expansion of the federal system. From a small bureaucracy in the early 1940s, the government had developed into an institution with 1.8 million functionaries. Eighty percent of its revenues were paid out in the form of wages and salaries totaling 100 billion pesos annually; only half of this was covered through taxation. Noting the direct links between such practices and the general inflation rate, Frondizi promised to curtail current expenditures.[47]

The president singled out the railroad system to exemplify abuse of deficit spending. As the most heavily subsidized state enterprise in the country, the railroad, according to the president, operated in the red, losing approximately 14 billion pesos each year from 1955 to 1958. The original agreement with the IMF called for a 60 percent cut in account expenditures; toward that end, rail fares were raised, and over 4,000 railroad employees were dismissed.[48] Still this was not enough, and in 1961 Frondizi proposed turning over certain parts of the railroad system to private enterprise. Aside from relieving the state of financial obligations, privatization would surely mean layoffs for the workers, who were not consulted about the proposition. News of the plan led to massive protests in November of that year as the rail workers were joined by millions of other laborers in a general strike. The security forces were sent in to quiet the rally, but the protesters held their ground long enough to exact a pledge from Frondizi to reconsider the plan before going back to work in December. The president lost this battle with labor (though he had gone to great lengths to make his point about fiscal austerity by trying to draft striking workers into the armed forces) and also lost a round with the military, who had misgivings about his handling of the railway workers.

The economy recovered somewhat in 1960 and 1961, primarily as a result of a massive influx in foreign investment. Real wages improved as well, by 8 percent in 1960 and 7.6 percent in 1961, *but remained below their 1955 levels*. Consequently, it would be wrong to interpret the drop-off in strike activity in these years (see Table 4.1) as evidence of labor's approval of the government. More likely, the rank and file had become demoralized after

**Table 4.1 Economic Policy, Repression, and Labor Protest: A Comparison of the Aramburu and Frondizi Years**

| Year[a] | Repression[b] (base year 1956 = 100) | Scope of Protest[c] |
|---|---|---|
| 1956 | 100 | 17079.8 |
| 1957 | 94 | 5432.3 |
| 1958 | 132 | 3302.2 |
| 1959 | 127 | 31356.9 |
| 1960 | 94 | 5001.7 |
| 1961 | 92 | 5499.1 |

*Sources*: Strike information is from the International Labor Office, *Yearbook of Labor Statistics* (Geneva: ILO), 1957–1962. Repression scores reflect a composite annual index of the following measures: arrest of leadership and rank and file workers, execution of rank and file workers, outlawing of labor parties and unions, denial of constitutional rights, legal restrictions on union activity, physical disruption of union activities, and intervention into labor affairs. Procedures for deriving scores are detailed in the appendix.
[a]Aramburu served from November 1955 to April 1958; Frondizi was inaugurated on May 1, 1958. Italicized years refer to orthodox stabilization policies.
[b]Highest score here reflects the use of preemptive repression in the fall of 1958, as the government's stabilization plan began to take shape.
[c]Figures represent the number of striking workers in each year divided by the number of strikes, producing a measure of the scope of labor protest.

one and one-half years of harsh repression and were no longer willing to risk the loss of jobs and personal safety. The real wage gains did not heal any wounds between the two sides: the workers would not forgive Frondizi for eroding the political freedoms that were granted in the first months of his administration or for moving from developmentalism to economic liberalism. In an effort to regain labor's trust, Frondizi permitted the Peronists to run in congressional elections in March 1962. Unexpectedly, they scored an impressive victory against Radical Party candidates. Fearful of a Peronist return to power, the military deposed Frondizi that same month.

## THE ILLIA-ONGANÍA TRANSITION: FROM REFORMISM TO MILITARISM

The interim military government that followed the Frondizi administration allowed, in 1963, limited elections that again excluded Peronist participation. Arturo Illia, the choice of the People's Radical Party (UCRP, the rival to UCRI), came to power with a weak political mandate and a host of economic troubles, including a large budget deficit, persistent unemployment, high inflation, and a huge foreign debt. At the advice of his ECLA team of economists, Illia abandoned the "shock treatment" advocated by Frondizi and chose a reformist-nationalist strategy. With the help of government financing and liberal credit schemes, domestically-owned industries would, according to this plan, be supported at the expense of larger, more efficient multinationals. Prices would be controlled and wages raised to generate demand. The peso would be devalued incrementally to boost exports while softening the blow on consumers.[49] Illia defied the IMF by canceling a standby loan and refusing to discuss the Fund's inflation remedies any further. It was not surprising that international loans to Argentina fell drastically during the Illia years.

Illia's nationalist strategy achieved promising results during the first two years. A series of record harvests produced export windfalls and trade surpluses. GDP increased and inflation was down. But deficits on the capital account grew, primarily as a result of repaying outstanding loans left from the Frondizi years; service payments on the external public debt alone, for instance, soared 66 percent from 1963 to 1966 and rose from 18 percent of exports in 1963 to 25.5 percent in 1966.[50] By September 1965, gold and foreign exchange holdings were in a precarious position, and an embarrassed Illia was forced to go to the Paris Club of creditors for debt relief. Inflationary pressures continued to build, compelling the government to tighten the money supply and to request voluntary wage restraint. Labor refused to cooperate; rather, a new militancy surfaced within the trade union movement, which was to undermine the Radical administration.

The origins of this militancy can be traced to January 1963 when the Peronist-dominated CGT regained its legal status, lost in 1955. The CGT drafted a *Plan de Lucha* that called for a series of strikes and factory occupations aimed at creating an entirely new economic and political system in Argentina. The plan blamed the government for relinquishing Argentine economic sovereignty to foreign capital and the IMF, and proposed to restructure economic relationships in the country: at a macro-level, workers would contribute to the formation of national priorities; at a micro-level, they would become partners with management in the administration and control of firms.

Illia's July election did nothing to assuage the concerns of labor. To the contrary, his victory only angered the union movement, which had been prevented from running its own slate of candidates. Illia's strategy was to win back labor's trust through a Keynesian spending program designed to raise living standards and purchasing power of the wage-earning sector. This approach actually worked economically: real wages increased steadily during the Radical Party's rule. In addition, wage-earners' share of the national income rose from 38.2 to 43.7 percent from 1963 to 1966. But the *Plan de Lucha* was implemented nonetheless, resulting in strikes by 3 million workers and the takeover of 11,000 factories.[51] Illia never challenged this impressive show of force. As predicted, his commitment to reformism inhibited the use of coercion. The hard-line elements within the armed forces argued that deteriorating economic conditions, coupled with subversive labor activities, were threatening the political order. Angered over Illia's failure to deal firmly with the Peronists, the military, led by General Juan Carlos Onganía, overthrew him on July 29, 1966.

The *Plan de Lucha* had undoubtedly helped to destabilize the Illia government, but it did nothing to solidify the trade union movement. The calls for far-reaching economic restructuring had rhetorical appeal but were never grounded in concrete objectives and strategies. The CGT leadership could not explain how the occupation of factories would produce the desired results in the long term or advance the interests of the workers in the interim. Bread and butter issues had always been and still were central to the Peronist worker. The improvement of living standards under Illia convinced many unionists that ideological combativeness was excessive and unnecessary, and that pragmatic negotiation would work just as well. This belief produced a formal split within the CGT between those favoring reconciliation and those desiring continued opposition. The former group was led by Augusto Vandor, the secretary general of the powerful metalworkers' union, who had risen to prominence in the underground during the Aramburu period. The rival faction was led by José Alonso and became known as the *62 de pie junto con Perón* (the 62-base organization, allied with Perón).

While labor would continue to disagree on many issues, it was clearly aligned on one point: support for the military coup that ousted the unpopular Illia government in June 1966. Labor's reaction to the coup was not so much eager anticipation, but rather a feeling of vindication against a democracy that had limited its participation. While Illia had remained remarkably restrained in his use of coercion, his declining political fortunes (most vividly displayed in the March 1965 congressional elections, which were won by the Peronists) and his fear of military intervention proved to be quite frustrating in the end. These prompted him to issue an antiworker decree (969) in 1966. Although never enforced by him, it laid the legal groundwork to weaken the trade union movement by approving the legalization of more than one confederation and prohibiting the intervention of second- or third-level organizations in union affairs. Labor hoped that the new military regime would defeat decree 969 and recognize the single confederation as "one of the genuine and representative institutions of national stature."[52]

For its part, the Onganía administration remained particularly guarded about its plans for economic reform during the first six months. Labor was optimistic, following a wage increase and the annulment of the 969 statute. The resignation in October 1966 of Felipe Fami, president of the Central Bank and a strong critic of monetarism, unveiled an apparent internal squabble. The nationalists within the military favored a closed economy and came face to face with "liberal" elements who argued for "openness."[53] It seemed that with Fami's removal the liberals had won, and with the appointment of Adalbert Krieger Vasena as minister of economy in January 1967, the labor movement's worst fears were confirmed. Krieger Vasena was a well-known proponent of monetarism. The CGT anticipated that the government would utilize its control over the collective bargaining process to bring wages into harmony with a stabilization program.

Finally, on March 13, 1967, Krieger Vasena appeared on national television to announce his "grand transformation" of the economy. The program had most of the trappings of an orthodox stabilization plan yet departed from it in several important respects: the peso would be sharply devalued to stimulate export revenues; import duties would be relaxed to expose domestic industries to foreign competition; government deficits would be lowered through cuts in current account expenditures and a reorganization of government administration and enterprises; and wages would be readjusted upward to match real purchasing power in 1966 but frozen thereafter. To avoid the recessionary impact of the plan, the government would free credit to the business sector by reducing its own reliance on credit through tax reform and aggressive external borrowing; and the state would increase capital expenditures to help stimulate growth. The state's participation in investment and its policy of liquidity expansion distinguished this plan from preceding orthodox stabilization efforts.[54]

How did the program affect the economy and state-labor relations? In macro-terms, the plan was a success. Real GDP growth rates rose steadily from 2.6 percent in 1967 to 8.5 percent in 1969, and inflation declined from 31.9 percent in 1966 to 7.5 percent in 1969. Argentina's international reserve position improved consistently, and the deficit of the central government was eliminated entirely.[55]

In distributive terms, the wage-earning sector lost out to capital. Real wages remained constant in 1967, dropped precipitously in 1968, and then rose slightly in 1969. By 1970, workers had only regained 1965 living standards. Furthermore, labor's share of national income increased in 1967 and then declined steadily.[56] In comparison with previous stabilization efforts in Argentina, labor's losses were not as severe. However, Frondizi's monetarism and Aramburu's structuralism were not the valid points of reference as far as the workers were concerned. History is not easily forgotten in Argentina. The Peronist unions still retained vivid memories of the Perón years when wage earners and not property owners set the national agenda and controlled the nation's income shares. They wanted a return to those days, and in that sense, there was much to be unhappy about.

In preemptive fashion, the military launched a repressive campaign against the CGT three months prior to the official enactment of the stabilization plan. It intervened in union affairs, outlawed some unions completely, and forcefully broke up strikes. Not all organizations were affected equally, however. The government's plan to trim the state sector guided its selective attacks. Krieger Vasena shared Frondizi's dislike for the overly subsidized state railroads. The 200,000-member union resisted the military's reorganization schemes, but this time the state overcame its resistance. As a result, the government was able to cut the wage and salary component of the current account budget by 2 percent in 1967 and 7.5 percent in 1968.

The government's use of force overall was considerably more effective than it had been under the stabilization program of 1959–1962. While strike activity expanded rapidly in 1959, labor dissent declined under Onganía. By comparison, during Illia's tenure, an average of 760,730 worker-days were lost annually to strike activity, while only 50,327 worker-days were lost under Onganía (see Table 4.2). In particular, during Illia's last year in office (1966), 236,000 workers participated in work stoppages, resulting in 1 million worker-days lost. In 1967, there were only 547 participants and 2,700 worker-days lost.[57] The CGT plans for public protests against Krieger Vasena's monetarism were cancelled for lack of participants. The movement was now badly divided. Those called participationists favored direct collaboration with the government. The Vandorists rejected collaboration but agreed to talks with Onganía. They were hesitant to engage in militant activity; by holding back, they hoped to deflect repressive action from their affiliate unions. These tactics were successful in the short term, as the brunt of the state repression fell on the more militant *62 de pie junto con Perón* faction, now led by Raimundo Ongaro. Yet, by 1968, it became clear that dialogue was not bearing Vandor's unions any economic fruits. The Onganía administration closed itself off to interest group pressures as it became more determined to see the stabilization plan through to completion.

In early 1969, Vandor called for the reunification of the CGT. By May, the CGT was on the verge of a general strike when the workers and students of Córdoba rose against the Onganía dictatorship in an unparalleled insurrection. The regime was caught completely off guard (as was the union hierarchy) and could not contain the uprisings. Other smaller disturbances followed, creating a politically unstable environment for investors. The confidence of private and international business had been shattered, and capital was expatriated abroad. These events undermined Onganía's authority, and he was replaced in June 1970 by a military government that pledged to return Argentina to civilian rule.

## THE RETURN AND FALL OF PERONIST RULE

The transition to democracy was not entirely smooth. General Roberto Levingston, Onganía's successor, envisioned continued military rule, and his stalling tactics cost him his position. In March 1971, General Alejandro Lanusse was named president. Since the early 1960s, Lanusse had been a member of the *azul* (blue), or soft-line faction of the armed forces. *Los Azules* considered themselves a coalition of military professionals in the old sense; their duty was to defend constitutional governments and not to engage in partisan politics. They clashed with the *Colorados* (reds), who favored long-term military intervention. Ironically, General Onganía had originally

**Table 4.2 Repression and Strikes under Illia and Onganía**

| Government | Annual Average Repression[a] | Annual Average Scope of Protest | Annual Average Days Lost[b] |
|---|---|---|---|
| Arturo Illia (July 1963– July 1966) | .4[c] | 7700.7 | 760,730.0 |
| Juan Carlos Onganía (August 1966– June 1970) | .76 | 2095.6 | 50,327.0 |

*Source*: Strike data is from the International Labor Office, *Yearbook of Labor Statistics* (Geneva: ILO, 1966), p. 710; (1975), p. 798.
[a]For calculations, see the appendix.
[b]Worker-days lost as a result of strike activity, averaged over the four-year period shown.
[c]The repression score for the Illia government is overstated because the figure for 1966 also reflected preemptive repression carried out by the military in the fall of that year.

been a soft-liner, only to reverse himself upon assuming the presidency in 1966. However, by 1970, many *Azules* who were disdainful of the "revolutionary government" decided to press for an expeditious return to democracy by legalizing all political parties. The officers were also mindful of the past. They wanted to avoid a "reckless" venture into democratic politics that might bring Perón himself back to power. By the same token, they could not exclude his party from the elections without rekindling enormous opposition and weakening any future non-Peronist incumbent. Therefore, Lanusse tried to piece together a moderate coalition that could defeat the Peronists, and then passed legislation to prevent Perón's own candidacy.[58]

Economic policy during this period was designed to win political approval. Government credit was liberally extended to domestic industry to help it compete with foreign capital. Nominal wages were periodically adjusted to insure support among labor. Unfortunately, inflation rates exceeded adjustments, and real purchasing power declined. In response, the CGT carried out a series of enormously successful national strikes in 1971 and 1972. The military avoided confrontation with the CGT. In fact, there were no reported incidents of violence between police and strikers, despite the fact that these work stoppages were illegal[59] and resulted in hundreds of millions of dollars in production losses. To the contrary, the military approved new wage increases after each national strike in a continual effort to placate the trade union movement.

The CGT's criticism of economic performance stopped short of a complete condemnation of the government. In February 1972, labor moderates won an important union vote that approved continued work stoppages but disapproved of militant protests designed to undermine the regime. The leadership had spoken, but not all of the rank and file were listening. Students joined regional and local trade unionist affiliates in violent protests and riots in cities such as Córdoba, Mendoza, and Tucumán. The military was already badly divided and demoralized and could not retaliate with sufficient force to end the disturbances. Its moderate use of coercion was enough to trigger greater waves of violence, and it contributed to the perception that the armed forces could no longer guarantee political stability. A labor communiqué released in June 1972 warned that if repression by the government did not cease, "neither the working class, nor the students, nor the people in general will be responsible for the chaos which could occur."[60]

This veiled threat had more significance than even the trade unionists themselves could have imagined. The birth of an armed unit called the Montoneros[61] raised the political stakes considerably. Although numbering no more than a handful in 1970, they had made their presence dramatically known by assassinating General Pedro Aramburu just ten days before the ouster of Juan Onganía.

Unlike other guerrilla movements, the Montoneros linked themselves to an established political party. As self-proclaimed Peronists, they eschewed class struggle as the *primary* form of resistance, instead advocating a form of national liberation laden with romantic notions of socialism. First and foremost, they considered themselves the vanguard of Peronism. They were convinced that once in power, Perón would follow a "revolutionary course." As the vanguard element, it was their obligation to demonstrate to workers the futility of nonviolent legalistic forms of struggle and the advantage of armed resistance. They were encouraged in this approach not only by the repeated historical tendency for the armed forces to sabotage democratic processes, but also by Perón's proclamation that "against brute force, only intelligently-applied force can be effective."[62]

The Montoneros attracted supporters and admirers, and they learned to perform military maneuvers with sophistication, though always at the expense of well-grounded political actions. However, they never made significant inroads with their alleged working-class allies and remained isolated from them. What held the Peronist movement together during this period was Juan Perón himself; he played his guerrilla "card" (or his special forces as they were called) to negotiate his own return to Argentine politics. Dramatic guerrilla raids on military installations and other symbols of authority went unanswered. This silence convinced the public that the armed forces were weak; it also reminded the nation that only such a popular authoritarian figure as Perón could restore peace. At the same time, Perón gave full support to labor conservatives such as CGT Secretary-General José Rucci. Rucci's proclamation of September 1972 suggested that avenues of cooperation be pursued with the military. Perón had a unique ability to manipulate and control this complex and contradictory movement.

As a politician, Lanusse was no match for Perón. He had hoped to win back some legitimacy for the military by successfully managing the transition to civilian rule. Instead, his futile efforts to mollify moderate labor elites and to contain the guerrillas left the armed forces without any popular base. The military candidate for president could muster only 2.9 percent of the vote in the 1973 elections, which were won easily by the Peronists. With the victory of the Peronist candidate Hector Cámpora, the party was restored to power for the first time in eighteen years. A Social Pact was formalized among labor, industry, and government in June of that year. The contract was supported by both conservative industrialists and more liberal small businesspeople. It established an across-the-board wage hike and price freeze to be followed by a voluntary wage freeze and selected price increases.[63] The sequential nature of the plan was devised to prevent wage-price spiraling. After the preliminary increase, wages could be annually adjusted by government decree, but only in line with productivity gains. To insure compliance, collective negotiations between unions and firms were suspended, and economically motivated strikes were prohibited. The plan hoped to achieve noninflationary growth and income redistribution at the same time. Cámpora confidently predicted that the pact would, within four years, restore wage-earners' share of the national income (48 percent) earned under the second Perón government.

Initially, the pact seemed successful: most economic indicators responded favorably. Juan Perón assumed the presidency from Hector Cámpora in a special election that fall, lending greater legitimacy to the agreement. External factors contributed as well, as export prices fór Argentine goods increased 65 percent from the year before, and imports declined, resulting in a current account surplus of U.S. $704 million in 1973.

With the cooperation of labor and the private sector secured, the "special forces" had outlived their usefulness to Perón. The Peronist leftists had hoped that once in power, their leader would deal blows to the capitalist class, fight dependence and imperialist monopolies, and eventually steer the nation on a course toward socialism. None of this came to pass. Perón's pact was simply an effort to make capitalist development more manageable through class compromise. He turned to his most loyal labor leaders, known as *verticalistas* (for their obedience to edicts from above), to guarantee the rank and file's cooperation with management and isolation from the Left. Perón's objective was no longer to hold together ideologically disparate members of his movement; instead he parted ways with the radical Left to secure his stature as the spokesman for reconciliation and compromise.

In 1974, problems surfaced that threatened the viability of the pact. The sudden increase in the price of oil raised Argentina's import bill significantly; profit margins had already been hurt by the price freeze and were narrowed even farther for businesses dependent on costly imports. Argentina's external terms of trade deteriorated sharply: price declines for exports were matched by lower demand, the result of a ban on meat imports by the European Common Market in July 1974. These constraints led many businesses to violate the terms of the agreement by absorbing costs through higher prices. Perón imposed sanctions against violators in May 1974, but the freeze was finally abandoned in the fall of that year, unleashing latent inflationary pressures. The problem was compounded by the government's provision of cheap credit to business. In the first sixteen months of the Perón administration, two and one-half times as much money was printed as had been printed in the previous 100 years.[64] The public sector deficit rose from 7.9 percent of the GDP in 1974 to 15.2 percent in 1975.

Maintaining a multiclass coalition at a time of economic downturn was difficult enough, but the Peronist government also had unanticipated problems with its working-class allies. Rebel unionists in Córdoba and elsewhere turned their attention from the military to the labor bureaucracy. These dissident workers were angered over the labor bosses' accumulation of excessive power, their negotiation of unfair wage agreements (which were then imposed on a defenseless working class), and their cooperation and collusion with previous authoritarian regimes. The unionists believed that the hierarchy had lost its right to defend the interests of the rank and file. Now it was time to decentralize the labor movement so that local leaders would be granted the authority to advocate on behalf of their constituents.[65]

Perón had always sympathized with the rank and file; this was his flock, and he would tend to their interests just as long as they remained obedient to him. The authoritarian nature of Peronist trade unionism now came face to face with internal rebellion. Perón responded with the Professional Association Law of November 1973. The law strengthened the hand of the labor bureaucracy by institutionalizing the right of federations and confederations to intervene in unions and overturn decisions made at lower levels.[66] What was mandated on paper, however, was more difficult to put into practice. Local strikes, which increased sharply from October 1973 to June 1974, effectively won concessions from management: suspended workers were rehired, back pay was granted, and pledges were made to improve working conditions. Candidates hand-picked by the bureaucrats were frequently rejected in union-level electoral contests. Perón was displeased with these developments yet reluctant to resort to state repression against his own constituents.

The same could not be said for his wife, Isabel Perón, who assumed the presidential seat upon Perón's death in July 1974. Isabel Perón was an inexperienced leader and depended upon, and indeed was manipulated by, the labor elite and an inner circle of advisers. She was quick to oblige the CGT leadership with state security assistance. Police accompanied armed right-wing unionists in assaults on local headquarters of the powerful steel and metalworkers' unions. Under a national security law passed to prevent industrial sabotage, the government prohibited all plant occupations and strikes that were economically motivated.[67] Labor protests declined from 39 a month prior to July 1974 to 11.6 a month by November of that year. By October, the major independent unions and dissident labor leaders had been purged: the national leadership appointed interim representatives who were compliant with directives from above.

The labor bosses had Isabel's ear, but not for long. Their authority was gradually usurped by a tight circle of right-wing Peronists. The conservative coup was led by José López Rega, Isabel Perón's chief adviser. A former police officer who dabbled in the occult, López Rega had managed to work his way into the family's inner circles during Perón's exile, becoming his confidant and personal healer. He was now Isabel's minister of social welfare and used his position to persecute political foes and pursue orthodox economic solutions.

López Rega orchestrated a broad and intensive state terrorist campaign against workers, students, guerrillas, and alleged sympathizers. He covertly and illegally sponsored a right-wing death squad called the Argentine Anti-Communist Alliance (AAA).[68] The AAA became the centerpiece of the state's security apparatus. Surrounding the AAA was the Ministry of the Interior under the direction of Alberto Rocamora, a close associate of López Rega. Rocamora had replaced Esteban Righi, who had used his authority to eliminate some of the coercive features of state rule. Rocamora was involved with efforts to revitalize coercive practices. The AAA also depended upon the cooperation and collaboration of the police. Alberto Villar, General Lanusse's police chief (who was later accused of torture), was quickly promoted to head the Federal Police Command. Under his guidance, the police provided the AAA with equipment and personnel. With its state network established, the AAA embarked on a ferocious campaign to liquidate Perón's "special forces;" by the end of 1975, it had carried out some 2,000 political assassinations.[69]

Initially, the government's repression against the guerrillas was more severe than that used against labor dissidents. Secure in the fact that her husband had already denounced the "special forces" in May 1974, Isabel Perón was prepared to tolerate excesses against these groups. However, she had to move with greater caution against trade unionists. Bearing the name of her legendary husband, she was unavoidably cast as the leader of the organized working class. She could not carelessly resort to force without trampling on Peronist tradition and undermining the state-labor alliance her husband had cleverly crafted.

The president was torn between her respect for that alliance and her deference to the social welfare minister; a tension that produced an ambiguity with respect to economic policy. López Rega convinced the president that she must abandon the Social Pact as a first step toward social and economic recovery. This she did in October 1974 with the appointment of Alfredo Gómez Morales as economics minister. Gómez Morales was a respected moderate who had executed Perón's stabilization program of 1952. He was committed to fighting inflation, but, to the disappointment of López Rega, he did not impose a wage freeze. In fact, the government raised real wages with an across-the-board adjustment of 15 percent in November 1974 and another 20 percent in March 1975. Gómez Morales satisfied some business interests with price decontrol and hoped to counter expected inflationary trends with restricted federal spending on personnel, low-cost housing, and a fixed exchange rate.[70] His mixed austerity package was clearly designed to administer austerity in a manner least offensive to labor.

This was a difficult balance to achieve. The fixed exchange rate hurt farm exports, caused trade deficits, and generated speculative activity against the peso. Fiscal restraint was not sufficient to stop the consumer price index from moving upwards, eroding wage gains with alarming speed: between November 1974 and February 1975, real wages plummeted 20 percent. Labor protested the loss of purchasing power, but it sounded more and more like a distant voice to a president isolated by López Rega. Labor leaders complained they were unable to get in to see her, a fact that was symptomatic of their complete loss of influence over government policy by the first part of 1975.

In that year, the government turned increasingly toward orthodox economic solutions and political repression of trade unions. The distinctions drawn earlier between guerrillas and workers seemed to fade as the "exceptional measures taken by the government to combat armed insurrection inevitably led to the repression of lawful trade union activity."[71] Raimundo Ongaro, the dissident leader of the Argentine printers' union, had been removed from his post in October 1974 and placed under arrest on a charge of illegal possession of firearms. A judge acquitted him in December, but the AAA wanted him out of the country. Its murder of his son in May 1975 forced Ongaro into exile later that year. This kind of state terror against organized labor became typical.

López Rega's hold on the president was now total. At his request, she fired Gómez Morales and replaced him with a committed rightist and economic liberal named Celestino Rodrigo. Rodrigo devalued the peso and raised the price of public goods and services by as much as 100 to 200 percent, while holding wage gains to 40 percent.[72] Workers had already lost confidence in the government and were now successfully negotiating salary increases directly with management. The labor bureaucrats found themselves in an embarrassing position: the minister's policies made it impossible for them to remain loyal to Isabel Perón while retaining the respect of a rank and file that had taken matters into its own hands. Ultimately they would have to choose, and they did. When the government cancelled all negotiated contracts and then reneged on a wage adjustment, the CGT sponsored a forty-eight-hour general strike on July 7 and 8—the first ever against a Peronist government.

Perón granted limited economic concessions to the strikers and fired Rodrigo and López Rega. The *verticalistas* anxiously lined up behind the president again, but time was running out. The middle class was hurting from an annual inflation rate that had reached 900 percent. It joined with industrialists, landowners, and segments of the armed forces to call for Isabel Perón's ouster. The situation deteriorated in early 1976 as the government, in a last desperate effort to salvage the economy, agreed in principle to an IMF-stabilization package in exchange for a sizable loan. Perón never had a chance to complete negotiations, as the military overthrew her on March 23, 1976.

## CONCLUSION

The golden years of Peronism (1946–1955) were important in two respects. Socially and politically, they meant the coming of age for the Peronist trade unions and their affiliated party. Economically, they represented the tremendous growth of the state bureaucracy and federal budget. The two processes were inextricably linked and mutually reinforcing: state expenditures generated economic growth, provided employment, and subsidized living standards for the working class; these benefits lured growing numbers of workers into the unions, until the labor movement grew powerful enough to extract even greater state intervention on its behalf.

Reformist administrations after Juan Perón's first administration did nothing to break the cycle, since they were convinced that liberal spending programs made economic sense (because they would fuel consumption and then investment), as well as political sense (because they would cultivate the support or, at a minimum, the cooperation of organized labor). These governments provided direct benefits to labor in the form of minimum-wage concessions, price subsidies, and public sector employment. Unfortunately for non-Peronist reformists, these economic rewards were not enough. The trade union sector remained fiercely independent and would not trade its material gains for political acquiescence.

Transitional governments such as Aramburu's dictatorship were more hesitant to spend since they were preoccupied with inflationary effects and determined to trim current expenditures so as to raise public savings for capital investment functions. By the same token, these governments were not prepared to launch stabilization programs that would place the full burden of economic recovery on the workers. They tried to strike a balance between redistribution and economic stability, devising a series of offsetting policies: they would devalue the currency (which raises the cost of living for low-income groups), then reform tax laws to ease the burden upon these same groups; or they would free prices, then retain subsidies on working-class commodities. Politically their aim was to create a compliant labor force fully divorced from Peronist influence, using co-optation and moderate levels of repression. All these strategies proved futile against a thoroughly defiant and insubordinate working class. Redistributive gestures were mere palliatives, and intermediate levels of coercion only persuaded the labor movement to become more combative.

Finally, governments guided by economic liberalism were the most committed to decontrol and deficit reduction. They realized that if the federal deficit were to be reduced, the power of organized pressure groups would have to be curtailed. They were determined to break the state-labor nexus with free market programs and higher levels of coercion against organized pressure groups. Still, the trade union movement was remarkably resilient throughout and was able to rebound from serious economic setbacks and state harassment. The authorities discovered the difficulty of demoralizing a movement that was determined to regain its previous stature, dividing a movement that had Perón as its figurehead, or silencing the protests of a movement whose pressure tactics had paid off in the past.

Although frustrated with the outcomes, the authoritarian-economic liberal government tried a bit harder. Convinced that the fault lay not in the design of the political-economic program but in the lack of political will to enforce it, it attacked those groups obstructing the policy process. Each succeeding administration hoped to correct past errors by resorting to increasingly higher levels of coercion. This "learning curve of repression" can be observed in Figure 4.1. The degree of repression from 1956 to 1980 dramatically increased in 1976, the year the military government of the Proceso de Reorganización Nacional (PRN) assumed power and embarked upon the most vigorous free market experiment in post–World War II Argentina.

**Figure 4.1 Repression of Organized Labor in Argentina: 1956–1980**

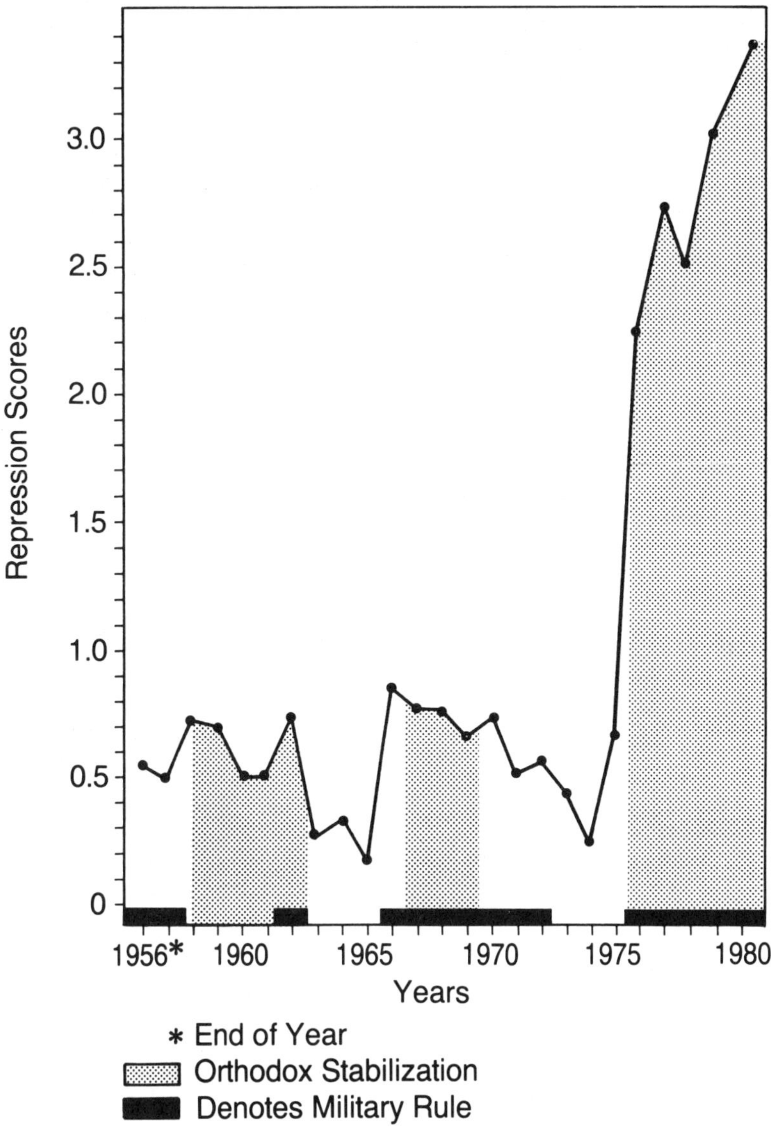

## NOTES

1. No doubt, the sheer force of numbers would have yielded sizable monetary gains for the rank and file. As the ratio of organized workers to the economically active population increased, so did labor's bargaining power. The movement spread quickly to hitherto uncontested sectors. Sugar refineries, packing houses, and transportation systems became exposed to a union presence for the first time. Its power also expanded within sectors, as the railroad union, the largest in Argentina, increased its membership by 25 percent in just three years. See the United States Department of Labor, *Foreign Labor Information: Labor in Argentina*, June 1959, p. 10. These developments were not a product of modernization, whereby industrial growth brings forth a larger proletariat force. In fact, the major industrialization drive began in the 1930s, under military rule. Yet by 1941, almost 80 percent of CGT affiliates came from *nonindustrial* regions. Though the objective conditions were ripe for unionization, the rural-based oligarchy feared the consequences and allied with the armed forces to check the mobilization of the working class.

2. Roberto Carri, *Sindicatos y Poder en la Argentina* (Buenos Aires: Editorial Sudestada, 1967), p. 32. A lower estimate of 2 million is provided by Samuel Baily, *Labor, Nationalism and Politics in Argentina* (New Brunswick: Rutgers University Press, 1967), pp. 70, 101.

3. United Nations Economic Commission for Latin America, *Economic Development and Income Distribution in Argentina* (New York: United Nations, 1969), p. 170.

4. No pretense is made to offer a comprehensive and in-depth account of the Argentine trade union movement. That has been done elsewhere. The focus is instead on the manner in which economic prejudices affect the treatment of organized labor at the hands of the state. For the pre-Peronist history of the Argentine labor movement, see David Tamarin, *The Argentine Labor Movement, 1930–1945: A Study in the Origins of Peronism* (Albuquerque: University of New Mexico Press, 1985); for a comprehensive treatment of Argentine labor history, see Baily, *Labor in Argentina*; Ruben Rotondaro, *Realidad y Cambio en el Sindicalismo* (Buenos Aires: Editorial Pleamar, 1971); Santiago Senen González, *El Sindicalismo Después de Perón* (Buenos Aires: Editorial Galena, 1971).

5. These measures are summarized in George Blankstén, *Perón's Argentina* (Chicago: University of Chicago Press, 1953), pp. 263–265.

6. Baily, *Labor in Argentina*, p. 102.

7. For instance, the index measuring export-dollar unit-values divided by import-dollar unit-values rose from 78 in 1940–1944 to 124 in 1947–1949, indicating improved external terms of trade. Balance of trade figures are from the United Nations, *U.N. Statistical Yearbook*. Terms of trade data is from Carlos Diaz-Alejandro, *Essays on the Economic History of the Argentine Republic* (New Haven: Yale University Press, 1970), p. 86.

8. Paul Buchanan, "The Institutional Faces of State Corporatism in Argentina: National Labor Administration Under Perón (1946–1955) and Onganía (1966–1970)," paper prepared for the Western Political Science Association Meeting, March 25, 1983; see Figure 1. This is an earlier version of an article that appeared in the *Latin American Research Review* 20 (1985) entitled "State Corporatism in Argentina: Labor Administration Under Perón and Onganía."

9. Ibid., pp. 17, 18.

10. Richard D. Mallon and Juan V. Sourrouille, *Economic Policy Making*

*in a Conflict Society: The Argentine Case* (Cambridge: Harvard University Press, 1975), p. 9.

11. Rotondaro, *Realidad y Cambio*, p. 180.

12. Statistics on subsidies and current expenditures can be found in Diaz-Alejandro, *Essays on Economic History*, p. 492. After 1949, the state permitted agricultural prices to rise relative to industrial prices. This would have meant higher consumption costs for urban workers had it not been for the policy of subsidy. It meant an increasing fiscal burden on the state, which had to make up a greater difference between the agricultural selling price and the urban purchasing price of these commodities.

13. Guido Di Tella and Manuel Zymelman, *Las Etapas del Desarrollo Económico Argentino* (Buenos Aires: EUDEBA, 1967), p. 122; Aldo Ferrer, et al., *Los Planes de Estabilización en la Argentina* (Buenos Aires: Paidos, 1969), p. 75; Diaz-Alejandro, *Essays on Economic History*, p. 403.

14. Baily, *Labor in Argentina*, p. 81.

15. Ferrer, *Los Planes*, p. 74.

16. Winthrop R. Wright, *British-Owned Railways in Argentina: Their Effect on Economic Nationalism, 1854–1948* (Austin: University of Texas Press, 1974), p. 258.

17. Ibid., p. 267.

18. For these statistics, see Diaz-Alejandro, *Economic Essays*, p. 496.

19. Labor membership information from Carri, *Sindicatos y Poder*, p. 28fn, and United States Department of Labor, "Foreign Labor Information: Labor in Argentina," June 1959, appendix A.

20. A discussion of Peronist trade union power and structure can be found in Daniel James, "Power and Politics in Peronist Trade Unions," *Journal of Interamerican Studies and World Affairs* 20 (February 1978):3–36.

21. Salvador Treber, *La Economía Argentina: Análisis, Diagnóstico y Alternativas* (Buenos Aires: Ediciones Macchi, 1977), p. 424.

22. Ricardo Jorge Ferrucci, "Doctrinas Económicas Filosofía del Liberalismo Argentino," *Realidad Económica* (July–September 1979): 63–64, 68–72.

23. On the stabilization plan, see Ferrer, *Los Planes*, pp. 77–83; Gary Wynia, *Argentina in the Postwar Era: Politics and Economic Policymaking in a Divided Society* (Albuquerque: University of New Mexico Press, 1978), pp. 70–73.

24. This analysis borrows from Mallon and Sourrouille, *Economic Policymaking*, pp. 9–14.

25. Edward Epstein, "Politicization and Income Redistribution in Argentina: The Case of the Peronist Worker," *Economic Development and Cultural Change* 23 (July 1975): 620.

26. For a discussion on the relations between the labor movement and the military, see Rotondaro, *Realidad y Cambio*, pp. 271–283.

27. A term borrowed from Alfred Stepan, *The State and Society: Peru in Comparative Perspective* (Princeton: Princeton University Press, 1979), pp. 74–79. Also see Guillermo O'Donnell, *Modernization and Bureaucratic-Authoritarianism: Studies in South American Politics* (Berkeley: Institute of International Studies, 1973).

28. The economic thinking behind the Prebisch plan for Argentina can be found in "The Problem of the Economic Development of Argentina," *Economic Bulletin for Latin America* 4 (March 1959): 13–24.

29. The depiction of this program as transitional is shared by Eprime Eshag and Rosemary Thorp, "Las Políticas Económicas Ortodoxas de Perón a

Guido (1953–1963)," in Ferrer, *Los Planes*, pp. 83–84.

30. Diaz-Alejandro, *Essays on Economic History*, pp. 198–207.

31. Real wage data computed from nominal wage and CPI figures found in *International Labor Organization Yearbook*, 1956–1958.

32. Aramburu's cabinet repeatedly refused to cut government spending and end subsidies in 1957, costing him the support of the IMF. *New York Times*, March 21, 1957, p. 1.

33. *International Labor Organization Yearbook*, 1965, p. 692.

34. Scores for particular forms of repression for the Aramburu period, along with scores for all of the Argentine governments, can be found in the appendix. A significant number of Peronist trade union leaders were arrested or forced to go underground during the Aramburu years. However, the rank and file were not as adversely affected.

35. Carri, *Sindicatos y Poder*.

36. Arturo Frondizi's general political and economic views are recorded in Arturo Frondizi, *Mensajes Presidenciales: 1958–1962* (Buenos Aires: Ediciones Centro de Estudios Nacionales, 1978).

37. A summation of Frondizi's economic plan by his most trusted economic advisor can be found in Rogelio Frigerio, *Los Cuatros Años: 1958–1962* (Buenos Aires: Editorial Concordia, 1962).

38. An analysis of the Frondizi plan can be found in Mallon and Sourrouille, *Economic Policy Making*, pp. 19–25.

39. Ibid., p. 71; a critical view of the Frondizi development strategy contends that the turn toward import substitution deepened Argentina's economic dependence since the country had to import capital goods to sustain domestic industry. See Clarence Zuvekas, "Argentine Economic Policy, 1958–1962: The Frondizi Government's Development Plan," *Inter-American Economic Affairs* 22 (Summer 1968): 45–73.

40. "Argentina Gets $329 Million in Aid," *New York Times*, December 30, 1958, p. 1.

41. "Economic Reform Set in Argentina," *New York Times*, December 1, 1958, p. 17.

42. Ibid., November 12, 1958, p. 1.

43. *International Labor Organization Yearbook*, 1960.

44. *The New York Times*, January 19, 1959, p. 1; January 22, p. 7.

45. *Plan Conintes* revived an old Peronist defense law that created internal zones of operation in the event of war. Most legal scholars at the time believed that *Plan Conintes* was in clear violation of the spirit if not the letter of Perón's defense measure. Perón had been careful to state that these provisions would only take effect if the nation was actually engaged in combat against a foreign enemy and were not designed for purposes of political repression. See *Clarín*, December 22, 1960, p. 5.

46. In describing the "subversive" content of the documents they had confiscated from the "terrorists," the military noted passages "inciting strikes and disorder" and expressing a "Peronist political tendency." *Notícias Gráficas*, April 23, 1960, p. 3.

47. Arturo Frondizi, *Mensajes Presidenciales: 1958–1962, vol. 1*, (Buenos Aires: Ediciones Centro de Estudios Nacionales, 1962).

48. Rosemary Thorp, "Economic Policies in Argentina in the Post-War Years," *Oxford University Institute of Economics and Statistics Bulletin* 27–28 (1965–1966): 21.

49. For an account of the Illia strategy, see Gary Wynia, *Argentina in the Post War Era: Politics and Economic Policy Making in a Divided Society*

(Albuquerque: University of New Mexico Press, 1978), pp. 115–117; Mallon and Sourrouille, *Economic Policy Making*, pp. 25–29. Also see various issues of the *Review of the River Plate*, 1963.

50. Inter-American Development Bank, *External Public Debt of the Latin American Countries*, Washington, D.C., July, 1982.

51. North American Congress on Latin America (NACLA), *Argentina: In the Hour of the Furnace*, (New York: NACLA, 1975), p. 13.

52. Rotondaro, *Realidad y Cambio*, p. 318.

53. John Thompson, "Argentine Economic Policy Under the Onganía Regime," *Inter-American Economic Affairs* 24 (Summer 1970): 54.

54. The economic philosophy and programs of the economics minister are found in Adalbert Krieger Vasena, *Política Económica Argentina: Discursos del Ministro de Economía y Trabajo*, February 1968–February 1969 (Buenos Aires: Marcos Victor Durruty, 1969).

55. GDP data from: The World Bank, *World Tables*, 1980. Inflation rates from: Ministerio de Economía, Instituto Nacional de Estadística y Censos, *Índice de Precios al Consumidor en la Capital Federal, 1968–1970*; deficit information compiled by the World Bank; reserve position from IMF, *International Finance Statistics Yearbook*, 1982.

56. Wage share information from ECLA, *Economic Development and Income Distribution in Argentina*, 1968, and Edward Epstein, "Anti-Inflationary Policies in Argentina and Chile, Or Who Pays the Cost," *Comparative Political Studies* 11(July 1978): 216.

57. International Labor Organization, *Yearbook*, 1968.

58. This section draws upon the following important analyses of the Lanusse years: Guillermo O'Donnell, *1966–1973: El Estado Burocrático Autoritario: Triunfos, Derrotas y Crisis* (Buenos Aires: Editorial de Belgrano, 1982); Ruben M. Perina, *Onganía, Levingston, Lanusse: Los Militares en la Política Argentina* (Buenos Aires: Editorial de Belgrano, 1983); Joseph Page, *Perón: A Biography* (New York: Randon House, 1983).

59. Lester A. Sorbel, ed., *Argentina and Perón: 1970–75* (New York: Facts on File, 1975), p. 46.

60. Ibid., p. 48.

61. The narrative on the Montoneros borrows from Richard Gillespie, *Soldiers of Perón: Argentina's Montoneros* (Oxford: Clarendon Press, 1982).

62. Ibid., p. 52.

63. Guido Di Tella, "The Economic Policies of Argentina's Labor-Based Government (1973–76)," in *Inflation and Stabilization in Latin America*, ed. Rosemary Thorp and Laurence Whitehead (New York: Holmes and Meier, 1979), pp. 181–216.

64. Gillespie, *Soldiers of Perón*, p. 142.

65. These developments within the labor movement are analyzed in Elizabeth Jelin, "Conflictos Laborales en la Argentina, 1973–1976," *CEDES, Estudios Sociales* no. 9, 1977.

66. Many provisions of the law were beneficial to all workers, including the right to establish associations, petition the authorities, elect their representatives and bargain collectively. For the complete text, see International Labor Office, *Legislative Series*, July–August 1974.

67. Elizabeth Jelin, "Conflictos Laborales," p. 25.

68. The fact that none of its operators were ever arrested for their atrocities sustains the theory that the organization had official endorsement.

69. Amnesty International, *The Amnesty International Report: 1975–1976*, p. 85.

70. This account of the Morales economic program borrows from Guido Di Tella, *Argentina Under Perón: 1973–1976* (London: Macmillan Press, 1983), p. 120–124; useful references for economic policymaking and policymakers during the entire Peronist administration are found in Juan Carlos de Pablo, *Economía Política del Peronismo* (Buenos Aires: El Cid Editor, 1980); Oscar Braun, *El Plan Económico del Gobierno Popular* (Buenos Aires: El Editorial Coloquio, 1974).

71. Di Tella *Argentina Under Perón*, p. 86.

72. Ibid., pp. 124–125.

# 5

# Security Ideology, Liberal Economics, and the "Dirty War" in Argentina, 1976-1983

*As many people will die in Argentina as necessary to restore order.*

—General Jorge Videla, Montevideo, 1975

On October 30, 1983, an ignominious chapter in Argentine history came to a close with the election of Radical Party candidate Raúl Alfonsín as President. The previous seven and one-half years under military rule were marked by repeated and flagrant violations of human rights at the hands of state security forces. In the first four months after the military coup of March 24, 1976, which deposed the elected government of Isabel Perón, more than 5,000 arrests were reported, and torture of detainees was commonplace. The Alfonsin-appointed human rights commission was able to document some 9,000 cases of individuals who had been abducted and had then disappeared at the hands of the security forces in the first three years under military rule. The commission estimates that "the true figure is much higher" but cannot be known since many families were unwilling to report human rights abuses for fear of reprisals.[1] Some figures run as high as 15,000 disappeared and an additional 5,000 murdered but identified and thus not counted as missing. Subsequent investigations of the disappearances have revealed that nearly all those victims also were executed.

Although many Argentines anticipated the 1976 coup, few could have foreseen the widescale state terror that was to follow. To some extent, the junta's opening proclamation was unexceptional in that it sounded the standard litany of charges leveled by Latin American dictators against their democratic opponents. Military men are frequently troubled by what they see as the lack of managerial competence and efficiency, the breakdown of order, and the erosion of Christian values under a democratic government. The Argentine armed forces claimed they had seized power to fill a vacuum left by the previous rulers, who had threatened Argentina with "dissolution and anarchy." They castigated the Peronist government for its "inability to provide cohesion," its "repeated contradictions apparent in measures of all kinds," its absence of "ethical and moral practices," and a failure to confront "subversion."[2] The military junta was particularly irked by the economic practices of the previous labor-dominated government, which it accused of a "manifest irresponsibility in the management of the economy which had destroyed the productive apparatus."[3] Their self-proclaimed mission was to rebuild the economy and eventually to restore effective, representative government, but that would not occur until they had achieved a thorough reorganization of the economic, social, and political life of the country. Aptly enough, the junta named their government the Proceso de Reorganización Nacional (Process of National Reorganization, or PRN). However, this antiseptic discourse disguised the fact that the regime would rely on mass terror to make that reorganization possible.

To come to grips with the harsh reality of the Proceso, it is essential to understand the military's motives. The Argentine generals subscribed to two fundamental ideologies: the first, a national security doctrine, provided the authorization for unmitigated state violence and guided the creation of an elaborate security apparatus; the second, a free market ideology, provided a focus for the selection of victims. As it turns out, the military forces were engaged in operations parallel to those of the military junta. The first, predating the coup and well-publicized, was the counterterrorist operation launched against leftist guerrillas. The second, clandestine and never acknowledged, was the repression of unarmed civilians. The junta easily and frequently lost sight of the distinction between armed and unarmed foes, thus earning their operations the name "Dirty War." Although many individuals were caught up in the government's web of assault, the junta placed special emphasis on its war against the trade union sector. Pursuant to the goals of free competition and decontrol, the government set out to deactivate those groups, such as the labor movement, whose interests were tied to a protective, interventionist, and expansionary state.

## SECURITY IDEOLOGY

The Argentine regime subscribed to what is known as the national security doctrine, or NSD.[4] This doctrine, in its various permutations, is an amalgam of resurrected concepts of geopolitics, counterinsurgency, and development, glorifying militarism, the state, and the nation. Although all states are security-conscious, security themes within the NSD become the yardstick by which all policies are measured. In fact, all "national politics," according to one Argentine general and former presidential adviser, "is to be understood and determined from the point of view of the national interest and national security."[5] The geopolitical aspect of the NSD suggests that the state, as the central institution of society, is the agent that must guarantee that security. The armed forces as ruling elite are charged with running the affairs of state and must be granted special rights. A triple identification is then made among the nation, the state, and the government: the military reifies itself as the only depository of the interests and values of the nation by virtue of its retention of state power; all dissent and denunciations of the military regime are viewed as attacks on the nation itself; conversely, attacks on the nation are considered to be direct challenges to the regime.[6]

The Argentine military regime sensed threats to its security nearly everywhere. As the target of increasing criticism domestically and internationally, it felt compelled to broaden its antisubversive campaign to include all real and potential government opponents, since they were by extension also enemies of the nation. The military perceived a comprehensive threat that grew in proportion to its own insecurities, but its sense of threat was also driven by the ideology to which it subscribed.

The Argentine variant of the NSD was, to a large extent, borrowed from other places and other times. Counterinsurgency principles, for example, first made their entry into Argentina during the late 1950s with the visit of French military missions. Officers who would later rule during the Proceso had their formative training and indoctrination into military life at about this time. The French were already entrenched in counterinsurgency operations in Algeria and Vietnam and could speak from experience. They were thus taken very seriously by these future heads of state.[7] A flurry of articles (many authored by French officers) soon appeared in Argentine military journals such as the *Revista de la Escuela Superior de Guerra*, warning of Argentina's vulnerability to international communism and preparing the country for countersubversive struggle. Writing in 1964, an Argentine colonel stated categorically that the hard-line French views had thoroughly penetrated the Argentine armed forces at every rank.[8]

The corps of French officers who participated in the colonial defense of Algeria believed that the Algerian National Liberation Front was simply the instrument for a larger and more ominous movement against Western civilization and its ideals. Shrugging off the suggestion that the resistance was a legitimate national effort to throw off the yoke of colonial subjugation, the French army treated their foes as disreputable foreign agents. The opponent was a terrorist who relied more on indiscriminate, excessive violence, and on the inculcation of fear than he did on ideological persuasion. Counterinsurgency would lose if it were not prepared to do likewise, according to Colonel Roger Trinquier, an important French theoretician of counterrevolutionary warfare. Colonel Trinquier was one of the first to acknowledge that proper identification of an enemy so well assimilated into society would be extremely difficult. Humanitarian assistance, propaganda, and education should come later, but in the interim, he said, they are wasted on a public that is "infected by clandestine organisms that penetrate like a cancer into its midst."[9] He was also the first formally to defend the practice of torture as a means to extract information about enemy intentions. His views were to provide a license for such less-discriminate campaigns of state violence as the "Dirty War."

The military's acceptance of French doctrine was remarkable, given how incompatible the ideas seemed to be with Argentine reality in the early 1960s. The revolutionary movements that began to flourish in Peru, Colombia, and Central America as a consequence of Castro's victory did not appear in Argentina. Few Argentines at the time had any sympathies with Communist parties or movements. The most progressive party with any clout was, of course, the labor-based Peronist Party. But its working-class followers had rejected socialist ideals long ago. Its allegiances were to Perón and his pragmatic vision of a reformed, but not overturned, capitalist system. Reading the military journals of the time, one would have thought that Argentina was on the threshold of a revolution. Nothing could have been further from the truth, yet the French ideas endured.

Of course, ideas are unlikely to stick unless they resonate with life experiences. Most assuredly, the emergence of the Montoneros and the People's Revolutionary Army (Ejército Revolucionario del Pueblo, or ERP) guerrilla forces in the early 1970s confirmed for the armed forces what the French had been saying years before. But how the military experienced and interpreted the guerrilla phenomenon was far more important than the phenomenon itself. From its point of view, the activities of these small bands of armed rebels represented a pernicious manifestation of a movement of global proportions. Argentina was one theater of operations in this ongoing confrontation.[10] This was an unconventional war whose practitioners were thought to operate in disguised form. Once having retreated from the battlefield, they would reorganize, penetrate, and then assimilate into the social and political mainstream to prepare for the next phase of their struggle. That struggle was multidimensional—the guerrillas were only one manifestation of a campaign that reached into the schools, factories, government offices, and homes. They could survive indefinitely under the protective cover of diverse legal organizations. Ramón Camps, chief of the Buenos Aires police during the height of the "Dirty War," and personally responsible for the disappearance and death of some 2,000 prisoners, stated, "You always have a latent element which awaits an opportune moment to reappear. . . . This is the thesis of Vo Nguyen Giap and of Mao Tse Tung."[11] Convinced that the enemy's chameleon-like transformations would help to widen their attack and prolong their life span indefinitely, the Argentine military thrust themselves into a war they perceived to be total and permanent.

Again, the idea was neither new nor Argentine. Erick Von Ludendorff, the World War I German general, first coined the term "total war." According to him, it meant that since war consumed all aspects of existence, the political realm must become beholden to military direction.[12] Ludendorff's dangerous inversion of Clausewitz's theories of war and politics were well-received within Latin American military circles. That the military regime had fully internalized the concept of a total war between East and West during a time of relative calm in U.S.–Soviet relations is remarkable in itself; that it had constructed policies predicated on the concept seems unfathomable. Jacobo Timmerman, the former editor of the Argentine daily newspaper, *La Opinión*, who was arrested and tortured by the security forces in 1977 and lived to write about it, comments:

> Even the most irrational being finds it necessary to formulate a certain coherence around his irrationality in order to be able to maintain its continuity. The Argentine military tapped their vast reservoir of hatred and fantasy so as to synthesize their action into one basic concept: World War III has begun; the enemy is left-wing terrorism; and Argentina was the initial battleground chosen by the enemy.[13]

To the extent that the armed forces believed in this new world war, they had not only grossly distorted the nature of the guerrilla movements but had prepared counterstrategies that were incompatible with Argentine realities. The largest guerrilla group, the Montoneros, was affiliated with the Peronist party and received no official or unofficial assistance or endorsement from Moscow. Although determined and well-armed, it was never a part of any international movement, nor did it ever successfully infiltrate mass organizations.

Ideologies that are conceptually flawed, anachronistic, or simply incompatible with contemporary realities are sure to "map" the political terrain incorrectly and thus generate serious misperceptions. The morc firmly perceptions are embedded in doctrine, the more glaringly discordant they become with the observable world. Exaggerated or implausible accounts of national conditions are then fully internalized, and mistaken options (such as the excessive use of violence against complacent populations) seem imperative.[14] This appears to have been the case with the Argentine armed forces.

It is tempting to pass the military's image of global conspirators off as a mere rationalization, devised to disguise its real goal of eliminating its political enemies. This argument will not wash for two reasons. First, the ideas that sustained the image of a regime and nation at risk were not conveniently invented just prior to the onslaught of terror. They had permeated the ranks of the military years before; they were elaborated upon in military journals, speeches, and hemispheric security conferences. Second, despite the defeat of guerilla forces in Argentina, the armed forces did not abandon their views when no longer needed. Even during current episodes of relative calm under democratic rule, officers have continued to repeat the same security themes. In an interview with this author in June 1984, former president General Roberto Viola expressed his alarm about the resurfacing of internationally connected "subversive" elements in Argentine society, even though he had announced the total defeat of the guerrillas in September 1977.[15]

The regime was determined to wipe out this "subversive" threat, but the term was used loosely to define those who were critics or potential critics of the regime, or those who resisted the political, economic, and ideological order. Given the expansive and enduring nature of the security threat, as perceived through the lens of the NSD, the military would have to extend its reach and remain forever vigilant. This could be achieved only by creating an elaborate security apparatus.

## The Security Apparatus

Impelled by its own security ideology, the military constructed a leviathan of terror that consumed vast financial and human resources. It had several distinguishing characteristics. First, it was geographically comprehensive, reaching into the most remote corners of the nation. From the tropical province of Misiones to the wind-swept and sparsely populated expanse of Patagonia, no part of the country was left unaffected. The armed forces established a set of security zones, subzones, and areas that effectively parceled the territory into increasingly smaller units.[16] These security units displaced normal political ones, and members of the armed forces assumed gubernatorial functions from elected officials.

The concept of security zones was not new to Argentina. As early as 1948, President Juan Perón's Law of National Defense stipulated that during times of war, the country would be divided into operative zones. Within these regions, martial law could be imposed, meaning that civil governors, administrators, and magistrates would lose their autonomy to the commanding officers in charge.[17] However, there were some important differences between Perón's version and that of the PRN. Under Perón's law, ultimate authority for these security arrangements resided with the chief executive officer, who was an elected official. That was naturally not the case with the military junta. Also, such an arrangement could only be instated during a period of declared war with another nation. The PRN government was never *officially* at war; it had turned a defensive device against foreign invasion into an offensive device to silence its domestic opposition.

A second characteristic of the junta's security apparatus was the organization of its chain of command. The zonal structure was mirrored by a pyramidal chain of authority that organized and regulated security affairs at each level. At the top resided the junta—the supreme political organ of the nation—composed of the commanders-in-chief from the army, navy, and air force. Answerable to it and just below it were commanding officers of the five army corps whose jurisdictions were congruent with the five zones.[18] Below them were infantry and cavalry brigade commanders who had responsibility for some thirty-five subzones, and beneath them were mid-ranking officers who led regiment and batallion divisions and had charge of some 210 areas. This was the official and overt arm of the security apparatus that, the military alleged, was devised to assist in the struggle against armed terrorists.

Actually, the security pyramid had another feature: the regiment and batallion commanders had immediate authority over some 100 documented clandestine detention centers (CCDs) scattered throughout the 210 areas.[19] Suspects were brought to these centers and detained—subject to inhumane conditions, repeatedly tortured, and often never heard from again. These centers were located on military premises or in police stations, and staffed by the police, army personnel, or federal penitentiary officials. Although most

CCDs were under direct army supervision, a few were placed in the hands of the air force, the navy, the police, and the Ministry of Interior.[20] In all, nearly 700 officers participated directly in their operation.[21] Consequently, by making sure that no armed service branch or relevant agency of state was denied participation in this aspect of the "Dirty War," the junta kept bureaucratic and institutional rivalries to a minimum.

The repressive designs of the junta are revealed not only by the mere existence of these concentration camps, but by their proximity to densely populated areas where masses of political suspects could be quickly processed. For example, Zone One of the First Army Corps was the second smallest geographically; but because it comprised Buenos Aires province and most of the city (where 40 percent of the country's population lived), it contained the largest number of identified CCDs (thirty-six), with seven in downtown Buenos Aires alone.

The terrorist operation was decentralized yet always under the firm grip of the military junta. This mixture of local action and central authority cut through bureaucratic red tape to expedite the elimination of political opponents without permitting the leviathan to get out of control. According to a secret directive of the junta, issued in 1976, all commanders were given wide latitude to intervene wherever and whenever they suspected "subversive" threats, and they were permitted to resort to any means necessary to achieve their objectives.[22]

Brigade commanders, for example, had the authority to assemble informal paramilitary units called *grupos tareas* or work teams. These were shadowy groups whose official ties to the state were publicly disclaimed by the junta for years. Although often recruited from the armed forces, their members wore no uniforms and drove in unmarked cars. They abducted citizens from their homes, transferred them to concentration camps, or eliminated them entirely. In the process, work teams would often confiscate the victims' valuables. Their method of operation was to cordon off urban areas, which they declared "free zones." Inside these zones, the police were instructed to desist from their normal activities and cooperate as needed with the terrorist operation. *Grupos tareas* had complete access to military personnel, hardware, and intelligence. In fact, privately, the military made no effort to disassociate itself from these groups. To the contrary, officers were frequently rotated in and out of the work teams so that everyone could "get their hands dirty," and profit from the "booty of war".[23] The *grupos tareas* epitomized the decentralized, yet institutionalized feature of the "Dirty War."

In this regard, the Argentine security state differed from the Brazilian one. In Brazil, the most unsavory acts of violence were performed by intelligence agencies who were operationally autonomous. Although staffed by military and police personnel, they had their own chain of command and were known to bypass or even overrule the armed forces' general staff. According to Alfred Stepan, Brazil's security apparatus became a feared state within a state.[24] In Argentina, the army, navy, and air force jealously guarded and closely monitored their respective intelligence agencies. Service rivalries always existed, but the junta managed these by partitioning government agencies and terrorist work among the separate branches, giving each a sense of autonomy and participation in the larger project.

In sum, the junta's campaign of terror was extensive, hierarchically organized, and decentralized. As vast a network as it was, it did not operate indiscriminately. There were certain focal points of terror, chief among them the organized labor sector. According to secret orders signed by army commander General Roberto Viola, top priority was to be given to the "elimination" of "subversive" elements at the factory level within manufacturing establishments.[25] This was a form of economically motivated combat, targeted against trade unionists who were perceived to be obstructing the achievement of economic objectives. To understand why the regime felt so threatened by labor, we turn to an examination of its economic ideology.

## ECONOMIC IDEOLOGY

### True Believers

In April 1976, the newly appointed economics minister, José A. Martínez de Hoz, announced a series of stopgap measures designed to lower inflation, generate growth, improve trade revenues, and eliminate the public sector deficit. Prices were deregulated, exchange controls eliminated, federal expenditures curtailed, credit tightened, and wages frozen.[26] The government's longer-term objectives were more ambitious: radically transforming the Argentine system by curtailing the state's role in the economy; exposing its industries to the pressures of international competition; and shifting resources toward Argentina's comparative advantage in agricultural exports. Fundamental to these moves was the premise that markets were stable and, if left alone, could allocate resources efficiently and rationally. The state's protection of highly unionized manufacturing firms through open and hidden subsidies, along with its regulation of competitors, had artificially distorted the market by shifting incentives away from the country's most able producers. The minister's objective was completely to rid Argentina of this "state nemesis." Martínez de Hoz summed up Argentina's economic problems this way:

> For the last 30 years, with the exception of a few interim periods, the prevailing system in Argentina could be defined as the promotion of an excessive state intervention in the economy . . . which unduly burdened the country with the social cost of such an action, and at the same time suppressed the possibility of an agile and efficient development of private enterprise to promote the growth of the economy.[27]

This was more than a matter of experience; for the minister it was a question of principle. Martínez de Hoz's views were embedded firmly in an Argentine free market, or "liberal" agrarian tradition that dated back to the nineteenth century. With the development of mechanized wheat farms and cattle ranches by the late 1800s, the emerging Argentine oligarchy was anxious to compete freely on international markets. Through the efforts of the then-powerful Sociedad Rural Argentina (SRA)—the association of wealthy wheat growers and cattle ranchers that best typified the purist devotion to free market ideology—the rural elites forced the federal government to strip away trade controls and disregard the protectionist cries of the modernizing industrial bourgeoisie. Born in 1925 into a family with vast agricultural and industrial holdings, Martínez de Hoz's father had been president of the SRA. As a former chair of the National Grain Board and secretary of agriculture and livestock, Martínez de Hoz fought for exchange rate liberalization, deregulation, and improved prices for farmers. For a short while in 1963, he served as economics minister for the interim government of José Guido. Guido supported an orthodox stabilization program, but his government's short life span frustrated the minister's efforts to launch a well coordinated economic strategy. Martínez de Hoz was now determined to complete the job he had left undone thirteen years before.

Martínez de Hoz shared his principles with a team of advisers and associates who were equally loyal to the monetarist cause. Guillermo Klein, the state secretary of economic planning and coordination and second in command, had served in the Krieger Vasena ministry during the Onganía dictatorship; Juan Alemann, the treasury secretary, was a long-time advocate of an unrestrained free market; and Alberto Diz, the governor of the Central Bank, was a doctoral graduate from the University of Chicago in 1966 and an acknowledged authority on monetary theory. Together, these economic technocrats formed one of the country's most ideologically cohesive ministries.

Why was Argentina's latest economic team readying itself to undertake an essentially free market strategy that had been unsuccessfully tried several times before? The minister and his associates were convinced for two reasons that the free market approach had never been given a fair test. First, the previous plans had been applied piecemeal. This was a mistake, since according to Martínez de Hoz, the success of one element was contingent upon the success of the others; the program would only be viable as a whole.[28] Second, these economists were bothered by the stop-and-go political cycles of the past, which had disrupted the smooth and thorough implementation of basically sound prescriptions. They claimed that once policy is adjusted, diluted, or delayed to satisfy special interests, it loses its effectiveness.

This time the economic team had reason to be confident. Its members were certain that they had in the armed forces the authoritarian backing to create the properly "tranquil" political climate necessary to insure success in the economic realm. They could count on General Jorge Videla's unswerving support for the program, as well as on other high-ranking army officers. Historically, the navy favored the neoliberal economics Martínez de Hoz preached and tended to go along. This left the more nationalistic-minded air force outnumbered and provided the economics minister with a manageable, predictable, and nearly "veto-free" environment in which to work. By most accounts, his bureau had became a "super ministry," with the power to design and execute economic policy without cabinet approval and repeatedly to override the objections of other ministries with overlapping interests.[29]

The economics minister in particular derived his power not only from his military superiors, but from his monopoly on expertise. With only limited economic understanding, but with a strong will to achieve technocratic (not political) solutions to problems, the junta continually deferred to Martínez de Hoz. He was by many accounts personally persuasive with the military, also. Even officers who disliked his economically liberal philosophy (and there were many) were impressed by his determination, style, logic, and command of the facts.[30] Referring to the minister's influence, Adolfo Canitrot remarked:

> From his position as Minister of the Economy, he led not only on economic matters; rather he made his mark on the entire conduct of government. He nurtured within the government the concept of a far-sighted and remote authoritarianism, possessed of a morality and discipline higher than that of a surrounding society made sick by years of mismanagement.[31]

## Comparative Advantage and Economic Openness

Argentina, so the economic team argued, had to rediscover its comparative advantage. The nation had lost sight of its status as one of the world's great grain producers. In a throwback to the pure liberalism of the pre-1930s, the economics minister claimed that agricultural progress was the key to industrial prosperity. A healthy rural sector would provide the foreign exchange needed to generate a dynamic and well-integrated industrial base—reversing Prebisch's logic of twenty years earlier that agricultural modernization depended on the manufacturing sector to provide important technological inputs.

Agricultural supremacy had not been achieved as yet owing to prejudicial state interference on behalf of the industrial sector. In an effort to "save" poorly run, highly unionized manufacturing establishments, the state had provided them with cheap credit and erected tariff walls on their behalf. Hiding behind these walls and unperturbed about cost overruns, these firms had rewarded wage-earners handsomely and had passed costs on to the consumers.[32] Industrial prices had grown relative to agricultural prices, raising input costs for farmers and thus placing them at an "artificially induced" disadvantage. The farmers' decline, according to the monetarists, meant ruin for the Argentine economy. For that reason, protectionism was a curse.

Martínez de Hoz proposed to solve this problem by opening the internal market to external competition, imposing a Darwinian formula: either survive through efficiency or go down in defeat at the hands of more competitive foreign firms. Martínez de Hoz explained:

> It has been our objective to eliminate all the sources of artificial distortion of our economy, to eradicate all the open or hidden subsidies, the overprotection and privileges existing for certain economic sectors. We have promoted a process of true exposure of the country's economy.[33]

To achieve this exposure, tariffs on imports with no domestic counterparts were reduced across the board to 10 percent. Cuts in tariffs on goods that could compete with Argentine goods were not as severe, but they were considerable and varied depending on the type of product. Export duties were lowered, exchange controls were lifted, and attractive foreign investment laws offered foreign businessmen free choice of sectoral location, unrestricted profit remittances, and equal treatment before the law.

These changes were dramatic, but still not sufficient as far as the monetarists were concerned. Aside from regulatory adjustments that would remove the barriers to the external penetration of the Argentine market, there also had to be internal fiscal and monetary adjustments to reduce the inflationary pressures that dissuaded investors. The agency that liberals considered most responsible for generating inflation was the state itself.

### Antistatism and the Working Class

In his first address to the nation on April 2, 1976, Martínez de Hoz pointed to the deficit as the "motor" force behind the nation's inflation.[34] In 1975, the inflation rate stood at 443 percent, and in that same year the public sector deficit equaled 15.2 percent of GDP. It was imperative, according to the minister, that the deficit be brought under control before the economy could be repaired further. The excess of public spending over income was bothersome, but even more so was the fact that most of this money had been squandered on consumer subsidies, wasteful and poorly conceived public works projects, overstaffed administrative offices, and, most importantly, inefficient state-run enterprises.

For the Argentine monetarists, the public companies best exemplified what was wrong with statist solutions to economic problems. They claimed that having diverged from its specific administrative functions and having interfered with the normal operations of the free market, the state had become an encumbrance upon the economy. It drowned the business sector in a sea of regulations and then substituted consumption and entrepreneurial activities that it was ill-equipped to carry out.

As shown in Table 5.1, the real expenditures of state firms rose appreciably through the first year of military rule, from 11.9 percent of GDP to 14.9 percent. These included salary payments for the 300,000 individuals, or approximately one out of six public sector employees who worked for the state enterprises during 1976. But, the income generated by these companies through public service had not kept pace with expenditures, as noted by the increasing proportion of income financed from other sources during 1975–1976, especially the treasury and Central Bank (see Table 5.2).

These state enterprises, as far as the monetarists were concerned, had become monuments to the "irrational" allocation of public resources and the politicization of price, wage, and managerial policy. Proper business decisions had not been made, leaving these deficit-ridden firms thoroughly dependent on disbursements from the state for their survival. Their deficits before transfers were larger than any of the other public institutions from 1961 to 1983, averaging three times that of the central administration, and almost twice that of all the provincial and municipal governments.[35] Naturally, the monetary emission necessary to save the firms from financial collapse contributed directly to the nation's inflation rate.[36] All these projects added nothing to the productive capacity of the economy, while diverting Central Bank credit away from potential producers.

These "irrational" expenditures had grown in proportion to the demands Peronist trade unionists had made upon the state. Collective pressures had (1) established the public sector and state enterprises as refuges for workers displaced by the market; and (2) politicized price, wage, and managerial decisions. Collective agreements signed between labor and management in the public firms had entirely ignored cost/benefit calculations, relying instead on political criteria. Management was itself to blame, since officials in these firms had been hired for their political suavity and not for their administrative expertise. Their appointments may have invited smoother relations between the state and labor but had done so at the cost of lowering the public sector's capacity to make "rational" economic choices. According to the Argentine monetarists, a classic example of this was the state power company, SEGBA.

SEGBA produces and transmits electrical energy to the greater Buenos Aires area, covering 12 million residents and 60 percent of Argentina's industrial and commercial establishments. Its 25,000 employees are represented by the Federación Luz y Fuerza, a historically militant union whose progressive leadership had won it important and unique privileges over the years, most notably status as co-manager of the company. Patterned after the concept of a classless "labor-capital community," SEGBA took the lead in the formation of co-managed firms. It appointed union members to serve on the board of directors and established labor committees that participated in administrative and financial decisions. Co-management also included the union's right to share in decisions regarding the hiring, firing, training,

**Table 5.1 Public Sector Spending and Personnel: A Comparison of the Perón and PRN Governments**

| | 1973–1975 | 1976[a] | 1977–1980 |
|---|---|---|---|
| Current Expenditure as a percent of Total[b] | 83.7 | 72.5 | 78.9 |
| Current Expenditure as a percent of GDP | 29.2 | 26.6 | 27.5 |
| Deficit as a percent of GDP | 10.2 | 11.6 | 3.9 |
| State Firms' Expenditure as a percent of GDP | 11.9 | 14.9 | 12.1 |
| Personnel (in millions) | 1.6 | 1.8 | 1.7 |

*Source*: all data is compiled from figures provided by the Ministry of Economics, Argentina.
[a]The PRN government came to power March 23, 1976.
[b]These figures are for central government only, which excludes expenditures of state enterprises and provincial governments.

**Table 5.2 Funding for Argentine State Enterprises[a] (billions of 1981 U.S. dollars)**

| | 1973 | 1974 | 1975 | 1976 | 1977 | 1978 | 1979 | 1980 |
|---|---|---|---|---|---|---|---|---|
| Current Income | 6.0 | 6.8 | 6.9 | 7.5 | 7.9 | 8.4 | 7.0 | 7.2 |
| Financing | 3.0 | 2.9 | 4.4 | 4.3 | 2.7 | 3.1 | 5.2 | 4.0 |
| Financing as percent of Income | 49.5 | 42.7 | 63.4 | 57.5 | 34.5 | 36.5 | 74.4 | 56.3 |
| Source of Financing | | | | | | | | |
| a. Loans | 1.3 | 1.5 | .7 | 1.1 | 1.2 | 2.3 | 4.6 | 3.3 |
| b. Central Bank Credit | .2 | .5 | 1.2 | .2 | | | | |
| c. Working Capital | .4 | –.6 | .7 | .5 | –.1 | –.3 | .1 | –.02 |
| d. Transfer | 4 | .5 | .4 | .3 | .4 | .6 | .6 | .6 |
| e. Treasury | .7 | 1.1 | 1.4 | 2.2 | 1.1 | .4 | –.1 | .1 |
| Loans as percent of all Financing | 44.1 | 49.7 | 15.4 | 24.7 | 46.3 | 76.8 | 87.5 | 81.2 |
| Central Bank Credit as percent of all Financing | 5.2 | 16.9 | 28.0 | 4.5 | 0 | 0 | 0 | 0 |
| Treasury Transfer as percent of all Financing | 24.8 | 37.5 | 31.9 | 51.3 | 40.5 | 13.9 | –1.0 | 2.8 |

*Source*: World Bank, *Economic Memorandum on Argentina*, June 22, 1984, pp. 330–331.
[a]Includes 18 major enterprises, 78 publicly-owned television stations, and 3 binational entities.

transfer, and promotion of personnel, as well as determination of salary levels and increases. These efforts culminated in June 1973 with the selection of long-time Luz y Fuerza chief, Juan José Taccone, as president of SEGBA.[37]

Although SEGBA had gone further than any other state enterprise to incorporate labor interests into management, for Martínez de Hoz it typified what he believed to be the general disruptive effects of the politicization of an essentially economic process. By vesting union-dominated management committees with decisionmaking power over budgets, investments, incomes, and promotions, the state had acquiesced to the pressures of the labor movement. These practices helped to perpetuate disguised unemployment in the public sector, preventing the natural flow of manpower into the more productive private arena. SEGBA's huge, redundant work force was nothing more than a built-in inflationary device, since the government could only shoulder these public servants through heavy borrowing from the Central Bank, and since these employees would create additional demand in the economy without contributing to savings and investment.

For these reasons, Martínez de Hoz claimed, the state enterprises had been transformed into a political asset for both the unions and the Peronist party in power, which facilitated the transformation of the companies. By keeping a ceiling on service charges to their users and expanding their payrolls, they had built support for the populist regime at the expense of the federal budget and efficient service for the public. As the minister explained:

> We are not inclined to tolerate that public service charges represent the cost of inefficiency of state enterprises . . . we are taking very serious steps to order and rationalize these enterprises and make them operationally efficient. Nevertheless, one must realize that the level of prices and service charges ought not to cover only operating costs but . . . ought also to cover a self-generation of funds within this system to finance expansion plans. The typical case is the electrical system. The system has lagged behind for many years and suffered many ups and downs as a consequence of *politically* set prices and has seen its expansion delayed so much so that electrical shortages are already a part of Argentine folklore [emphasis mine].[38]

These views were sharply contested by SEGBA's management. Juan Taccone insisted that the firm had become a model of effective state entrepreneurship, with no labor disruptions during his tenure, high productivity, a 130 percent increase in the sale of energy to 30 percent more users, and, consequently, a lowering of the firm's deficit.[39] The facts of the SEGBA case can probably still be argued, but facts were not really the point for the military's economic team. It was convinced as a matter of principle that state-managed firms were less viable than privately run companies; much less so once "victimized" by labor co-management.[40]

By way of example, the sobering "facts" about public enterprises such as SEGBA were meant to demonstrate that the state's role in the economic life of the nation would have to be curtailed. Although the state should establish the general parameters within which private enterprise was to play the game, it could not, for the most part, itself participate in that game.[41] It should act as a subsidiary to the private sector, engaging in entrepreneurial endeavors only in those limited areas where business could not. The minister explained, "The State should not invest in those sectors in which private capital is available, with the few exceptions of areas such as security or national defense."[42]

The government proposed to privatize the state, turning entrepreneurial functions over to the business sector.[43] In those instances where transfer was not possible owing to the complexity of the system or to its massive indebtedness, the firm would be rationalized: deficits would be gradually eliminated by raising public service and utility rates, cutting back operating costs, eliminating surplus employees, and hiring new executives. Restrictions on state activities would achieve the ultimate objectives of lower deficits, less monetary emission, and lower inflation.

The privatization and rationalization of the state was also an attack on wage earners, who would lose jobs once nonpolitical criteria were employed to assess the viability of public sector firms. A weakened public sector would halt the march of populist labor politics in Argentina.[44] Political leaders could no longer dip as easily into the public trough of personnel budgets in hopes of geometrically expanding their political base, as Perón had once done. By allowing the market to determine what would be produced, and who would be employed and at what cost, the populists would lose their appeal, and power would permanently shift from them toward a more conservative, antilabor leadership. Consequently, the economic project as envisioned by the government had far-reaching political repercussions. In proposing radically to transform Argentina from a state-centered to a market-centered economy, the military's economic planners were also proposing to redesign the country's political future. Those designs could come to fruition only with the support of a coercive state.

## POLITICAL CONSEQUENCES OF ECONOMIC CHOICE

> *So long as there exists a stable government that is able to supply complete political support for the necessary continuity in the implementation of the economic program, we consider that we will be able to close the cycle of recovery with the achievement of the established goals.*
>
> —Dr. José Alfredo Martínez de Hoz,
> speaking at the opening of the International Industrial Conference,
> San Francisco, September 12, 1977

As unfocused as the "Dirty War" appeared to be, it was not an exercise in random terror. Individuals affiliated with intermediary organizations (such as unions) were more likely to become victimized than those who were independent. Of the total number of "disappeared," 48 percent were union members; of these, 30 percent were blue-collar workers and 18 percent white-collar.[45] A pattern to union-directed repression quickly emerges: it is apparent that those who were members of particularly large or powerful collectives in the industrial and public sectors were more likely to become targets of state abuse than those who belonged to smaller unions outside those sectors, or to no unions at all, according to one sample of detentions and disappearances of local trade union leaders, delegates, and militants from thirty-four organizations. The ten federations in the country with membership of 100,000 or over represented just 4.7 percent of the associations registered with the Ministry of Labor, yet accounted for 53 percent of the detainees. Table 5.3 presents select data from this same sample; industrial and public sector unions stand out as overrepresented. One out of three unionists persecuted was an industrial worker; nearly one out of four was a public servant. If union teachers and construction workers who worked in the public sector were included, the figure would be higher. Six of the fourteen organizations most severely affected by political repression represented public sector employees, and three represented employees from state enterprises.

To associate with collectives was therefore dangerous, especially if those organizations resided in the industrial and state sectors. Because such organizations engaged in monopolistic practices to (1) safeguard private and public sector employment; and (2) defend artificially high wage structures with the connivance of the "interventionist state," their members were culpable, in the minds of the liberals. Larger unions tended to have greater monopoly power, making them even more threatening to this free market–minded dictatorship. The military was anxious to cripple these unions because it believed they had intentionally undermined the foundations of the economy. Whether workers actually engaged in protest against the monetarist plan, or only intended to, was not the point. The regime's economic ideology told it that as collectivized agents with an inherent motive to protect their own interests, they held ultimate responsibility for wreaking havoc on the free operations of the market.

In the public sector, the military's strategy was to strip public employees of the job security they had enjoyed before, and the make any forms of resistance against these measures extremely costly. The economics ministry designed a series of overlapping decrees that institutionalized the arbitrary dismissal of employees; these decrees were as political as they were economic with punitive consequences for those found guilty of "wrongful acts." Its Ley de Prescindibilidad (law 21274) declared public employees dispensable and dismissible without warning, for reasons of "service," "national security," or "redundancy." As early as April 1976, Juan Taccone was ousted from his post at SEGBA, and some 260 employees fired under this provision. Four years later, the economics minister boasted that the

**Table 5.3 Argentine Union Affiliation and Political Repression: March 1976–June 1979**

| Union | Number of Members[a] | Sector[b] | Detained or Disappeared | Rank | Percent of Total |
|---|---|---|---|---|---|
| Metalworkers | 267,000 | IND | 129 | 1 | 20.1 |
| Mechanics | 54,000 | IND | 85 | 2 | 13.3 |
| Teachers | 189,000 | M | 75 | 3 | 11.8 |
| State Employees Association | 86,000 | PUB | 31 | 4 | 4.9 |
| Electric Power* Workers | 70,000 | PUB | 30 | 5 | 4.7 |
| Bank Workers | 125,000 | SER | 30 | 5 | 4.7 |
| Civil Service Employees | 133,000 | PUB | 24 | 6 | 3.8 |
| Railway Workers* | 143,000 | PUB | 22 | 7 | 3.5 |
| Construction Workers | 187,000 | M | 22 | 7 | 3.5 |
| Rural Workers | 73,000 | AGR | 18 | 8 | 2.8 |
| Printers | — | — | 18 | 8 | 2.8 |
| Textile Workers | 74,000 | IND | 18 | 8 | 2.8 |
| Telephone Workers* | 40,000 | PUB | 17 | 9 | 2.7 |
| Municipal Workers | 250,000 | PUB | 12 | 10 | 1.9 |
| All Others | | | 106 | | 16.7 |
| Total Detained/ Disappeared | | | 637 | | 100.0 |

*Sources*: Repression data is from Arturo Fernandez, *Las Prácticas Sociales del Sindicalismo (1976–1982)*, (Buenos Aires: Centro Editor de América Latina, 1985) pp. 115–134. Union size is from *Clarin*, September 8, 1986, *informe especial*, p. 4.
[a]Rounded off to nearest thousand.
[b]IND = Industrial; PUB = Public; AGR = Agricultural; M = Mixed; SER = Service.
*State enterprise unions.

same law had made possible the firing of some 200,000 public servants. For SEGBA in particular, this meant a 26 percent decline in its work force between March 1976 and June 1979, marked when compared with figures for the decimated manufacturing sector as a whole, which showed a 20 percent reduction in employment for the same period. The decline is yet more significant when contrasted with data that indicate a slightly improved employment rate for all of Argentina between 1976 and 1980.[46]

The law revoked elements of a 1975 labor stability law prohibiting dismissal of employees except for job irresponsibility. The old statute said that in those isolated instances where jobs had to be eliminated or where new skills were required, a just form of compensation would be paid.[47] Other clauses in the old statute that set minimum work-force levels in the public enterprises were also annulled. Related decrees sharpened the political focus by allowing employers to interrogate applicants about their political loyalties before hiring them,[48] and by making permissible the firing of public servants engaged in activities of a "subversive" or "disruptive" nature.

Historically, laws similar to these had been invoked only in times of emergency, when the cooperation and discipline of public sector personnel (on whom the nation's communication, transportation, and energy needs depend) were absolutely essential. It is significant that law 21274 was renewed annually for five years, thus institutionalizing this form of discrimination against public employees for the first time. Moreover, these decrees were so worded as to raise significantly the level of uncertainty for all those affected. Few could tell where strictly economic criteria ended and political criteria began. Ostensibly, dismissals would occur under the redundancy clause once a calculation of manpower and production needs was made, and yet workers might be terminated for improper service, disruption, or subversive activity—none of which was ever clearly defined by the regime.[49] It became virtually impossible for employees to know whether it was their job performance, political orientation, or union affiliation that was the cause of their release, or whether their fate rested with an across-the-board decision of management. Consequently, they could not predict when they would be found in violation of the law.

Some sought legal counsel but found that many attorneys were reluctant to provide services, since those who helped accused state employees had themselves become victims of state harassment. The accused were presumed to have committed "wrongful acts" before being declared guilty by the courts and were thrown out of work before a legal defense could be mounted.[50] Their uncertainty was heightened by the fact that financial remunerations were offered to those who denounced fellow workers. The distrust that developed among the rank and file was a predictable consequence of a law whose purpose was to sow discord. Finally, a series of punitive sanctions were promulgated, most notably an industrial security law with stiff penalties against all forms of direct action aimed at interrupting or slowing down the rhythm of the work place. Those who organized strikes or direct actions could receive three-to-ten-year sentences, and those who simply participated could receive one to six years.[51]

By casting doubts about the utility of collective action or even affiliation, the government could trip up those special interest groups who in the past had succeeded in diluting or reversing economic policies before they could take effect. That was particularly important for an economic model that was not to bear fruit for some time. In the interim, it was imperative that "policy continuity" be maintained, according to Martínez de Hoz, and that the process be carried out with "faith, perseverance, disciplined effort and broad social solidarity, with private interests subject to the general welfare."[52]

On October 5, 1976, SEGBA's management, now in the hands of the military, fired an additional 200 light and power workers. They counted this as part of the economic minister's overall objective to remove "redundant" employees from the public sector. Employees were carefully selected to include important members of the union's executive committee and plant delegates, confirming fears that Luz y Fuerza was about to lose its participatory status and much more. With President Jorge Videla's signature of a new labor contract law, its worst fears were confirmed. In all, the junta's decree revoked or modified 125 of the 300 articles contained in the 1974 *Contrato de Trabajo* (Worker's Contract).[53] Although a few provisions pertained to private sector employees, including the revocation of wage indexing, most of the law was directed toward public sector employees—in particular, SEGBA employees. It stripped labor of its right to co-manage and its decisionmaking authority to set promotions, pay levels, and budget priorities. It also canceled the stipulation that a minimum number of workers be assigned to specific posts, lengthened the work week from thirty-five to forty hours, reduced vacation time, and eliminated time off for union officials.[54] According to the labor minister, this decree "revokes rules that made possible the existence of special situations in the public sector and in state enterprises . . . *contributing to their financial deficits*" (emphasis mine)[55], leaving little doubt that this was part of the government's austerity package.

Luz y Fuerza declared a work stoppage in retaliation for the firings, but the military was ready. The commander of the First Army Corps invoked the industrial security law and pledged to "preserve order, the security of personal property and that of the state" and to "assist the overall national reorganization process." He then ordered his troops to occupy the offices of SEGBA and the electrical plants. A day later, 135 light and power workers were detained, followed by the arrest and torture of three important union leaders.

At first, the union was not deterred. Luz y Fuerza called for a work slowdown (*trabajo a tristeza*) that continued for the duration of the year. On January 26, 1977, the union held the first public demonstration against the junta, as 5,000 of its numbers gathered outside the federation's capital headquarters. Walkouts continued, and acts of sabotage and arson against power installations were also reported. At the same time, the union showed restraint, making clear that its job stoppages and slowdowns were strictly directed against company policy and were not designed to undermine the regime. It stated:

> Labor union organizations have been, are and always will be an invincible barrier to subversion. . . . We do not want to be left out of the process of National Reorganization to which all Argentines are committed; we only ask to be heard; we only ask for justice.[56]

The strike dragged on through February, as the military prepared written warnings to 20,000 SEGBA employees threatening dismissal should they not return to work. Finally, the union entered into difficult negotiations with the junta. On the eve of the settlement, unidentified security agents abducted and assassinated Oscar Smith, the widely respected head of the Federal Capital branch of Luz y Fuerza.[57] His death was particularly frightening because it pointed up the fact that no one within the labor movement, regardless of his stature, was immune from state terror. Shortly thereafter, the strike ended and the light and power workers reluctantly returned under an agreement that raised salaries a meager 16 percent (prices would rise by 170 percent in 1977) and kept in force the new labor contract law.[58]

Notwithstanding Luz y Fuerza's courageous defiance of the regime's security apparatus, the fiscal priorities of the state were just too great to permit the power workers to set an example for other public employees. A short while later, the economics minister confidently predicted that by the end of the year personnel in the state enterprises would be reduced by 20 percent. He also maintained that

> legal and management reorganization of the state enterprises, especially in the power sector [had commenced,] transforming them into state-owned stock companies, with the purpose of giving them the operative effectiveness of a private enterprise as well as the consequent responsibilities regarding efficiency and fulfillment of their objectives.[59]

In 1979, the military were confident enough to believe that the Proceso had reached the moment of institutionalization. With individual trade unionists cowed into submission through physical coercion, it was now time legally to transform the labor movement as a whole. In November of that year, the junta issued its new and long-awaited Professional Association Law.[60] The law, like most of those promulgated by the military, overturned the progressive features of labor legislation written during the previous Peronist administration: first, it strengthened the subordination of the movement to the state by augmenting the power of the labor minister to intervene at a whim in order to close unions, disqualify union leaders, seize funds, or modify union statutes; second, it stripped the CGT of its associational status, leaving the pyramidal trade union structure without a third-tier organization and bringing to an end a fifty-year-old tradition of uniconfederational movement, first established in 1930. Although second-tier organizations (federations) were left intact, they could not intervene in the affairs of affiliate unions. That brought to a close a Peronist regulation designed to insure that unions conform to the dictates of labor elites. These structural changes decapitated a movement that for forty years had been organizationally "top heavy" and vertically ordered.

The Professional Association Law was also intended to fragment the labor movement: first-tier organizations were hampered by a provision that confined their activities to zones; unions whose activities had extended beyond the limits of these zones were dissolved and their activities assumed by locals operating within the narrower geographic limits established by the state. While such decentralization risked the radicalization of locals, the state was prepared to assume this risk, believing that the greater benefit was a fully segmented movement—one incapable of coordinating efforts at a regional or national level.

The law's financial provisions reinforced the structural dimension. Previously, federations received a portion of employee withholdings that were used to finance union-run social services called *obras sociales*. These services were a source of enormous status to the federations and, by most accounts, a source of enormous wealth and power for the labor aristocracy. This privilege was revoked. Additionally, normal union dues, which formerly went directly to federations, were now withheld by employers, deposited in official bank accounts, and then sent to the separate unions. Only by mutual agreement among the unions could a percentage of these dues be given to the federations and then only to cover operating costs.[61] Federations were prohibited from receiving any form of assistance from employer associations or foreign trade unions, nor could they undertake any for-profit activities. By reducing and then concentrating financial resources at base levels, the regime could fragment the movement even further. The law was rounded out with stipulations that (1) union membership be voluntary, (2) union representatives be elected directly and by the entire work force, including nonmembers, and (3) workers could be charged with "unfair practices." This last provision was previously pertinent to employers only, but now included any attempt by workers to force employers to discriminate against other workers for failing to join a union.

The government's statute marked the official insertion of its social plan into the larger economic plan. The latter was designed to create a competitive system, free from the fetters of state control; the former was meant to restructure social relations to conform with those of the economic system. By curbing its organizational and financial wherewithal at national and regional levels, the movement's monopolistic control over the supply of labor and the political orientation of the Argentine work force would be shattered. Since union membership was voluntary, the labor supply would be regulated not by the coercive power of unions but by the demands of employers. Individuals would be free to sell their labor power as they pleased on the open market. And since nonunion members had voting rights, the entrenched labor elite could be challenged by a new slate of candidates appealing to a more heterogeneous constituency, inaugurating a kind of union-styled pluralism. These stipulations were remarkably consistent with the goal of forcing worker relations into the mold of a competitive economy.

Once "liberated" from union shackles, skilled workers would, so the junta's economic team calculated, market themselves more effectively and hence be more easily discovered by firms in need of their abilities. In addition, they would be more quickly promoted, thus raising general income levels for employees. According to Martínez de Hoz, this would invert the pyramidal shape of the labor movement entirely, widening the ranks of the upwardly mobile white-collar sector and narrowing the blue-collar base. He was convinced that this plan had won his government many working-class admirers, particularly after 1978 when real wages inched upward for the first time since the coup.[62]

As deluded as he may have been by his own doctrine and about the extent and voluntary nature of this support, the minister's views prevailed within the regime. He still had the ear of his military superiors for one very important reason: the junta was in missionary search for an economic formula that would not only lead to recovery but that would automatically induce support for the Proceso, sparing it the burden of political discourse and practice. The military had repeatedly discarded plans proposed by individual officers and their civilian advisers to politicize the Proceso in one form or another. In 1976, under the penmanship of navy Commander-in-Chief Almirante Emilio Eduardo Massera, it was proposed that a Movement of National Opinion (MON) be created. With unmistakable fascist overtones, the MON's purpose was to forge an alliance with the masses by creating the military's own political party. Hard-liners in the armed forces quickly rejected this idea, fearing that someone like Massera would use the party as a personal vehicle for power as Perón had done in the 1940s. (President Roberto Viola had made a feeble and unsuccessful effort to resurrect the idea in 1981.)

In 1977, Ricardo Yofre, the civilian subsecretary general to the presidency who served under General Juan Villareal, authored a three-staged plan to legitimate the military at their moment of supreme power. He proposed that (1) politicians be brought into the cabinet and government at federal, regional, and local levels, (2) a constituent assembly be held to draft constitutional amendments and to select a military official to serve as president, and (3) after three to four years, open elections be held.[63] With modifications and with no commitment to a timetable for implementation, the plan was quietly approved by Videla in January 1978, only to be turned down by hard-line commanders later that fall.[64] According to Yofre, Martínez de Hoz had his hand in this decision. The Yofre plan would have "civilianized" the cabinet and was clearly a threat to the minister who, at the time, was the only civilian to hold ministerial rank. Moreover, Martínez de Hoz feared that the plan would put an end to the Proceso and his economic agenda. In the end, Videla went along, betting that the new legal and economic order would be sufficient to create a base of legitimacy for his government. He made a terrible miscalculation: just two years later, the Proceso would come unraveled for want of any popular appeal, and the armed forces would plunge themselves into war with Great Britain to resuscitate the faltering authoritarian order.

## ALTERNATIVE EXPLANATIONS

### Repression on Behalf of Local Industrialists

Because repression was particularly acute within the industrial sector of Argentina, it is logical to ask whether government policies were conducted on behalf of industrial entrepreneurs. In negotiations with management, Argentine workers had their own natural advantage: the country's low population growth and limited reserve army of labor meant greater bargaining power for their trade unions. To "even the score," was the state called upon to crush the labor movement? Indeed with the initial ban on collective bargaining, the removal of restrictions on prices, and the imposition of a tight wage freeze, it appeared that the junta was intending to do just that.

It is unlikely that the industrial business class was behind state terror in Argentina. First and foremost, the regime's economic policies were more sectorally prejudicial than they were class-prejudicial. Both labor and management were penalized by a program that led to the "progressive destruction of the productive apparatus in the industrial sector."[65] From the revaluation of the currency, to the across-the-board reductions in tariffs and import duties, to the elimination of subsidies on importation of inputs, the government's economic program showed no mercy in its relentless attacks on domestic firms. The "open" economy left industrial producers helplessly vulnerable to international competition. As a consequence, some of the steepest declines in growth were registered in those sectors with the highest levels of political repression. Shortly after the coup, the armed forces began systematically to sweep through the manufacturing belts surrounding Buenos Aires, Córdoba, and other major cities. Factories were seized and occupied by military force; hundreds of unionists were abducted and executed. Metalworking, automotive, and textile plants were among those most adversely affected. If the intimidation of trade unionists had the effect of disciplining the work force, that in itself contributed little to the vitality of these manufacturing firms. Of the nine major economic sectors in Argentina, manufacturing fared second to worst, averaging annual growth rates (at factor cost) of 1.1 percent between 1976 and 1979, compared with rates of 1 percent in restaurants and hotels, 3.2 percent in agriculture, 7.1 percent in construction, 5 percent in mining, 4.8 percent in electricity, and 2.3 percent in transportation and communication.[66]

The decline in growth meant that industry's relative share of value added in the economy also declined, from 27.3 percent in 1974–1975, to 25.5 percent in 1979–1980, and to 22.3 percent by 1981. All this contributed to an unprecedented 15 percent reduction in manufacturing establishments and a 140 percent increase in bankruptcies between 1975 and 1980.[67] This decline was not part of a secular trend, since industrial manufacturing had grown at an impressive 5 percent annual rate between 1971 and 1975; nor did this decline limit itself to medium and small firms, since giant auto, iron, and steel industries such as Sonrisa, Acindar, Fiat, Chrysler, and GM experienced significant losses.

Industrial entrepreneurs were quick to realize that the fundamental threat to business was not high wages but inadequate demand. Initial gains made through price-wage differentials were soon offset by shrinking markets. By 1977, owners were searching for ways to circumvent the governmental wage limitations in order to improve income levels for striking employees. Wage increases exceeding governmental ceilings by 62 percent were achieved by year's end through production bonuses and advances on salaries never discounted for future earnings.[68] Ironically, the government's program had made strange bedfellows out of management and labor.

The military's economic advisers knew full well what they were doing to domestic firms, but they were not perturbed. They were sure that more competitive transnational corporations would displace those faltering domestic companies. To what extent, therefore, did political repression safeguard foreign capitalists against disruptive labor practices? Were terrorist policies taken at the behest of the transnational corporations, and if not, did they serve their interests nonetheless?

### Repression on Behalf of Transnational Corporations

Transnational corporations (TNCs) were in a weak position to influence the course of political events in Argentina just prior to the coup. By the mid-1970s, foreign firms had lost interest in Argentina. Investor confidence had been shaken by the explosive Cordobazo riots of 1969; huge amounts of capital left the country never to return; the cycles of violence and counterviolence, the canceling of oil contracts, and the nationalization of some firms during the Peronist years of 1973 to 1975 conspired to dissuade investors from coming to Argentina. The country's share of continental TNC investment dropped from 10 percent in 1967 to 7 percent in 1975 as companies shifted operations to larger and faster growing markets in Brazil and Mexico. At the time of the coup in 1976, TNCs represented only 0.7 percent of all industrial establishments in Argentina and employed approximately 2.2 percent of the country's urban workers. What direct or indirect role, if any, these firms had in shaping the political events leading up to the coup is not known; but it is unlikely that either they or their own governments were deeply involved, given their diminished enthusiasm for and contributions to the Argentine economy.

The military regime made concerted efforts to lure TNCs back into Argentina. A 1978 law established new rules for foreign investors that were among the most liberal in Latin America. TNCs were given the same rights as domestic investors: no limits were placed on repatriation of capital or profits, and there was only a modest tax on remittances exceeding 12 percent; TNCs had complete access to local capital; and all transfers between local subsidiaries and parent companies abroad were treated as "arm-length transactions."[69]

The results were unimpressive and deceptive. The figure of U.S. $2.42 billion in new capital contributions to Argentina between 1977 and 1983 disguised the fact that nearly a third of this went to the exploration and production of oil and natural gas. Historically, industry had accounted for 90–95 percent of direct foreign investment in Argentina; its share now plummeted to 48 percent. Most of the rest went to the financial sector and business services. Only 17.5 percent of the new firms established as a result of foreign capital inflows were in manufacturing. More significantly, much of the funds went to purchase additional shares in local firms owned by parent companies, to buy out already existing firms (e.g., Volkswagen's takeover of Chrysler), or to capitalize loans (e.g., the auto industry). Those ventures added nothing to the productive capacity of the nation, nor did they send a vote of confidence to the Argentine economy.[70]

Those TNCs that made productive investments in Argentina generally did quite poorly. The few that performed well were those with diversified holdings (with seven or more subsidiaries) and operations in numerous markets (including financial ones). Still, their cumulative annual growth rate between 1973 and 1983 totaled 0.16 percent.[71] The bulk of TNCs continued to operate in restricted, oligopolistic markets. Although their share of the value of total production equaled 41 percent by 1983, that represented a decline from 48 percent in 1973. More importantly, they suffered a negative, cumulative annual growth rate for the same period (–3.4 percent), which was worse than that of domestic Argentine industrial firms. Consequently, if the purpose of state terror was to insure a better growth environment for these firms, it certainly failed to meet its goal.

More to the point, it is abundantly clear that most TNCs during this period had qualms about making long-term commitments under the prevailing conditions. Theirs was a timid, noncommittal strategy, evidenced not only by the trivial flows of new capital into the country but by the declining reinvestment of profits. Instead of choosing to invest in Argentina's future, they preferred to repatriate capital abroad at a quickened pace; often, they closed shop entirely. Faced with recessive conditions, the exhaustion of market opportunities, and new regulations denying them all but the most minimal forms of protection, automotive manufacturers in particular (such as GM, Chrysler, and Citroen) chose to flee rather than fight the regime. They appeared to be much more intimidated by the government's free market policies than they were by organized labor's wage demands. In fact, in April 1978, a meeting was held between ministers of the Argentine government and over 100 executives from leading U.S. and European banks and corporations. At that meeting the executives asked the officials how they could expect workers to subsist on U.S. $50 a month, and whether continued wage restrictions would not result in social upheaval. No direct replies were made by the embarrassed Argentines.[72] Moreover, the operations of all TNCs affected an extremely small percent of the Argentine urban work force, so that it is unlikely that the labor-intensive character of state terror was initiated on their behalf in the first place.

### State Terror as a Reaction to Protest

Despite the explicit policy of the state to weaken the labor movement, stoppages, demonstrations, factory seizures, and even sabotage occurred under military rule. In fact, some 680 strikes involving 1.6 million workers took place between 1976 and 1980.[73] Could protest have precipitated repressive action on the part of the state?

I am inclined to think not for the following reasons: first, though strikes were common, they were nearly always scattered and localized—without a coordinated and wider focus, they created little anxiety for the regime;[74] second, strikes were overwhelmingly limited to wage demands. Actions against general economic conditions or those that were politically inspired could be construed as antigovernmental. Yet these occurrences were rare: of 325 conflicts examined between 1976 and 1978, only 11 percent were focused on unemployment and a mere 2 percent were politically inspired.[75] Even in those instances, it appears that state repression was not retaliatory. Arturo Fernandez, Bernardo Gallitelli, and Andres Thompson concur that the railroad strikes of October 1977 and November 1978 were politically charged and designed to protest the loss of fellow workers. However, according to my figures, there was no noticeable increase in the disappearance of railroad employees during or immediately after the union walkouts.[76] The worst occurrences of state terror against the railroad workers took place in June and August 1976 and then again in April and June 1977, when the union was relatively inactive.

For the labor movement as a whole, the highest frequency of nationwide strike activity took place in 1979 and 1980, after state terror had diminished considerably.[77] Generally speaking, mass repression was unprovoked by striking workers. In fact, strike action could be interpreted as an accomplishment of the regime itself. The junta knew full well that unions would attempt to take advantage of the fact that employers in the private sector had been given some discretion to exceed wage guidelines set by the state. They also knew that because unions varied in strength, some would achieve larger pay increases than others, thus sowing divisiveness within the movement. Those with larger gains would protect their winnings rather than risk losing it all by joining with disadvantaged sindicates in regional or national stoppages.[78] If the fractured patterns of labor strikes subsequent to this time were any indicator, the junta's strategy had indeed succeeded.

## CONCLUSION

The monetarist program remained intact, though by no means did the economic team achieve all it had set out to do. The minister's vision of the stateless economy, with a complete return to the market, was no doubt clouded by the armed forces, whose reluctance fully to endorse the stateless principle is easily explained by the fact that they had held on to their controlling shares in the state-subsidized arms industries, known as Fabricaciones Militares. What started out on paper as a complete commitment to monetarist principles ended as something less than that. Nonetheless, the departure from the original blueprint was a matter of degree only, since the basic contours of the liberal approach remained, and its principles were respected—even by key, high-ranking officers. The continuity of the Argentine monetarist experiment and the strong backing it received from a significant portion of the high command within the armed forces are what distinguish it from the stabilization program adopted in Peru from 1976 to 1979.[79]

## NOTES

1. Argentine National Commission on the Disappeared, *Nunca Más* (New York: Farrar, Straus & Giroux, 1986), p. 5.

2. *Review of the River Plate* (Buenos Aires), May 31, 1976, p. 405.

3. Ibid.

4. For important discussions of the NSD and the Argentine interpretation of it, see Genaro Arriagada Herrera, *El Pensamiento Político de los Militares* (Santiago, Chile: Centro de Investigaciones Socioeconómicas, 1981); David Pion-Berlin, "The National Security Doctrine, Military Threat Perception and the "Dirty War," *Comparative Political Studies* 21 (October 1988): 382–407.

5. Osiris Villegas, *Políticas y Estrategias para el Desarrollo y la Seguridad Nacional* (Buenos Aires, Argentina: Pleamar, 1969), p. 34.

6. For this interpretation and an account of the NSD, see Roberto Calvo, "The Church and the Doctrine of National Security," *Journal of Interamerican Studies and World Affairs* 21 (February 1979): 81.

7. At the time, public condemnation of atrocities by the French Army forced De Gaulle to grant independence to Algeria. The Argentine junta were deeply respectful of French doctrine but also determined not to be pressured into losing their war.

8. Colonel Mario Horacio Orsolini is quoted in Arriagada, *El Pensamiento Político*, p. 186.

9. See Roger Trinquier, *Modern Warfare: A French View of Counterinsurgency* (New York: Frederick A. Praeger, 1964), p. 49.

10. These views were expressed by General Ramón J. Camps, former chief of police for the Buenos Aires province, who often posed as an unofficial spokesman for military ideology. Indeed, his views were shared by the majority of Argentine officers at the time. For Camps's specific statements, refer to Daniel Frontalini and Maria Cristina Caiati, *El Mito de la Guerra Sucia* (Buenos Aires: CELS, 1984), pp. 13–15.

11. Ramón C. Camps, interview in *La Semana*, June 2, 1983, p. 8.

12. General Erich Von Ludendorff, *La Guerra Total* (La Paz, Bolivia: Editorial Renacimiento, 1941), p. 99.

13. Jacobo Timmerman, *Prisoner Without a Name, Cell Without a Number* (New York: Alfred Knopf, 1981), p. 101.

14. For example, Arendt powerfully described how the Nazis' fictionalized accounts of demoniacal Jewish plots were turned into cardinal principles of state, turning the extermination of Jews into a matter of historical necessity. See Hannah Arendt, *The Origins of Totalitarianism* (New York: Harcourt, Brace,1951), p. 352. In fact, scholars lament the fact that *Mein Kampf* was not taken seriously enough at the time it was published. An early appreciation for the importance of Hitler's exaggerated and implausible world view may have sent warning signals to the rest of the world about his future intentions.

15. General Roberto Viola, interview with author, Buenos Aires, July 17, 1984. These extreme views were also shared by the military's economics minister, Martínez de Hoz, as revealed in an interview with the author in June of the same year.

16. For further detail on the terrorist structure, see Centro de Estudios Legales y Sociales, *692: Responsables del Terrorismo de Estado* (Buenos Aires: CELS, 1986).

17. See Proyecto de Ley, Camara de Diputados de la Nacion, May 3, 1948, pp. 84–92.

18. As an essentially land-based operation, the army naturally assumed the greatest responsibilities; the air force and navy played more minor though not insignificant roles.

19. This figure represents only those centers for which adequate documentation was available. The Argentine National Commission on the Disappeared estimates that the actual number of CCDs was 340. See the Commission's *Nunca Más*, p. 51.

20. Ibid., p. 63.

21. Centro de Estudios Legales y Sociales, *692: Responsables del Terrorismo.*

22. See the annex to President Videla's Secret Order 504/77, reprinted in *El Diario del Juicio 31* (August 1985): 585.

23. See Eduardo Luis Duhalde, *El Estado Terrorista Argentina* (Buenos Aires: El Cabollito, 1983), pp. 94–95.

24. For a more complete account of the Brazilian intelligence system, see Alfred Stepan, *Rethinking Military Politics: Brazil and the Southern Cone* (Princeton: Princeton University Press, 1988).

25. Annex to Secret Order 504/77, pp. 583–585.

26. República Argentina, *Memoria: March 29, 1976–March 29, 1981*, vol. 3 (Buenos Aires: Ministerio de Economía, 1981).

27. "Dr. Martínez de Hoz at San Francisco," *Review of the River Plate* September 21, 1977, p. 441.

28. República Argentina, *Memoria*, vol. 3, p. 3.

29. General Horacio Liendo, who at the time was minister of labor, was one officer with little enthusiasm for the monetarist program. However, he was sure that his government's stiff wage guidelines and suspension of labor contracts were temporary and that, with labor's good faith effort to cooperate, the normalization process would be speeded up. Martínez de Hoz was quick to head off any hints of wage concessions. Both ministers jockeyed for position with the ruling junta. On this occasion, like most others, the generals sided with their chief economic advisor. The labor minister's frustrations were reported to the author in an interview in June 1984.

30. In an interview with this author in Buenos Aires in July 1984, former president Roberto Viola demonstrated considerable contempt for Martínez de Hoz and his ideas. Viola represented a group of nationalist-minded officers seeking a rapprochement with labor and opposed to "liberal" economic models. Nonetheless, even he admitted that initially he was quite impressed by the minister's expertise and was willing to give him a chance to prove that his economic ideas could work.

31. Adolfo Canitrot, "Discipline as the Central Objective of Economic Policy: An Essay on the Economic Programme of the Argentine Government Since 1976," *World Development* 8 (1980): 916.

32. Ibid., pp. 913–928. This source gives a related and more complete analysis of the Argentine liberal model.

33. José A. Martínez de Hoz, speech before the Argentine Chamber of Commerce, *Economic Information on Argentina*, March 1980, p. 7.

34. República Argentina, *Memoria: Marzo 3, 1976–Marzo 3, 1979*, vol. 3, pp. 1–15.

35. World Bank, *Economic Memorandum on Argentina* (Washington, D.C.: World Bank, 1984), p. 37.

36. It is also interesting to note the cutoff of Central Bank funding after 1976. At this point, the government turned to noninflationary financing of these companies by borrowing from abroad. Unfortunately, repaying the loans pushed these firms to the brink of insolvency, and, ironically, the treasury had to retire their debt.

37. Luz y Fuerza's accomplishments are detailed in Juan José Taccone, 900 *Dias de Autogestion en SEGBA: Una Experiencia Argentina de Participación* (Buenos Aires: Fundación, 1977); also see Leonardo E. Dimase, "La Política Económico-Social Inaugurada en 1976 y Sus Efectos en los Sindicatos que Nuclean Trabajadores de Empresas Estatales," *Revista del Centro de Investigación y Acción Social* 30 (1981):58–59.

38. República Argentina, *Memoria*, vol. 3, p. 147.

39. Taccone, *900 Dias*, pp. 156–158.

40. Jorge Schvarzer also argues that the minister's objections were largely a matter of principle and not objection to specific practices. See *Expansión Económica del Estado Subsidiario: 1976–1981*, *Ensayos y Tesis* 3 (Buenos Aires: CISEA, 1983), p. 125.

41. *Review of the River Plate*, September 21, 1977, p. 441.

42. *Economic Information on Argentina*, April 18, 1978, p.8.

43. From 1976 to 1980, approximately 120 firms were privatized under this formula. José A. Martínez de Hoz, *Bases Para una Argentina Moderna: 1976–1980* (Buenos Aires: Compañía Impresora Argentina, 1981), p. 51. Far fewer firms were privatized than planned, and some argue that the subsidiary state actually expanded under military rule. See Jorge Schvarzer, *Expansión Económica del Estado Subsidiario: 1976–1981* (Buenos Aires: Centro de Investigaciones Sociales Sobre el Estado y la Administración, 1984).

44. Similar points are made by Canitrot, "Discipline as an Economic Objective"; Francisco Delich, "Desmovilización Social, Reestructuración Obrera y Cambio Sindical," in *El Poder Militar en la Argentina: 1976–1981*, ed. Peter Waldmann and Ernesto Garzón Váldez (Buenos Aires: Editorial Galerna, 1983), pp. 101–115.

45. Argentine National Commission on the Disappeared, *Nunca Más*, pp. 5, 448.

46. Figures for SEGBA found in Dimase, "La Política Económico-Social,"

p. 43; data on unemployment in the manufacturing sector and nationwide from The World Bank, *Economic Memorandum on Argentina*, pp. 143, 285.

47. On labor stability legislation, see Dimase, "La Política Económico-Social," pp. 40–45.

48. This was law 21297, which annulled twenty-seven articles in the old Labor Contract Law. See Bernardo Gallitelli and Andres A. Thompson, "La Situación Laboral en la Argentina del 'Proceso,' 1976–1981," in *Sindicalismo y Regimenes Militares en Argentina y Chile*, ed. Bernardo Gallitelli and Andres A. Thompson (Amsterdam: Centro de Estudios y Documentación Latinoamericanos, 1982), pp. 147–148.

49. See Arnold Spitta, "El Proceso de Reorganización Nacional de 1976 a 1981: Los Objectivos Básicos y su Realización Práctica," in Waldmann and Valdez, *El Poder Militar*, p. 82.

50. Gallitelli and Thompson, "La Situación Laboral en la Argentina del 'Proceso,' 1976–1981," p. 148.

51. Santiago Senen González, *Diez Años de Sindicalismo Argentino: De Pérón al Proceso*, (Buenos Aires: Corresidor, 1984), p. 63; *Arturo Fernandez, Las Prácticas Sociales del Sindicalismo (1976–1982)* (Buenos Aires: Centro Editor de América Latina, 1985), p. 59.

52. *Economic Information on Argentina*, April, 1978, p. 9.

53. Alvaro Abós, *Las Organizaciones Sindicales y el Poder Militar (1976–1983)* (Buenos Aires: Centro Editor de América Latina, 1984), p. 17.

54. These provisions found in *Review of the River Plate*, February 9, 1977, p. 156.

55. Ibid.

56. "More Trouble Coming," *The Review of the River Plate*, October 29, 1976, p. 707. The military never tried to abolish unions, apparently convinced that union structures provided a form of control by regulating the flow of manpower in and out of industry. The military could use these organizations to order and monitor the behavior of the rank and file and to check the tide of radicalism. Unlike General Aramburu, who purposefully encouraged the formation of rival associations (by eliminating the Professional Association Law clause permitting only one representative union per sector), General Videla discouraged rival groups entirely, preferring to dominate those which already existed. Interestingly, and despite all its anti-Justicialist rhetoric, the junta made no effort to recruit new labor leadership to displace the much-hated Peronists. Labor's first tack was to use the military's arguments to its own advantage, as evidenced in the Luz y Fuerza statement. Claiming that the movement had always stood as a bulwark against communism, they urged the government to retain their free trade union status. A fully operable union, run by experienced workers, could effectively guard against plant level disruptions by "outside influences." The junta never agreed to trade union freedom, although they were persuaded that existing union structures added an element of predictability to labor behavior and lowered the chances that "anarchical" violence would spread. Hard-liners within the armed forces who wanted to destroy union structures were clearly outmaneuvered.

57. Information on the strike and the abduction of Oscar Smith can be found in González, *Diez Años de Sindicalismo Argentino*, pp. 65–73; Abós, *Las Organizaciones Sindicales*, pp. 22–28; *Review of the River Plate*, October 21, 1976, pp. 637–639, and October 29, 1976, pp. 707–708.

58. Juan José Taccone estimated that his union members suffered a loss in real wages of 58 percent between December 1975 and July 1980.

59. *Economic Information on Argentina*, June 6, 1977, p. 7.

60. The text can be found in *Review of the River Plate*, November 30, 1979, pp. 871–889.

61. Ibid., pp. 875, 895.

62. The minister's views were expressed to the author in an interview conducted at his residence in Buenos Aires on June 28, 1984.

63. This plan was revealed to the author in an interview with Ricardo Yofre in Buenos Aires on October 6, 1986.

64. Included in this group were division generals Carlos Suárez Mason, Luciano Benjamín Menéndez, Santiago Omar Riveros, and Ramón Genaro Diaz Bessone.

65. Victor E. Tokman, "Global Monetarism and Destruction of Industry," *CEPAL Review* 23 (August 1984): 109.

66. Fundación de Investigaciones Para el Desarrollo, "Coyuntura y Desarrollo, Anexo Estadístico XIV" (Buenos Aires: FIDE, April 1983) p. 18.

67. Tokman, "Global Monetarism," pp. 108, 110, 112.

68. *Latin America Economic Report* 5 (November 4, 1977): 200.

69. Ibid., 4 (August 20, 1976): 125.

70. Daniel Azpiazu, Eduardo Basualdo, and Bernardo Kosacoff, "Transnational Corporations in Argentina, 1976–1983," *CEPAL Review* 28 (April 1986): 102.

71. Ibid., p. 129.

72. Julian Martel, "Domination by Debt: Finance Capital in Argentina," in *NACLA Report on the Americas* 12 (July–August 1978): 36.

73. Ronaldo Munck, *Argentina: From Anarchism to Peronism* (London: Zed Books, 1987), p. 229.

74. According to Munck, of 482 strike calls, only 63 or 13 percent were taken up at the regional level, and 5 percent at the national level. There were no sympathy strikes in 1976–1977, one in 1978, and 17 in 1979. The view that the strikes were not anxiety-provoking is shared by Bernardo Gallitelli and Andres A. Thompson, eds., *Sindicalismo y Regimenes Militares en Argentina y Chile* (Amsterdam: Centro de Estudios y Documentación Latinoamericanos, 1982).

75. Ricardo Falcón, "Conflicto Social y Régimen Militar: La Resistencia Obrera en Argentina (Marzo 1976–Marzo 1981)" in Gallitelli and Thompson, eds., *Sindicalismo y Regimenes Militares*, p. 101.

76. This assessment was made by chronologically sorting data on the "disappeared" made available to me by the Argentine Permanent Assembly of Human Rights. The data included occupational and union affiliations for over 2,000 victims of the "Dirty War" between 1975 and 1979. Thus, I was able to identify railroad employees who were victimized, record the dates of their disappearances, and match these with the dates of known railroad union protests.

77. Munck, *Argentina*, p. 229.

78. Falcón, "Conflicto Social y Régimen Militar," p. 107.

79. That would remain true until the spring of 1981, when a financial crisis in Argentina raised troubling questions about the free market plan and set off a dispute that would do irreparable harm to the regime.

# PART THREE
# PERU

# 6

# The Limits to Democratic Rule: "Beltranismo" and the Politics of Austerity

State-labor negotiations under democratic rule can be strained by the government's choice of a national economic program. Peru's democratic government, under Manuel Prado (1956–1962), lost the flexibility necessary to bargain with its political opponents once it committed itself to a monetarist economic program. Its hands were tied by a program that reduced the available resources and options needed to reach peaceful accords with the trade union movement.

Prado's administration came to power in 1956 after eight years of dictatorship under General Manuel Odría.[1] A lawyer by profession, conservative in his views, and a member of one of Peru's richest families, Prado preserved the traditional upper-class economic dominance. He also restored many of the political rights lost under the dictatorship. His electoral victory was made possible through the support of APRA (Alianza Popular Revolucionaria Americana—American Popular Revolutionary Alliance), the populist party of the middle and working classes founded by Víctor Raúl Haya de la Torre. APRA was a powerful, ideologically radical, and sometimes violent political force, which had suffered under the Odría dictatorship. The general's Internal Security Law of 1949 turned APRA members (Apristas) into second-class citizens. Many were tortured and executed, and the party's leader was forced into five years of internal exile. APRA's affiliate labor confederation, the CTP (Confederación de Trabajadores Peruanos—Confederation of Peruvian Workers) was outlawed and its leaders imprisoned.

The party was pleased by Prado's pledge of political amnesty and repeal of the repressive legislation of the past six years. APRA had been outlawed for all but four of its twenty-five years, and now was quite anxious to regain legal status. They were prepared to support Prado's candidacy and, by voting for a historical opponent, hoped to strengthen the constitutional democracy. In fact, they issued a manifesto to the Peruvian people in May 1956 that was decidedly moderate in tone and pluralist in conviction, calling upon everyone to rally "behind a leader whom all branches of democratic opinion can accept."[2] Prado in turn relied on APRA's vote to defeat his two rivals, Hernando de Lavalle and Fernando Belaúnde Terry (Belaúde Terry became president of Peru in 1963). For those reasons, and despite their clear differences in class constituencies, Prado and APRA came together in an electoral alliance known as the Convivencia (coexistence).[3]

From the moment he took office, Manuel Prado was exposed to a vocal and strident defense of free market economics. Pedro Beltrán, editor and major shareholder of Peru's major daily *La Prensa*, used the newspaper's editorial columns to preach the virtues of the free enterprise system. He had resigned from his position as director of the Central Bank in 1934, in order to head a consortium that purchased *La Prensa*. In 1944, he was appointed ambassador to Washington and also served as Peru's representative at the Bretton Woods Conference. In 1946, Beltrán returned to private life to take over the management of the paper, transforming it into the right wing's most opinionated tabloid. Beltrán's views became widely known, and for years the free market ideology within Peru was referred to as "Beltranismo."[4]

Setting up an opposition not unlike the monetarists' depiction of rational and irrational governments, Beltrán referred to sound versus unsound administrations. The former were characterized by cautious spending, refusal to print money or borrow excessively, and an appreciation for the laws of supply and demand. Unsound governments permitted excessive expansion of liquidity and deficit spending—the perfect recipe for inflation. Beltrán's obsession with inflation was typified by his use of the *maquinita* (printing machine) to symbolize the Prado government's alleged irresponsible spending habits. The image of a man cranking out bills to keep pace with the lavish consumption habits of government eventually was noticed when prices began to rise.

At first, Beltrán's views did not sit well with the Odría or Prado administrations nor were they validated by objective conditions. From 1950 to 1956, Peru enjoyed solid growth, averaging 6 percent a year. Prices were suppressed with cheap food imports and wage restrictions. The balance of payments was also strong, as evidenced by successive trade surpluses and heavy inflows of foreign capital. Taxes from exports and imports provided the government with an important source of revenue for fiscal spending. Odría used this surplus to build social services and to provide employment in the public sector. Prado made moderate departures from Odría's program, cutting back public investment and leveling off expenditures.

In 1957, the demand for Peruvian exports on world markets weakened and led to declines in foreign exchange earnings. Mineral production, which accounted for nearly 13 percent of Peru's GNP, was particularly hard hit, and industrial production as a whole dropped. As a result, overall growth rates declined by 3.9 percent. Peru had adopted a fluctuating exchange rate policy, so that internal prices depreciated the nation's currency, the sol. Unfortunately, trade deficits mounted, caused principally by declining earnings for cotton and sugar. The government then tried to preserve the sol's value with foreign currency sales, depleting its reserves even further. As export taxes declined, the government resorted to deficit financing of its programs. Deficit-induced inflation brought "I told you so's" from Beltrán; even though inflation could have been attributable to supply rigidities and cost-push factors, it seemed to many that "Beltranismo" was a philosophy whose time had come.[5]

Prado's political situation was tenuous. He was caught between non-Aprista unions who were bidding up wage rates through strike activity and a dissatisfied export-oligarchy whose labor costs had risen as world prices for its commodities had fallen.[6] Rumors surfaced of impending military efforts to oust him. Reluctantly, the president went to the IMF to sign a standby loan to gain access to foreign credit. Shoring up Peru's reserve position would, he thought, help the economy overall and in turn stabilize the political situation.

This was not the first time Peru had been to the Fund. In 1954, the government and the Fund signed an accord that was renewed annually for three years. That agreement was made in economically auspicious circumstances; furthermore, the Fund was pleased with Peru's fluctuating exchange rate policy and consequently not so concerned with the government's spending habits. The new accord in January 1958 was reached in the midst of a declining world market for primary goods and under less-than-favorable internal conditions. The IMF laid down precise guidelines for domestic readjustment: Peru was required to ease inflationary pressures through a reduction of government spending and an increase in revenues; to exhibit caution in meeting the demands for new Central Bank credit; to avoid major liberalization of reserve requirements; and to resist wage and salary increases.[7]

The agreement proved impossible to fulfill. The government could not keep the lid on wages or restrain fiscal expenditures; public outcry over attempts to eliminate subsidies and cut wages prevented trimming the then-current account. Instead, Prado borrowed more money from the Central Bank. In June of that year, Beltrán was asked to form a new cabinet after the previous two had resigned. Only then did the government show resolve in its application of the austerity plan. What had held the administration back during the preceding year and a half?

As has been stated, Prado won the 1956 election in large part thanks to the backing of the Apristas. His tolerance of APRA activity and political liberalization unleashed tremendous pressures that had been building under military rule. Previously, the incorporation of multinational capital into the extractive and manufacturing sectors had prompted impressive growth rates in production, requiring a larger work force. Hundreds of thousands of laborers were added to the payrolls; the proletariat class grew in size, but unions were largely prohibited.[8] With the return to civilian rule, Peru became a signatory to the 1949 International Labor Organization (ILO) Convention, which provided freedom of association for trade unions. In 1955, there had been 493 officially recognized unions in Peru; by 1961, that figure had climbed to 1,093.[9] The growth of the organized labor movement brought forth claims for services, goods, income, and jobs.

In this context, Prado was hard pressed to justify fiscal restraint and decontrol: any advance in that direction brought swift responses from labor.

As James Payne described the situation, labor utilized the threat of militant violence as a bargaining chip with the state.[10] When the authorities failed to show sufficient flexibility, labor raised the stakes and created politically unstable conditions. An insecure administration feared military intervention and thus submitted to workers' requests. APRA mediated the conflict by both disciplining the work force and encouraging a moderate level of resistance. Payne's analysis is a fairly accurate portrayal of Peruvian politics during the early and later Prado years; but the years in between saw a changing economy and new policy responses, which reduced government flexibility in its negotiations with labor. This change is exemplified by the government's handling of bank employees' strikes from 1957–1959.[11]

On May 6, 1957, the Federation of Bank Employees called a strike that attracted over 7,000 members.[12] In January, the federation had presented to the banks a list of twenty-three demands, including a 40 percent salary hike, family allowances, and fringe benefits. The banks offered a 5 percent pay raise. Weeks of fruitless negotiations followed, and the two sides finally took the matter to the Ministry of Labor. After deliberation, the ministry issued a resolution calling for stepwise increases totaling 30 percent. The owners grudgingly accepted this compromise, but the federation rejected it. The ministry reconsidered and finally granted an attractive package of fringe benefits including bonuses, family allowances, and extra vacation time. It also overruled a 1945 decree that forbad unionization of state employees. The final agreement was signed on May 12 and was estimated to have increased bank payrolls by 13–26 percent. This was a situation in which the government had made every effort to head off potential disruption by the bank employees; quickly reaching a settlement that was on balance more favorable to the workers than the employers.[13]

Two years later, on April 12, 1959, the bank workers walked out, demanding a 40 percent increase.[14] The owners remained firm at 5 percent. The Ministry of Labor issued a resolution ordering a 9 percent increase on the first 2,000 soles, plus a minimum-wage hike. This offer was quickly rejected by the federation, which demanded that in addition to pay raises, striking workers should receive compensation for lost time. Rather than renegotiate a compromise, the Prado regime made their final offer and urged the employees to return to work or face dismissals. Violence erupted when employees desiring to return to work clashed with those remaining outside. The police intervened, and more serious confrontations ensued between the strikers and the authorities.

On April 16, Prado suspended constitutional guarantees, obstructing all trade union gatherings. He justified the suspension by claiming that the strike was not called to express legitimate economic grievances but instead was "part of a program for the subversion of public order in which elements outside the federation had intervened."[15] After accusing the federation of Communist affiliations, Prado closed several union headquarters, arrested twenty-eight bank union leaders, declared the strike illegal, and renewed the suspension for another thirty days. Finally, by the end of May, the strikers reluctantly agreed to the ministry's firm offer plus a small additional increase. On June 2, they returned to work, having failed to extract concessions on most points. As Francois Bourricaud put it, "the outstanding aspect of this affair is the extent to which the bargaining process was politicized."[16] The government purposefully cut short the legal mediation process, resorting to coercive measures to gain labor compliance. Rather than back down in the face of labor militancy, it retaliated with a strong show of force.

It appeared as if the pressures to conform to the Fund's program had, by the spring of 1959, forced the government to take a harder line against labor. Still, Prado moved hesitantly. Fiscal expenditures continued to rise as efforts to slash bread subsidies and lift gasoline controls met with significant public resistance. Furthermore, the strike had so upset operations at the Central Bank as to make credit restraint impossible. Pressures from various sectors forced Prado's hand, and for the third time in two years his cabinet resigned. A new one was formed, this time under the leadership of Prado's principal nemesis—Pedro Beltrán. The president's unlikely choice made political sense: should Beltrán's policies work, the administration would reap the rewards as well; should he fail, Prado would have vindicated himself against the free market advocates.

The move firmed up Prado's position with important social and political sectors. Members of the oligarchy were generally pleased—particularly those tied to exports and oil. Beltrán's family and close associates held controlling shares in a major petroleum company. The APRA representatives in Congress were surprisingly supportive.[17] *La Prensa* had launched angry tirades against APRA during the reformist government of Bustamante. Now, the party was able to forgive, recognizing the mileage gained from Convivencia. The potential to consolidate forces in a politically open environment outweighed any losses attributable to free market policies—which APRA had historically opposed.[18]

Most importantly, Prado had the support of the military. The stabilization program, drawn up under Beltrán's supervision, won praise from the generals who were pleased to collaborate with the new finance minister. The government signed the standby agreement in July 1959, confident that it had leverage of its own against recalcitrant labor groups: failure of labor to comply with ministerial arbitration would bring the military to the side of the civilian rulers in confrontation with the workers.

Payne has argued that insecure civilian leaders had to tolerate wage-price spirals to satisfy labor demands (assuming slow productive growth); high inflation was the price for political stability. With Beltrán's entrance into the cabinet, the game changed: now, deflationary strategies would generate security for the heads of state, since the Beltrán–IMF plan had the coercive backing of the armed forces.

There was virtual unanimity between Beltrán's and the IMF's proposals. The Fund was particularly pleased at Beltrán's insistence that government borrowing from the Central Bank be prohibited. Both parties agreed that: the bank's extension of credit to state and commercial banks would have to be curtailed; legal reserve requirements would be strictly enforced to prevent a buildup of liquidity; budget deficits would have to be reduced, food subsidies terminated, and wages frozen.[19]

The wage proposals had important implications for state–labor relations. If the wage freeze was to be enforced, workers could no longer appeal to government for favorable arbitration or mediation settlements. Labor's pressure tactics would risk direct confrontation with the authorities. In other words, the austerity program raised the stakes for both sides. How did the Prado government respond, once the Beltrán–IMF nexus was formalized?

In July 1959, cab drivers called work stoppages to protest the increase in gasoline prices. The government again suspended guarantees, rounded up the cabbies, and quickly put an end to the strike without granting concessions.[20] In October, collective actions by state postal and telegraph employees were met with mass dismissals. Custom house employees in Calloa walked off the job in solidarity with other state employees, and the authorities sent the navy to occupy port facilities.[21] Shortly thereafter, the postal strike was called off with none of the strikers' objectives having been reached. In May 1960, iron and steel workers in Chimbote walked out in a dispute with the SOGESA Company. The company refused to comply with a 5 percent cost-of-living allowance that had been written into a negotiated contract about to expire. The union, after repeated efforts to engage management in talks, asked the government to mediate. Beltrán's orders were to ignore union pleas. The minister's callousness precipitated protests in Chimbote. Police and troops were called in to clear the streets, and the confrontation that ensued between workers and the authorities left four dead and twenty-seven injured.[22]

Several observations can be made about the overall sequence of events during the Prado years:

1. *The turn toward orthodox prescriptions for economic maladies tied the government's hands in its dealings with labor and management.* Accommodation to labor demands would have swiftly eaten into the heart of the austerity program. Pressures that generated greater fiscal expenditures could not be tolerated; wage gains would raise income levels and consumption capacity; wage and employment benefits in the public sector would aggravate current account deficits; subsidies and controls would shift relative prices against the agricultural sectors and stymie efforts to free prices. Consequently, the 1958–1960 period brought a greater willingness by the government to short-circuit negotiations. Issues that were formerly decided in the offices of the Ministry of Labor were now resolved in the streets. Changes in economic strategy, therefore, weakened the political bargaining process.

2. *Government insecurity in the face of labor resistance declined.* With the military solidly behind the Beltrán strategy, the government could deal more firmly with organized labor. Beltrán's entrance into the government also solidified oligarchical support for the austerity program, which gave Prado added assurance that his policies could be carried out.

3. *APRA's leadership within the labor movement was compromised.* In a spirit of cooperation, and with the hope of preserving political freedom, APRA lent support to the orthodox program. The party also disassociated itself from worker actions during 1959–1960, applauding the government's crackdown against unaffiliated and militant unions (such as the bank employees). While gaining certain concessions for the CTP affiliates in the short term, APRA's Convivencia with the oligarchy weakened its hold on the labor movement in the long run. The economic crisis and the orthodox response to it accelerated rank and file exodus away from APRA and CTP leadership, thus opening opportunities for radical influence. Metal and construction workers, bank employees, and teachers demonstrated greater receptiveness to leftist ideologies as a result of APRA's support for orthodox measures and selective repression during these years.[23]

Labor's political bargaining strategies, as elucidated by Payne, were effective during times of economic expansion when concessions could be easily granted. But once the economic crisis took hold, and the government's commitment to anti-inflationary programs was firmed up, the effectiveness of these strategies declined.

Despite pressures, the state remained reluctant to comply fully with IMF stipulations until Beltrán's entrance into government. It was then that the convergence of domestic and internationally sponsored economic strategies provided the impetus for change. Naturally, it is difficult to assert that without Beltrán's intervention, Prado would have resisted austerity; worsening economic indicators lead one to believe that he could not have held out for long. Nonetheless, Beltrán seems to have provided the government with a "home-grown" certification of the orthodox doctrine. The rather confused and floundering Prado administration was formidably influenced by Beltrán's aggressive insistence on the correctness of his position, his confidence in laissez-faire principles, the remarkable convergence between his plan and the Fund's, and his impressive standing with the oligarchy and mass media. His stature with the international financial community undoubtedly helped augment the monetary value of the 1959 standby package, the largest Peru would see for ten years.[24]

Although it is only speculation, the IMF's precise and elegant mathematical formulas to alleviate trade and budget deficits probably generated further support for Beltrán's position. Hence, both Beltrán's authoritative style and the Fund's arrogant claims to fiscal and monetary knowledge likely were two significant factors that pulled the government into the monetarist fold. Ultimately, the rapid recovery that followed in late 1959 and 1960 convinced many inside and out the government that orthodoxy did indeed make sense (though the cause of that recovery is still very much in dispute).[25] In sum, both international and domestic doctrines were important elements in shaping relations between government and organized labor.

The Prado years provide a useful, though sketchy, introduction to the politics of Peruvian orthodoxy. Little has been written about that period in Peruvian history, despite the important lessons that can be drawn from it. In some sense, the late 1950s served as a prologue to a more lengthy and dramatic narrative: the years of military rule from 1968 to 1980. No doubt, familiarity with events during Fernando Belaúnde Terry's administration from 1963 to 1968 is essential for a complete understanding of the political and economic dynamics leading up to the October 1968 coup. However, given the important parallels between the crisis years under Prado (1956–1962) and those following the departure of General Velasco (1975–1980), this earlier slice of Peruvian history can help to set the stage for and illuminate more recent events and processes.

## NOTES

1. Scholarly work on the Manuel Prado years is very limited. The following are some of the sources that were drawn upon by the author: François Bourricaud, *Power and Society in Contemporary Peru* (New York: Praeger, 1967); Frederick Pike, *The Modern History of Peru* (New York: Praeger, 1967); James L. Payne, *Labor and Politics in Peru: The System of Political Bargaining* (New Haven: Yale University Press, 1965); Manuel Prado, "El Mensaje Presidencial de Año Nuevo," *Informaciones Comerciales* 8 (January 1957): 2–5; República de Peru, Ministerio de Hacienda, "Mensaje Presentado al Congreso por el Doctor Manuel Prado, Presidente Constitucional del Peru," Lima, 1959, 1960; various issues of *La Prensa*, *El Comercio*, and *The Peruvian Times*.
2. Quoted in François Bourricaud, *Power and Society in Contemporary Peru* (London: Faber and Faber, 1970), p. 265.
3. A favorable view of the Convivencia is offered by José Barba Caballero, *Historia del Movimiento Obrero Peruano* (Lima: Ediciones Signo, 1981), pp. 135–145.
4. The ideology of "Beltranismo" can be gleaned from reading editorials in the Sunday edition of *La Prensa* during the 1950s.
5. A useful analysis of economic practice and outcomes in this period is provided by Rosemary Thorp, "Inflation and Orthodox Economic Policy in Peru," *Bulletin of the Oxford Institute of Economics and Statistics* 29 (August, 1967): 185–210.
6. This view is shared by Thomas Scheetz, *Peru and the International Monetary Fund* (Pittsburgh: University of Pittsburgh Press, 1986), pp. 95–97.
7. International Monetary Fund, *Staff Report and Recommendations 1958 Consultations* (Washington, D.C.: IMF, February 8, 1959).
8. Denis Sulmont, *El Movimiento Obrero Peruano 1890–1980: Reseña Histórica* (Lima: Tarea, 1980).
9. Ibid., p. 212.

10. Payne, *Labor and Politics in Peru*, pp. 1–26.

11. Information on the strikes is sparse. This analysis relies upon the following sources: Bourricaud, *Power and Society*; newspaper accounts in *El Comercio* and *The Peruvian Times*.

12. *Peruvian Times*, April 18, 1958, p. 1.

13. Ibid.

14. Bourricaud, *Power and Society*.

15. *Peruvian Times*, May 1, 1959, p. 2.

16. Bourricaud, *Power and Society*, p. 108.

17. Pedro G. Beltrán, *La Verdadera Realidad Peruana* (Lima: Editorial San Martín, 1976).

18. In fact, the Aprismo doctrine had strongly emphasized state-led development. Haya de la Torre went so far as to suggest that the state comprised a third factor of production after labor and capital. Robert J. Alexander, *APRISMO: The Ideas and Doctrines of Víctor Raúl Haya de la Torre* (Kent, Ohio: Kent State University, 1973).

19. The nature of the stabilization plan is discussed in Pedro Beltrán, "Plan Económico 'Beltrán' para el Perú," *Espejo* 1 (March 1960); Beltrán, *La Verdadera Realidad*; International Monetary Fund, *Staff Report*, February 8, 1959.

20. *Peruvian Times*, August 14, 1959, p. 3.

21. Ibid., October 23, 1959.

22. Bourricaud, *Power and Society*, pp. 108–114.

23. Denis Sulmont, *El Movimiento*, pp. 84, 85.

24. Thomas Scheetz, *Peru and the IMF*, p. 100.

25. For a critique of the Beltrán plan, see Thorp, "Inflation and Economic Policy," p. 205.

# 7

# The Revolution Unraveled: The Morales Bermúdez Government and Monetarist Policy

By Latin American standards, Peru's experiment in military rule, from 1968 to 1980, was exceptional. Led by General Juan Velasco Alvarado, the officers who toppled the democratic government of President Fernando Belaúnde Terry on October 3, 1968, were determined fundamentally to alter the course of Peruvian development through a program of sweeping structural transformations of the state and society. Unexpectedly, the military embarked upon a progressive, sometimes radical, and certainly nationalistic policymaking course that led to the expansion of state ministries, the reform of land tenure, the nationalization of certain foreign-owned firms, and the creation of industrial communities whose workers had a voice in the management of firms. Although there was public sentiment in favor of many of the proposed changes, the programs themselves were to be independently chosen by military elites (and their civilian advisors), not pressured into existence by the masses. For that reason, this chapter of Peruvian history became known as the "revolution from above."

There were two phases to this revolution. The first began with the October 1968 coup and ended in August 1975, when the Velasco government was overturned by a group of fellow officers loyal to General Francisco Morales Bermúdez. Inaugurating the second phase, President Morales Bermúdez promised to maintain the "revolutionary" direction established by his predecessor, but many observers at the time were skeptical. The generals were forced to come to terms with a deepening economic crisis, and were under considerable pressure to choose alternatives that would curry favor with the international lending agencies. Reluctantly, the government "swallowed the pill" of economic monetarism in order to restore to health their afflicted economy. Once that dose was swallowed, the body politic had to succumb to the logic of orthodox management, as many of the first-phase reforms were shelved. This chapter will focus on the relation between that economic reorientation and the state's selective use of political repression against two important labor groups: the mine workers, who were thought to be obstructing export performance; and public sector teachers, who, the government claimed, stood in the way of fiscal and monetary adjustment.

## THE FIRST PHASE

In a proclamation delivered on October 3, 1968, the day of the coup, the military stated it had seized power to "transform social, economic and cultural structures" and to defend "national sovereignty and dignity."[1] For decades,

Peru had been run by a powerful coalition of landowners, exporters, and international capitalists. The landowners, operating in semifeudal mode, extracted a profit at the expense of tenant farmworkers; exporters exchanged raw materials on the world market for finished goods; and North American investors sent profits back home through controlling interests in mining and manufacturing. These groups held economic and political power and, together, effectively deprived the majority of Peruvian peasants and workers of sufficient income or representation. Julio Cotler describes the oligarchical-dependent status of the nation:

> The open, semicolonial character of the Peruvian economy, linked with the precapitalist sector, resulted in a high degree of concentration of economic, social, and political power, oriented around the institutional network controlled by primary foreign capital (principally North American) and secondarily by local capitalists. This latter group maintained the peasant population at the margin of political participation through the gamonal system. Within this system of linkages with foreign capital, the native bourgeoisie had to content itself with whatever spoils were left then by North American enterprises. These spoils allowed the native bourgeoisie to perpetuate the system of political domination. Yet under this system, the potential for internal capitalization was very limited, and the capacity for distributing resources to the middle and lower classes was relatively small.[2]

Trade surpluses in the post–World War II era, combined with shifts in investment patterns, permitted an acceleration of capital accumulation directed toward industrial and consumer production. This gave rise to the social mobilization of middle- and lower-class elements and to new demands for political participation. Despite economic progress, Peru remained under the leadership of a privileged class that refused to legitimize its rule through democratization. It was in this context that the military, sensing that the frustrations of politically and economically marginalized groups could boil over into radical revolution, decided to overturn the Belaúnde Terry government. Declaring that their revolution would pursue a "humanistic" middle path between capitalism and socialism, General Velasco and his colleagues embarked on a program of land reform, regulation of foreign investors, and development of the state infrastructure.[3]

As ambitious as these reforms were, the major ideological orientation of the new regime was nonetheless centrist,[4] and its intellectual model was structuralist. The centrists converged with the radicals regarding the need for reform of land ownership patterns, but only to release the productive capacity of the farm sector, not to empower a hitherto exploited class. Consequently, these officers saw no purpose to social mobilization in support of this state-directed "revolution." The structuralists believed in planning, not politics. Progress was possible if left in the hands of a military and technocratic elite that would rationally design an industrial-agricultural strategy. The "revolution" could be achieved without foot soldiers; it began and ended in the ministries of state.[5]

Substantively, the centrists modeled themselves after the structuralists. Although the economic program was plagued by inconsistencies, its calls for state-led investment, agrarian reform, industrialization, protection for domestic firms, and control of foreign investment were mostly consistent with ECLA doctrine.[6] Peru's policymakers were quick to attribute economic problems to external forces. Inflation, they believed, was a derivative of overpriced manufactured commodities from abroad flooding the domestic Peruvian market. The government's price control program was a necessary, defensive reaction to externally induced inflation.[7] Food subsidies would lower costs for urban consumers, and pressures on the central budget could be relieved through foreign borrowing. External indebtedness also helped to sustain a vital public sector investment program, and besides, such indebtedness was not troublesome for a government that anticipated oil discoveries and accelerated export growth.[8] So, though much was blamed on the international environment, Peruvians were still prepared to do business with foreign lenders just so long as they, and not foreign agents of capitalism, could decide how to allocate the funds. While acknowledging Peru's continued dependence, policymakers were proud that the regulatory and entrepreneurial activities of state had lessened the harmful effects of that reliance, or so they thought.

The military's promise to find a noncapitalist, nonsocialist path to development foundered economically because the state could not accumulate a sufficient surplus with which to finance its "revolution"; it ran aground politically because Velasco could not popularize his program.[9] The deficit on the then-current account of the balance of payments had increased from U.S. $807 million in 1974 to U.S. $1,537 million in 1975.[10] Dramatic declines in the anchovy catch, supply constraints in cotton production, and dry oil wells all contributed to the unanticipated loss in export revenues. These export shortfalls were serious for a state whose reliance on foreign exchange to support ambitious domestic programs was still considerable. Moreover, the seizure of some domestic and international corporations did not produce the expected windfall for the state, since many of these firms were run down or seriously decapitalized. The government was now heavily indebted, running short of cash, and had few noninflationary financing alternatives left. State spending increased to compensate for declining export performance. By June 1975, inflation had reached 23.6 percent, the highest in recent Peruvian memory; real wages had fallen by 13 percent since 1973 and the GDP had declined from 7.5 percent in 1974 to 4.5 percent in 1975.

With dwindling resources and lacking a strong political base, the first military government became unstable, isolated, and internally fragmented. From the start, the generals differed ideologically, but Velasco's adroit political skills held the regime together and gave the progressives the advantage.[11] The economic crisis, however, widened these fissures, which eventually turned into unmanageable disputes. Also, the regime's failure to generate a strong and loyal constituency to back its radical reforms both weakened and isolated the more progressive officers surrounding Velasco.[12] Finally, the center and center-right forces prevailed, clearing the way for an as-yet-unspecified departure from the original revolution.

## THE SECOND PHASE

Ultimately, the military opted for an economically liberal and politically coercive strategy.[13] The break from phase one was not easy to make. Even as Morales Bermúdez inched his way toward economically unpopular positions, his concerns about legitimization remained. At Velasco's funeral, Morales Bermúdez witnessed an impressive outpouring of sympathy by the masses for a leader who had at least come to symbolize Peru's struggle to free itself of dependence. While President Morales Bermúdez had no illusions of popular grandeur, he was careful not to dissociate himself from the rhetoric of the "revolution" Velasco had helped create. His persistent references to the first phase and pledges to faithfully carry forward the revolutionary goals of the 1968 revolt were all designed to popularize his program.[14]

It is significant that few fundamental changes in economic policy were made until 1976. During the transitional period, January to June 1976, Morales Bermúdez's references to humanism, nationalism, and pathways between capitalism and communism were more frequently spliced with free market promotions and warnings about state interference and unlimited consumer spending. Peruvian elites and masses alike heard the president admonish them for irresponsible consumption and lack of dedication to productive, disciplined work. Changes in language were bumpy; so were changes in policy. The transition from structuralism to monetarism was uneven and at times confused, with important setbacks along the way. Military officers intermittently blocked austerity measures for bureaucratic and institutional reasons; ministerial heads were reluctant to go along with budget cuts that would reduce their own allotments; and officers inside and outside of government wanted to protect budget shares to continue arms purchases from abroad. Still, between 1976 and 1979, monetarist principles were advocated with increased regularity.[15]

The austerity measures announced by Luis Barúa Castañeda on June 30, 1976, marked the clearest departure yet from structuralist doctrine and set the policymaking tone for the next three years. Barúa Castañeda shifted blame from the international environment to the Peruvian state: public spending was driving inflation and discouraging private risk-taking. A freeze on current account expenditures and hiring of new administrative staff was imposed. Most commitments to government-sponsored production were dropped; credit to the social property sector and subsidies to state firms (which were told to become self-financing) were lowered and in some cases terminated. In the spirit of greater market reliance, the government announced on July 16 that the state fishery company, Pescaperú, would sell off its anchovy fleet to the private sector.[16] Pescaperú had been operating with a subsidized deficit budget of U.S. $215 million that supported the payrolls of 15,000 workers. The government declared that subsidies had robbed fishermen of their incentive to work. Fiscal conservatism could not succeed alone; a balanced budget in a country like Peru depended on trade to bring in taxable exports. To encourage export sales, the government devalued the sol by 44 percent, the largest devaluation since 1967.

### The Retreat: July–August 1977

In the first week of July, 1977, Peru was on the verge of signing an agreement with the International Monetary Fund that would have freed up U.S. $300 million in credits. The agreement had been worked out between Fund officials and the newly appointed Peruvian finance minister, Walter Piazza Tanguis. The plan was not all that the Fund desired since it contained modest wage increases and a high end-of-year inflation target. However, the bulk of the proposal was to the Fund's liking. It called for a 50 percent increase in the price of gasoline, elimination of food subsidies, an 8 percent reduction in ministerial spending, and a freeze on hiring new personnel.[17] Piazza brought this plan to the cabinet for its endorsement on July 5; the military refused to sign on, and the next day Piazza resigned.

The military's turnabout reflected the growing influence of a presidentially appointed commission headed by General Gastón Ibañez Obrien, a former minister of industry and tourism. Ibañez was a political conservative and an economic nationalist strongly in favor of industrialization. He believed that Peru could grow out of its economic crisis through demand stimulation, which would come about were government to spend more, supply credit to local manufacturers, and permit real wage increases. He also favored a return to a fixed exchange rate between the Peruvian sol and the U.S. dollar.[18]

The commission's only concession to fiscal frugality was to limit public sector spending, though that excluded arms purchases from abroad. The air force in particular was anxious to complete a purchase of $250 million worth of Russian helicopters and military transport aircraft, a sale that meant greater prestige for the armed forces and attractive commissions (as much as 10 percent of the purchase price) for individual officers.[19] By reversing Piazza's 8 percent cut in ministerial budgets, the military leaders were acting as bureaucrats as well, hoping to stem the rebellion of angry civil servants whose positions were becoming increasingly more expendable.[20]

The commissions's suggestions apparently had worked their way into the military cabinet during the spring of 1977, leading to the resignation of Finance Minister Luis Barúa Castañeda. At the advice of the influential

Council of Presidential Advisers (COAP), which had endorsed the Ibañez report, Morales Bermúdez did nothing to bolster the position of his own hand-picked finance ministers, leaving them with no choice but to resign. The expansionary program of July and August 1977 was particularly irritating to Central Bank President Carlos Santistevan, since it had overturned the cornerstone of the bank's liberalization plan: the mini-devaluation. The mini-devaluation represented a historic break with the nearly sacrosanct policy of leaving unchanged the sol's exchange rate with the dollar unless and until sudden economic downturns made major devaluations necessary. Santistevan was convinced that these periodic mini-devaluations (also called a crawling peg) would restore Peru's trade balance and attract foreign credit without triggering price inflation and social unrest at home. Unfortunately, the military was persuaded that any form of devaluation was inflationary and would simply further erode the living standards of wage earners. Once the military government abandoned the crawling peg, Santistevan also resigned. The shakeup in personnel and the return to an expansionary economic model marked the sharpest break yet with the trends of the previous year and a half.

### A Return to the Fold: September 1977–October 1978

As quickly as the regime had beat a retreat from the monetarists in July 1977, they returned to their fold in September. Morales Bermúdez's cabinet endorsed an arrangement between the IMF and Peru that would, among other things, substantially trim the budget deficit and result in wholesale dismissals of public employees.[21] The government now argued that the present levels of employment in the public sector could no longer be maintained since the bloated state budget was thought to be the principal obstacle to price and trade stability. Government expenditures were placing excessive amounts of liquidity in the hands of consumers who were purchasing imports and threatening the balance of trade. Credit to the public sector was to be strictly controlled, forcing interest rates up. Previously subsidized public firms were now asked to raise prices to cover their own costs. Real wages would be frozen, even though the return to mini-devaluations of the sol would raise the cost of living.

The government's dramatic reversal could be explained as follows: where one government faction lacks a well-conceived strategy, a rival faction equipped with such a strategy will prevail. The retreat of July 1977 could not be sustained because it was inconsistent, ad hoc, and confused. Lacking a more solid fall-back position to rely on, the military was more easily persuaded by the IMF, Central Bank, and minister of economy and finance to go ahead with the monetarist option. Those in favor of expansion could not convincingly demonstrate that their short-term adjustments would lift Peru out of its crisis. Why, for instance, would more productive investments be made by the private sector at a time when wages were being adjusted upward?

How could economic expansion generate a sufficient surplus quickly enough to rescue the nation from its foreign reserve deficit, which in July 1977 stood at nearly U.S. $1 billion?[22]

Perhaps the military should have taken a turn to the Left: declare a debt moratorium, increase state control over the economy, and build an alliance with the working class. These options were never considered, since any hope of consolidating a mass base had waned. The military had insured its own isolation through a rigid, hierarchical mode of governance that did more to demobilize popular groups than to endear them to the goals of the revolution.[23] And besides, populist economics could only buy back lost political legitimacy were the rewards sufficiently high. The generals were not prepared to unleash the kind of spending program required to attain that objective, nor could they explain how they would do so in a manner that would free Peru from its international debt bondage. Not surprisingly, their position was indefensible.

## MONETARISM AND REPRESSION UNDER MILITARY RULE

The second phase of the Peruvian "revolution from above" was Janus-faced. On the one hand, it was a transitional period marked by liberalization in preparation for democratic restoration. The military government must be credited for recognizing its own political inadequacies and for permitting a renewal of the democratic process. On the other hand, the period was also punctuated by increased and selective political repression aimed at the social sector. Organized labor bore the brunt of it, as all forms of political repression directed against workers increased over 300 percent between 1975 and 1978 (see Table 7.1). By declaring curfews and sectoral states of emergencies, suspending constitutional guarantees, transferring civilian trials to military courts, and arresting thousands of workers, the armed forces were doing more than insuring a timely and orderly transfer of power. In fact, such measures—which would normally have been warranted only by extensive public disorder—seemed excessive in the face of only intermittent protests.[24] The military had a second agenda: to fulfill new economic goals. The reduction of fiscal deficits, the restoration of payments equilibrium, the recovery of lost reserves, and the lowering of the nation's indebtedness made it imperative that certain groups be made to comply with state objectives. The following case studies of Peruvian mine workers and teachers are designed to demonstrate the linkages between these economic preferences and the use of state terror.[25]

### The Balance of Payments and the Mine Workers

Peru has been described as *un pais minero* (a mining nation). Its Central Sierra region is blessed with one of Latin America's most abundant and diverse stores of minerals. Between 1901 and 1971, mining codes placed much of this national treasure beyond the reach of Peruvians and in the hands

**Table 7.1 Monetarist Stabilization and Political Repression Under Military Rule in Peru: 1968–1980.**

| Year | Repression Score |
|---|---|
| 1968 | .63 |
| 1969 | .58 |
| 1970 | .31 |
| 1971 | .27 |
| 1972 | .69 |
| 1973 | .69 |
| 1974 | .47 |
| 1975 | 1.00 |
| 1976 | 1.91 |
| 1977 | 3.28 |
| 1978 | 4.17 |
| 1979 | 2.05 |
| 1980 | .36 |

Repression scores reflect a composite annual index of the following measures: arrest of leadership and rank-and-file workers, execution of rank-and-file workers, injuries to the rank and file, denial of constitutional rights, legal restrictions on union activity, physical disruption of union activities, and intervention into labor affairs. Data was accumulated for each year for each of these activities to produce separate indices of repression; indices were standardized and then combined into a general index. For a more complete explanation of the derivation of repression scores, see the Appendix. Italicized figures are for those years with monetarist stabilization programs.

of foreign-owned conglomerates. Having authored the mining legislation, those firms were able to extract considerable wealth at low cost. Even during the decades of plunder, however, foreign exchange earnings from this sector helped to pay for imports; taxes on property and outgoing commodities provided a source of revenue for the central government. With the revision of mining codes in 1971, the state became the marketing agent for its own mineral exports and assumed entrepreneurial and regulatory powers over mining operations, turning ore extraction into an even more valuable asset.

The true measure of the importance of mining is not found in its contribution to tax revenue, GNP, or employment, but in its commanding share of the value of Peruvian exports. Immediately after World War II, copper, silver, lead, and zinc—the four major metals mined in Peru—accounted for 15 percent of the value of its exports. By 1960, their share had increased to 36.4 percent and in 1973 to 55.4 percent. Peru's other major exportable products are sugar, cotton, coffee, and fishmeal, but their contributions declined steadily from 54 percent of all export earnings in 1950 to just 18 percent in 1972.[26] So dependent had the nation become on mining production by the early 1970s that Rosemary Thorp has described Peru at that time as a virtual mono-export economy.[27]

Labor's cooperation is required if the mining sector is to produce abundantly. Historically, a single day lost as a result of work stoppages in the mines has meant well over a $2-million shortfall for Peru. All Peruvian governments have been aware of this fact, but not all have reacted with equal urgency to labor insubordination.

*Velasco and the politics of concession.* The military government of Velasco pursued a conciliatory policy toward the mine workers. First, it forged a tactical alliance with the Peruvian Communist Party and its affiliated labor confederation, the CGTP (Confederación General de Trabajadores del Perú, or General Confederation of Peruvian Workers) in order to moderate the demands of striking workers. Since the days of the José Luis Bustamante y Rivero government (1945–1948), and with few interruptions, APRA and its affiliate labor confederation, the CTP (Confederación de Trabajadores Peruanos or Confederation of Peruvian Workers) held a steady grip on the mining sector. APRA had not only an organizational edge over its competitors, but special access to state ministries as well, which it used to win settlements for its affiliates. When the military regime came to power, that grip was weakened sufficiently to create a vacuum that was filled by more radical, left-wing parties and confederations. The Communist Party in particular was anxious to solidify relations with the rank-and-file miners who were disaffected from the Apristas. As official go-between, the Communist Party hoped to receive credit for having arranged wage settlements by keeping *los pliegos* (demands) confined to apolitical and manageable issues in exchange for favorable state mediation. Ministerial offices became very accessible to mine worker delegates and all sides preserved an atmosphere of openness and congeniality. Later, the Communist Party lost favor with the mine workers, who were won over to a more radical independent federation, but the military under Velasco continued to court the miners nonetheless.

Worker demands remained moderate, but strike activity did not. During the first three years of the Velasco government, the number of man-hours lost to strikes in the mining sector climbed 121 percent, from 2.8 million in 1968 to 6.2 million in 1971.[28] In the Gran Minería (the largest mining operations in the country) in particular, there was a 170 percent increase in man-hours lost in just a two-year period. These stoppages resulted in considerable export production losses.[29]

Production slowdowns had serious repercussions in a country where mining's share of total export value averaged 46 percent. The military government accepted virtually all the demands of striking miners. One study of state-labor relations between 1969 and 1974 indicates that in no instance were union demands totally rejected,[30] and in most cases, the majority of demands were fulfilled. Fixed-term contracts were normally not part of the settlements, meaning that unions were not bound to live with a certain wage level for the year; not surprisingly, workers struck repeatedly against the same firm. Companies of the Gran Minería reported an average increase of 20–25 percent in labor costs during this period.[31]

Since the government usually agreed to the strikers' demands and since fixed-term contracts were not enforced, it appeared that the military had encouraged labor insubordination. Knowing that the military was generally sympathetic to their grievances, the miners came to rely less on direct talks with the companies and more on direct action, betting that the state would eventually arbitrate on their behalf. They were usually right. Undeniably, the results were beneficial to them, as their real wages rose at a considerably faster rate than those of industrial workers in Lima.

Some scholars have argued that Third World governments must exhibit caution in dealing with organized labor within the extractive industries. They must strike a delicate balance between preserving a vital source of foreign exchange and winning the sympathy of powerful labor federations.[32] The state must insure the output of metals without sacrificing the miners' welfare, and likewise arbitrate on their behalf without jeopardizing the receipt of export revenues. Achieving that equilibrium is often difficult, if not impossible.

For President Velasco, the balance tilted in favor of the miners, for two reasons. First, the president anticipated Peru's becoming less dependent on exportation. (In fact, exports as a percent of GDP did decline from 21 percent in 1968 to 13 percent by 1975.) The state, he thought, would import less by developing industries of its own and would accumulate a surplus through the acquisition of domestically and foreign-owned enterprises. Velasco's hope was that such an industrial strategy would ease the pressure to perform consistently well in a highly volatile international commodity market. Meanwhile, corporate repatriation of profit would be tightly regulated so as to lessen the burden on the nation's current account. For these reasons, Velasco was convinced that with or without a large export surplus, the state would find the resources it needed to carry out its ambitious "revolutionary" objectives. Of course, things did not turn out the way Velasco had envisioned, but, certain that they would, the president was more willing to look favorably upon miners' grievances, and he refrained from coercive retaliation against recalcitrant strikers.

Second, the mine workers were not to blame for Peru's economic ills, according to the structuralist and dependency critiques that Velasco embraced. These workers were victims, inadvertently trapped in an exploitative national and international system beyond their control. Peru had been tightly inserted into the capitalist orbit in centuries past. Prior to the military takeover in 1968, Peru was a veritable shopping center for foreign mining companies interested in selecting from a diverse stock of important metals. The Peruvian state was weak and subordinate, easily relinquishing control of the nation's resources while exposing its labor force to the designs of foreign enterprises.[33] These firms would suppress Peruvian wages to keep mineral extraction costs down, then export the raw materials cheaply to parent firms abroad, permitting larger profits once finished goods were sold on the world market.[34] The revolution's obligation was, according to Velasco, to reverse this process by recovering control of the mining sector and placing its wealth at the service of the national economy. In doing so, the state would also "protect the dignity of the mine worker and improve his job safety conditions and his material welfare."[35]

By encouraging a moderate level of resistance against foreign-owned firms, the government could emphasize its anti-imperialist themes and touch responsive chords in a working class anxious to redress historically and internationally rooted inequities. When it came time to negotiate an end to strikes, the minister of energy and mines could be heard frequently exhorting the miners to return to work "for the sake of the revolution" and "not to play the game that the oligarchy and imperialists would like to see played."[36] The military's endorsement of structuralist and dependency critiques drew it closer to the miners.

Even a deterioration in Peru's economic standing between 1970 and 1972 (as shown in Table 7.2) did not appreciably alter the government's position. During the latter part of 1971, Peru was suddenly faced with a sharp decline in the world price for copper, a collapse of the giant fishmeal industry, and a balance of payments deficit of U.S. $65 million. Still, the government acted with remarkable restraint in its handling of the Cobriza miners' strike of October–November 1971.[37] The federation of unions representing workers in the Cerro de Pasco (CPC) mines had set a list of comprehensive demands before the company in September, including wage hikes, prohibition on closings, reinstatement of dismissed workers, and recognition of the CPC miners' federation. A month later, the company, which was Peru's largest single employer of mine workers, rejected these demands, claiming that no money was available.

The CPC federation called for a strike, prompting the Velasco government immediately to call for negotiations between the strikers and the state. The two sides were on the verge of signing an agreement when two miner delegates returning from Lima were arrested by state security forces. An embarrassed Velasco dispatched a delegation from the Ministry of Labor to La Oroya to repair the damage and insist that a settlement was possible. During their stay, a skirmish between miners and company security officials ended in violence. Two company officials were taken hostage. Soon thereafter, 300 workers occupied a local university in protest. A second round of negotiations commenced between the mine workers and the ministers of labor and internal affairs, but to no avail. Finally, nearly a month after the strike had begun, police and national guardsmen moved in to forcibly release the hostages, and several casualties were reported. Two days later, the government declared the strike illegal.

The state's threshold for labor violence was higher than one might have

**Table 7.2 Mine Workers' Strikes and Export Performance in Peru: 1970–1979**

| | Number of Strikes | Man-Hours Lost to Strikes (millions) | Total Export Value ($U.S. millions) | Trade Balance ($U.S. millions) | Terms of Trade[a] |
|---|---|---|---|---|---|
| 1970 | 66 | 4.3 | 1034.0 | 335 | 103.1 |
| 1971 | 76 | 6.3 | 889.0 | 160 | 90.6 |
| 1972 | 33 | 1.0 | 945.0 | 133 | 83.8 |
| 1973 | 80 | 3.8 | 1112.0 | 15 | 96.6 |
| 1974 | 38 | 1.9 | 1503.0 | –403 | 135.3 |
| 1975 | 57 | 2.6 | 1330.0 | –1,098 | 104.0 |
| 1976 | 29 | .5 | 1341.0 | –740 | 108.3 |
| 1977 | — | — | 1726.0 | –438 | 101.6 |
| 1978 | 53 | 4.6 | 1972.0 | 340 | 86.8 |
| 1979 | 40 | 1.2 | 3676.0 | 1,566 | 117.2 |

*Source*: Number of strikes and man-hours lost to strikes are from David Becker, *The New Bourgeoisie and the Limits of Dependency: Mining, Class and Power in Revolutionary Peru* (Princeton: Princeton University Press, 1983), p. 301. Total export value is from Banco Central de Reserva del Peru. Trade balance is from International Monetary Fund, *International Financial Statistics Yearbook*, 1982. Terms of trade are from *Statistical Abstract of Latin America*, vol. 24, 1985, p. 479.
[a]Export unit value divided by import unit value (base = 100).

expected, given Peru's precarious balance of payments position at the time. National guard units were held in reserve and called upon only after all negotiations had broken down. The government remained accessible to the miners at all times and at all levels: the ministers of labor, internal affairs, and energy and mines all met with the workers, as did the president on two occasions.[38] This, the worst confrontation between the authorities and the mine workers during the Velasco years, underscores the point that the political payoffs to conciliation were perceived to be greater than the economic costs to export decline. With the beginning of General Morales Bermúdez's regime in 1975, that perception would change.

*The Morales Bermúdez government and economically motivated repression against mine workers.* Prices for most of Peru's export commodities began their descent a year before Morales Bermúdez assumed power in August 1975. Since there was still sufficient international demand for Peruvian goods, export revenues could be augmented, but only by increasing the volume of production. The prospects for supply increases in the fishmeal, agriculture, or livestock sectors were not promising, throwing the burden on the mining sector.[39] The government was banking not only on the successful expansion of copper output in the Gran Minería, but on labor's cooperation as well. This is not to say that the government's tolerance or intolerance of labor dissent was simply a function of objective export performance. If that were the case, one would have predicted the worst repression of mine workers from 1974 to 1976, when Peru's trade balance suffered the most. Repression against the miners did not escalate until 1976–1979, even though copper prices had stabilized, prices for other metals had risen, and trade surpluses were restored for the first time in four years. What had changed were priorities and perceptions, so that *any* interruption of the smooth flow of goods to international markets became much more threatening. Once demand management and balance of payments equilibrium took on added significance for the new government, labor disruptions of any magnitude were sure to cause (and did cause) considerable consternation among ruling elites.

Morales Bermúdez's policy addresses of March and April 1976 set the tone for the new, more conservative administration. To insure the advance of capitalism, workers would have to come to grips with their obligations to respect authority in the work place and to maintain levels of production and productivity. The president insisted that with the country in the midst of an economic crisis, the labor sector, which had recently enjoyed the spoils of the "revolution from above," would now have to demonstrate "a true social and political discipline."[40] Those undisciplined workers who "sabotaged" the production process (and the president mentioned mining in particular) were committing intolerable acts of "subversion" and "treason."[41]

These harsh words coincided with sectoral legislation promulgated on April 6, 1976, declaring a state of emergency and suspending the Labor Stability Law in the mining industry. A federal law passed in 1924 had permitted owners to terminate job contracts without justification or advance warning, allowing entrepreneurs to regulate costs by keeping workers off balance, since unions could not guarantee employment stability for their members. With the passage of the Ley de Estabilidad Laboral (Labor Stability Law) by the Velasco government, all of this had changed.[42] Arbitrary dismissals were outlawed; dismissal could only arise from serious negligence or misconduct, or as a result of general work force reductions authorized by the labor authority. Negligent conduct was defined narrowly to include a failure to fulfill job responsibilities or a refusal to carry out orders. Employers had to justify layoffs to the authorities, and if the government decided that justification was inadequate, the worker had to be reinstated and paid for lost time.

The law was one means by which the Velasco government could follow through with its desire to increase employment. In 1969, the year before the law's enactment, overall unemployment stood at 5.9 percent; by 1974, it had dropped to 3.9 percent. As the size of surplus labor pools declined and larger numbers of unions became officially recognized, the wage-earning sector became a more formidable foe of management.

During the second phase of military rule, private enterprises clamored for more flexibility in labor contracts, claiming that workers were taking advantage of job security laws by slacking off. Heightened insecurity, they reasoned, would foster greater attentiveness to the job and thus stimulate production. The more efficiency-minded Morales Bermúdez administration agreed: anyone found participating in work stoppages in the mining sector would be summarily dismissed. A further rationale was provided by the minister of interior, General Luis Cisneros Vizquerra:

> The suspension of the (labor) stability, that was first declared in the fishing sector and then in mining activity, is owed to reasons of an economic nature. In a country that is in crisis, we cannot permit political labor activity to reach the extremes of paralyzing the economic life of the country.[43]

The suspension, coupled with the ongoing national recession, placed miners' wage and employment gains of the last decade in serious jeopardy. The FNTMMP (Federación Nacional de Trabajadores Minero Metalúrgico del Perú—National Federation of Metal Mining Workers of Peru) called a strike for August 4, 1978. The response was impressive: 50,000 miners from virtually all regions participated in demands for wage adjustments and reinstatement of some 320 dismissed labor chiefs. The military refused to yield to either demand, declared the strike illegal, and rounded up scores of mining leaders. This was a significant act, since five of the unionists were also leaders in the newly formed and recently convened Constituent Assembly, which was to be the first step toward redemocratization.

Political considerations would have logically dictated that the armed forces not interfere with the assembly, particularly in its early stages. The armed forces had pledged themselves to democratic transition and were hoping to salvage some respect by backing out of power gracefully. Economic concerns, however, compelled them to take vigorous measures to prevent labor disruption of production in the export sector. The government was nearing an agreement with the IMF. The Fund's stipulations included a revival of production in strategic sectors,[44] a restoration of balance of payments equilibrium, and a deceleration of inflation. Hence, even as the delegates were filing into the assembly hall for the first time, the military government was initiating a period of severe repression against the mine workers.

At this moment, the state had a tremendous investment in both the stabilization program and the crushing of the miners' strike. One interesting indicator of this is the out-of-character remarks made by certain state ministers. The minister of economy and finance, who normally confined his comments to general macroeconomic trends without singling out particular groups, could not refrain from noting that the strike was "an act of aggression against the national economy."[45] Manuel Moreyra of the Central Bank joined in, stating publicly that the walk-out was costing Peru $2 million a day in lost export revenues and was undermining the standby agreement with the Fund. He was reported to have offered his resignation to the president out of frustration at being hamstrung in negotiations by the miners' action.[46] At one point in the summer of 1978, the minister of labor declared the miners' strike an "act of treason" against the state. This represented a dramatic turnabout for a ministry that several years before had applauded similar labor actions.

Undaunted, the miners took their grievances directly to Lima, as they had done on previous occasions. Eight years earlier, la Marcha de Sacrificio (the March of Sacrifice) was warmly embraced by officials bent on demonstrating their unswerving loyalty to Peru's working class. This 1978 march to Lima of over 10,000 workers faced a different reception, which graphically demonstrates the change in attitude between the first and second phases of the revolution. The workers assembled at the campus of San Marcos on August 6, 1978, having come to negotiate with the government and asking the church to mediate on their behalf. The government answered their call by sending national guardsmen onto the campus to forcibly remove the workers. In the wake of the attack, several workers lay dead, and many others were injured. The rest were put on buses and sent back to their respective provinces. The mining sectors were then occupied by national guardsmen, who cordoned off the areas to prevent food and supplies from entering and cut off communication and coordination between the workers and organizers on the outside. All constitutional guarantees were suspended, and further work stoppages prohibited.

The following year, the price of copper soared, and Peru enjoyed its largest trade surplus in years. These gains in trade did not augur a period of political freedom. To the contrary, the IMF targets were now within reach, and with the military under pressure to meet the Fund's timetable to insure the rescheduling of future loans,[47] the government had less flexibility to negotiate with the mine workers and more resolve to punish any labor disruptions in the extraction industry.

The government's repressive measures became more comprehensive and increasingly more effective. Attacks were launched on the national executive committee of the FNTMMP in order to "sever the head" of the labor movement. The committee was charged with coordinating all union activities nationwide; at the behest of the state, many of its members were thrown out of work, thus losing their trade union status. Those who retained their status had difficulty convening. When a plenary session of the FNTMMP approved a work stoppage in February; it could not be ratified because local delegates were unable to assemble.

The government directly terrorized the rank and file. Under a "plan of national defense," the military split the territory into battle zones, dispatching troops to occupy key mining centers, cutting all traffic between mines, and sending police from door to door to intimidate truck drivers and shovel operators, who were critical to the production process. These workers returned to the job, and the government's preparation of 110 additional dismissal letters persuaded union leaders to call off a March 27 strike. The use of mass dismissals and terror against leadership and rank and file alike seriously weakened the organic structure of the federation, making mass mobilization virtually impossible.

The military called on other institutions to exert psychological and moral pressure on the miners. The state-controlled media launched a disparaging campaign to turn public opinion against the workers. As part of the campaign, the national rivalry with Chile was resurrected; the press charged that the mine workers were responsible for giving Peru's historic competitor the advantage in prosperous world copper markets. Even the church joined in, exhorting the miners to settle and go back to work, stating that they had "profoundly alarmed and preoccupied all Peruvians in circumstances in which Peru faces a difficult economic situation and when the price of copper is at its highest level."[48]

Government officials were quick to minimize their actions. In a candid interview with the leftist weekly *Marka*, Economics Minister Javier Silva Ruete defined the government's crackdown against the miners as the "minimal use of force" under difficult circumstances, intended to prevent the further erosion of social and economic order.[49] Peru, he claimed, was in the midst of a national emergency, and if several hundred mining jobs must be sacrificed, so be it, since it would contribute to the restabilization of the Peruvian economy. Morales Bermúdez alleged that the use of coercion in this instance was an insurance plan for transition to civilian rule. With a strong show of force against the miners, he and other moderates (Morales Bermúdez was a self-proclaimed member of this group) were able to appease rightist officers within the armed forces and avert a reactionary coup. Although his rationale was plausible, it is also likely that Morales Bermúdez exaggerated the strength of *golpista* elements within the army (those ready to launch a coup) as a pretext to continue repressing mine workers for the reasons that his finance minister had enumerated.

No doubt, government attacks on labor could have been worse. By comparison with similar actions in Argentina from 1976 to 1981, the Peruvian response was mild. But, while absolute levels may have been lower, relative changes within Peru were rather dramatic. The new economic program had unleashed repressive forces against labor not seen in Peruvian society since the days of the Odría dictatorship (1948–1956). During the first phase of the "revolution from above," Peruvian sovereignty and national security were linked to the successful completion of structural changes. Land reform, expropriation of foreign-owned firms, and redistribution of income would set the foundation for a secure and stable future, and would "steal the thunder" from more radical movements. Now, Peru's very survival was being measured in foreign exchange earnings; external balance had become the apparent cure for Peru's economic woes. The miners stood in the way of this recovery; they had to be removed.

In the monetarist view, the miners were not the only obstacles to recovery. External balance had to be matched by internal balance. Export performance could only help when government spending was kept within manageable limits to prevent demand pressures from spilling over into imports. The salaries of public sector employees are, of course, fully dependent upon state disbursements. In that regard, the military's behavior and attitude toward public sector employees becomes significant.

*The federal deficit and repression of teachers.* The majority of Peru's teachers are state employees. For that reason, changes in budgetary allocations have had a profound impact upon educators, and, conversely, union activity among teachers has had an equally serious influence on the budget. For many years, educational expenditures had been, next to defense, the single greatest line item in the central government budget, averaging 21.4 percent of all state spending, compared to defense's 24.1 percent share (see Table 7.3). Education was by far the largest item among social sectors (with health running a distant second at 7.7 percent of the total), and easily surpassed governmental allotments to any single productive sector (agriculture, mining, industry, etc).

The overwhelming share (about 97 percent) of educational expenses were found on the current account. In turn, 66 percent of current educational expenses were composed of teachers salaries (annual figures are shown in Table 7.4), and remunerations for educators in Peru accounted for approximately 16 percent of all central government expenditures between 1970 and 1980. Of course, these salaries contributed directly to the government deficit, which grew steadily from 1.2 percent of GDP in 1970 to 6.9 percent of GDP in 1977.[50] The deficit was financed largely through the internal banking system and the rest through external borrowing. Since bank contributions serve as a broad gauge for inflationary financing, one can conclude that education had contributed significantly not only to the state's deficit, but also to general inflationary trends. It comes as no surprise that the state's economic officers kept a careful watch over the educational sector. Nonetheless, not all Peruvian administrations have been equally sensitized to the fiscal ramifications of educational spending.

During the Velasco administration, the military relied on noncoercive policy instruments to thwart the influence of the independent teachers' union, SUTEP (Sindicato Único de Trabajadores de la Educación Peruana—the Single Union of Peruvian Education Workers). SUTEP was formed in 1971 as a rank and file challenge to the political leadership of the pro-Moscow Communist Party. Many teachers had been angered over the Communist Party's critical support of the Velasco regime, and control had passed to the Maoist Communist Party (Partido Comunista del Peru—Patria Roja), which was anything but enthusiastic about the military government.

In classic corporatist fashion, the military set up its own parallel teachers' union—SERP (Sindicato de Educadores de la Revolución Peruana—Educational Union of the Peruvian Revolution). SERP was

**Table 7.3 Government Expenditures on Education in Peru: 1970–1980 (millions of current intis)**

| Year | Total Current Expenditure | Education: Current Expenditure | Education as a Percent of Total Current Expenditure | Education as a Percent of GDP |
|---|---|---|---|---|
| 1970 | 34.4 | 8.8 | 25.6 | 3.3 |
| 1971 | 39.0 | 10.2 | 26.1 | 3.4 |
| 1972 | 43.6 | 11.9 | 27.3 | 3.6 |
| 1973 | 53.2 | 14.9 | 28.0 | 3.8 |
| 1974 | 62.0 | 17.2 | 27.7 | 3.5 |
| 1975 | 93.2 | 22.4 | 24.0 | 3.6 |
| 1976 | 126.8 | 28.7 | 22.6 | 3.5 |
| 1977 | 176.9 | 35.3 | 20.0 | 3.1 |
| 1978 | 234.3 | 46.8 | 20.0 | 2.5 |
| 1979 | 340.1 | 82.9 | 24.4 | 2.4 |
| 1980 | 769.0 | 177.3 | 23.1 | 3.2 |

*Source*: Banco Central de Reserva del Peru, 1986.

**Table 7.4 Government Expenditures on Education and Teachers' Salaries in Peru: 1970–1980 (millions of current intis)**

| Year | Current Expenditure on Education | Number of Teachers | Teachers' Salaries | Salaries as a Percent of Current Educational Expenditure |
|---|---|---|---|---|
| 1970 | 8.8 | 108,225 | — | — |
| 1971 | 10.2 | 63,542 | 7.5 | 73.6 |
| 1972 | 11.9 | 66,526 | 8.8 | 73.7 |
| 1973 | 14.9 | 66,562 | 10.2 | 68.2 |
| 1974 | 17.2 | 118,889 | 11.6 | 67.4 |
| 1975 | 22.4 | 118,375 | 14.6 | 65.1 |
| 1976 | 28.7 | 120,517 | 18.6 | 64.7 |
| 1977 | 35.3 | 124,142 | 22.4 | 63.4 |
| 1978 | 46.8 | 130,177* | 29.3 | 62.7 |
| 1979 | 82.9 | 137,180* | 49.2 | 59.3 |
| 1980 | 177.3 | 144,217* | 105.3 | 59.4 |

*Sources*: Current expenditures are from Banco Central de Reserva del Peru, 1986. Number of teachers and teachers' salaries are from UNESCO, *Statistical Yearbooks*, 1972, 1979, 1980, 1982, 1983.
*These are estimated figures.

government-subsidized, its leaders hand-picked by Velasco. Velasco then tried to win educators away from SUTEP by denying it legal status and by arguing that SERP could more effectively defend the interests of the rank and file, since the union was in a nonadversary relation with the state.

Unfortunately, the strategy backfired. The educators looked upon SERP as a form of state intervention that violated government's traditional neutrality with respect to the free association of trade unions.[51] Additionally, the government's decision to place SERP under the jurisdiction of the Ministry of the Interior was a costly mistake, since wage earners associated that ministry with the creation and implementation of coercive policies. In May 1974, SERP lost badly to SUTEP in an election for control of thirteen teacher cooperatives. Out of 60,000 votes, SUTEP won 90 percent to SERP's 10 percent.[52] The government recognized that its parallel union was going nowhere and consented to negotiations with SUTEP. Despite the clear ideological differences between Peru's major teachers' union and the state—and notwithstanding the military's failure to incorporate the movement—the Velasco government resisted the use of high levels of coercion.

The Morales Bermúdez government pursued a mixed policy of coercion and concession with the Peruvian teachers. From the government's point of view, SUTEP's strike call for May 8, 1978, could not have come at a worse moment. SUTEP was demanding a 100 percent wage increase, reinstatement of dismissed employees, and greater job security. The economic team was readying its austerity proposal (to be announced May 14) and was jittery about meeting fiscal targets so that an accord could be reached with the IMF. Peru was to enter negotiations with the Fund for a standby loan of U.S. $184.5 million. This would help cover payments on its onerous debt obligations, which equaled 55 percent of the country's export revenues for that year.[53] The Central Bank was reportedly out of foreign exchange at the time, and the first monthly installment of amortization and interest payments of U.S. $70 million was falling due.[54]

By mid-May, the deficit was running well ahead of projected levels, and the minister of education remarked that the pay increase demanded by the teachers would more than double the state's educational payroll. The minister of economy, Javier Ruete, slashed subsidies and announced upward adjustments in food and gasoline prices at a time when workers' purchasing power had already declined by 25 percent since the first of the year. This touched off labor protests nationwide, culminating in the massive national work stoppage held on May 22–23.

A confrontation between the government and the teachers seemed inevitable. In anticipation of disruptions, the minister of education canceled all classes and placed riot police on alert for student protesters. A meeting of striking teachers at the University of San Marcos was forcibly dispersed on June 2. Two hundred teachers were arrested and warrants were issued for the detention of an additional 700 activists. Meanwhile, talks being held between

SUTEP leaders and the ministry of education broke off after the government refused to agree to any of the union's demands. On June 7, the minister of interior warned that he would continue to use force against a walkout that he charged was politically inspired and he accused the rank and file workers of being "duped by ultra leftists."[55]

By July, the government's position had softened considerably for two reasons. First, support for the teachers' strike had grown immensely, and in unexpected social and political quarters. Twenty-four-hour sympathy work stoppages by other unions in Cuzco, Arequipa, Puno, and Ayacucho proved to be 100 percent effective. Private school teachers, who were conservative and distrustful of SUTEP's political leadership, were making gestures of solidarity with the strikers. As more diverse social sectors of Peruvian society took up the teachers' call, political support for the strike soon spread beyond the narrow confines of the extreme Left to assume national dimensions. Such mainstream parties as APRA and the right-wing Partido Popular Cristiano (Popular Christian party), who were to participate in the newly formed Constituent Assembly, could no longer ignore this impressive display of solidarity and hopped on the bandwagon.

The second reason was the installation of the Constituent Assembly, due to take place on July 28. The assembly, charged with reforming the Peruvian constitution and establishing procedures for subsequent presidential and congressional elections, represented the first step toward Peru's redemocratization. By offering the mainstream parties an electoral formula, the military reasoned that they would reciprocate with support for the stabilization plan. Meanwhile, the competition for seats in the assembly would sharpen the divisions within the Left, thus complicating its efforts to resist the economic plan in a unified manner.[56]

Unfortunately, the military had not anticipated the SUTEP strike becoming a significant focal point for the Left, and any further escalation of repression against the teachers would simply have been counterproductive. The military also wanted to strengthen the hand of the moderate APRA, which had won 35.3 percent of the vote and twenty-five seats (compared to the right-wing Popular Christian Party's 23.7 percent of the vote and twenty-five seats, and the seven separate parties and electoral fronts on the Left that combined for 36.3 percent of the vote and thirty-four seats). APRA's venerable leader of fifty years, Víctor Raúl Haya de la Torre, had been appointed president of the assembly. Haya de la Torre's adroit political maneuvers had won APRA control of the assembly's internal commissions, allowing the party to set the agendas and focus discussions narrowly on constitutional reform and away from wider social and economic issues.[57]

To win the Left's cooperation, APRA had, at least on a rhetorical level, given approval for elements of the Left's socioeconomic platform, which included issues of income redistribution and wage adjustments for workers. In the process, APRA prevented the Left from turning the assembly into an ideological forum to denounce the military and "bourgeois system." It expected the military to show appreciation by not interfering in the assembly's operations *and* by not cracking down on the teachers. The miners had been more easily isolated geographically and politically and had therefore been coercively controlled with less political damage. But, the teachers' strike was national in scope, and at least for the moment, the military had to weigh the economic benefits of repression against the political costs of democratic betrayal.

Hurriedly, the military announced a general amnesty for political prisoners and exiles that included some 200 teachers, dropped its plans to prosecute striking educators, and renewed its negotiations with the union. This led to a settlement on July 27, 1978—just one day before the assembly was to convene. Virtually all of SUTEP's seventeen demands were agreed to, including (and most important) a nominal wage increase of 26 percent, official recognition of the union and the reinstatement of teachers victimized during previous strikes.[58]

The wage settlement with SUTEP would surely have exceeded IMF limitations on federal expenditures, prompting the military to negotiate with Fund officials for greater flexibility. An agreement between Peru and the Fund was signed in the first week of August, and, to the surprise of many at the time, the IMF team permitted a higher-than-expected ceiling on bank credit to the central government—primarily to pay an extra 6 billion soles to cover the teachers' pay increase.[59] Despite these moves, the government had by no means abandoned its austerity commitments. To the contrary, its IMF-approved austerity package still called for a reduction of the deficit from $750 to $350 million over the next year. Moreover, the military's economic team won approval for a budget law that for the first time would permit the dismissal of civil servants for economic reasons alone. At the time, it was estimated that some 30,000 out of Peru's 450,000 public sector employees could be affected.[60]

From hindsight, it is clear that the state conceded less to the teachers than it appeared at the time. Although wage adjustments were made, these were quickly eaten away by an inflation rate of 75 percent. By year's end, virtually no other aspect of the accord had been fulfilled: official recognition of SUTEP had not been granted, and fired teachers had not been reinstated. Apparently, the Morales Bermúdez administration simply decided to postpone its showdown with the teachers until after the installation of the assembly. With the Constituent Assembly off the ground, with APRA's tacit cooperation assured, and with an IMF agreement signed, the government felt more confident about pursuing its stabilization plan—uninterrupted by political protest.

A positive sign as far as the military was concerned was the failure of a general strike call in January, 1979. The CGTP refused to have anything to do with the far Left, fearing that they would turn the strike into a violent confrontation with the military to provoke a rightist coup. Left to their own devices, the radical fronts such as FOCEP (Frente Obrero, Campesino, Estudiantil y Popular), UDP (Unidad Democrático Popular), and SUTEP could not coordinate the strike or pull together sufficient support. Many workers were intimidated by the armed forces' strong show on the scheduled first day of the work stoppage and urged organizers to call it off.[61] This convinced the military they could move against SUTEP which they did, with greater ease.

In May, SUTEP called for another walkout, to win concessions on demands that had been previously ignored and to press for a 100 percent pay increase. This time, with the Constituent Assembly behind them, and with no further wage concessions possible given the IMF's fiscal stipulations, the armed forces moved swiftly and unmercifully against the teachers. Preemptive raids were made by the Civil Guard against 200 teachers on May 26 at a delegates' conference, followed shortly thereafter by the detention of 700 educators and the dismissal of 1,200 more.[62] Army and police battalions quickly seized control of Lima; tanks occupied positions near the schools and universities to prevent disruption of classroom activities; SUTEP rallies were swiftly broken up by antiriot squads; and numerous raids were launched by the authorities on SUTEP bases of operation. The government refused to negotiate, calling the strike illegal and unpatriotic. The minister of the interior explained that the "extremist acts" of the teachers were thwarting Peru's economic recovery.

Central Bank President Manuel Moreyra set the new tone for the government when, in reference to the austerity plan, he stated that "the success of the efforts of the next decade could depend on the decisions taken in the next few months."[63] Failure to achieve a balance on internal and external accounts and to restore price equilibrium would have a lasting deleterious effect on the Peruvian economy. No sector loomed as significantly as did education. Even small wage concessions to a work force whose salaries drew 16 percent of state revenues would seriously interfere with deficit reduction and overall economic recovery. For this reason, the president, minister of finance, and Central Bank president were determined to hold tightly to monetarist guidelines. The armed forces followed suit by slashing their annual requests for armaments.

Actually, the orthodox plan had already started to yield results. Projections in 1979 were for a budget savings of 36 billion soles. Some financial planners were now going so far as to contend that after several years of recession, inflation persisted as a result of expectations and not simply excess demand. However, the economic facts were not guiding government policy—perceptions were. At no time in recent memory had the authorities shown so much resolve to stay the course in hopes of coming out of the crisis by 1980.

By the middle of June, the teachers, like the miners before them, sought the services of the Catholic church in hopes of bringing the military to the bargaining table. These efforts proved to be fruitless, and state terror escalated in July and August. It was apparent that the military's stubborn adherence to the austerity plan was behind its repudiation of church mediation efforts. Linking the government's refusal to negotiate with its cruel disregard of the economic plight of the teachers and school children, the bishop of Cajamarca, Monseñor José Dammert Bellido, said that "the economic demands of the IMF have produced hunger, infant malnutrition, sickness, lack of education and work, in a word, misery for numerous Peruvians."[64] The church called on the government (1) to stop crushing resistance with antipopular repression and economic programs, (2) to respect the right of teachers to work, (3) to restore civil liberties and protect human rights, and (4) to comply fully with the 1978 agreement. Political parties across the ideological spectrum joined the church in a chorus of protest against the state's treatment of its employees. A petition signed by Acción Popular, Democrática Cristiana, and the Partido Popular Cristiano, asking for flexibility on the part of the minister of education, was ignored. Twenty-one leftist politicians, including members of the Constituent Assembly, responded with a hunger strike.[65]

The military seemed indifferent to these protests, and its coercive strategies grew more ruthless. A state of siege was imposed in the south, where miners at the Southern Peru Copper Corporation joined the teachers' protests. Amnesty International described the government's response:

> In order to disperse the mass mobilization of the people and the teachers, the special forces of the Guardia Civil used police dogs, submachine guns and buckshot, which caused the death or serious wounding of many people.[66]

These measures weakened the resolve of the strikers, and the government returned to the bargaining table in its strongest position. SUTEP was embarrassed when the military refused to meet directly with its representatives; the teachers were forced to send a nonunion delegation on their behalf. The military granted moderate salary increases but refused to release imprisoned teachers, reinstate dismissed teachers, or recognize SUTEP.[67] When SUTEP pressed for more, the government abruptly terminated the talks and proceeded to reorganize the education sector; hundreds of SUTEP-affiliated staff were replaced with nonunion workers, many of them students.

Finally, on September 29, 1979, SUTEP called off its four-month-old strike, after having failed to achieve most of its objectives. By the strike's end, Amnesty International estimated, between 30 and 100 people had been killed, 350 wounded, and 1,500 imprisoned. Over 6,000 professionals were forced out of their jobs in what was surely the worst single period of political repression under military rule.[68]

## ALTERNATIVE EXPLANATIONS

Why had the military regime abandoned all normal recourse to mediation with labor opposition? Possibly, it was determined to destroy the Maoist political arm of SUTEP, the Partido Comunista del Peru–Patria Roja (PC-PR), and re-establish APRA's control. This is plausible, given the strong ideological divide that separated Patria Roja from the armed forces. On the other hand, the PC-PR had been a thorn in the military's side from the start; why did the regime wait eight years to crack down on this radical party?

It can be said that any government would have reacted as harshly in the face of huge budget deficits, but this is simply not convincing when one compares the military regime with the civilian government of Fernando Belaúnde Terry that preceded it. Until the very last moment, President Belaúnde resisted austerity measures. He turned to the Central Bank to finance his programs, having been unable either to borrow from the public by selling bonds or to raise taxes. Reserves fell precipitously from U.S. $135.7 million in January 1967 to U.S. $69.7 million in August of that year (owing to the loss of export revenues), and the bank was forced to print currency to support the president's request.[69] The bank urged the president to lobby hard for tax increases and to limit his expenditures. Belaúnde Terry rejected the advice, believing that the bank technocrats were economically alarmist, and that fiscal deficits were not likely to have serious consequences for the economy. Many in Congress were equally unconcerned and, rather than pass tax measures, simply overstated revenues and understated expenditures; fiscal discipline was not a priority. No "objective" assessment of fiscal imbalance of the Belaúde Terry period could have explained presidential or congressional behavior.

## CONCLUSION

The views of Morales Bermúdez and his close economic advisers were different from those of the Belaúde Terry government, and they persuasively shaped the unfolding drama between the state and the teachers. Could the armed forces fulfill their monetary and fiscal obligations, while maintaining political order? The outcome was predicated on the regime's firm handling of the state sector employees. The 1979 teachers' strike served as a critical test for the military, measuring its resolve to "stay the economic course" as Moreyra had urged. The prestige and integrity of the armed forces hung in the balance. The generals had turned away from the original revolutionary goals of the Velasco years and toward the monetarist models of the IMF. In doing so, they based their ability to perform competently as heads of state on their capacity as tough financial administrators rather than social innovators.

The military was determined to return to the barracks, having established itself as an institution capable of effective leadership. Once fiscal austerity and deflation became valued, their achievement became imperative. In this respect, the government's battle with SUTEP was a strategy of legitimization to prove to itself and to Peru that it could execute desired policies.[70] The escalation of state-inflicted violence was predictable, owing to the inherent conflict between demands for greater income and the requisites of monetarist management.

## NOTES

1. The complete proclamation of the new government is reprinted in Henry Pease García and Olga Verme Insua, *Peru: Cronología Política*, vol. 1 (Lima: Centro de Estudios y Promoción del Desarrollo, 1974), pp. 19–20.

2. Julio Cotler, "The New Mode of Political Domination in Peru," in *The Peruvian Experiment: Continuity and Change Under Military Rule*, ed. Abraham F. Lowenthal (Princeton: Princeton University Press, 1975), pp. 47–48.

3. Important accounts and interpretations of the Juan Velasco government can be read in Abraham F. Lowenthal, ed., *The Peruvian Experiment: Continuity and Change Under Military Rule*; Abraham F. Lowenthal and Cynthia McClintock, eds., *The Peruvian Experiment Reconsidered* (Princeton: Princeton University Press, 1983); Alfred Stepan, *The State and Society: Peru in Comparative Perspective* (Princeton: Princeton University Press, 1978); E. V. K. Fitzgerald, *The Political Economy of Peru, 1956–1978: Economic Development and the Restructuring of Capital* (Cambridge: Cambridge University Press, 1979); George D. E. Philip, *The Rise and Fall of the Peruvian Military Radicals: 1968–1976* (London: Athlone Press, 1978).

4. Liisa North reports, on the basis of interview data and content analysis, that the overwhelming majority of Peruvian officers occupied moderate ideological positions, while a small minority took extreme leftist and rightist views. The ideological spread is: progressives, 12 percent; Center Left, 14 percent; Center, 34 percent; Center Right, 30 percent; and extreme Right, 10 percent. The moderates were developmentalist in their views. See Liisa North, "Ideological Orientation of Peru's Military Rulers," in Lowenthal and McClintock, eds., *The Peruvian Experiment Reconsidered*, p. 252.

5. Liisa North described the centrist view: "A voluntaristic notion of social and economic transformation was inherent in this centrist perspective. It was a logical component of both the faith in technology and rational planning and of the incapacity to perceive the sectoral and class power at stake in a process of fundamental reform." Ibid., p. 261.

6. See Jane Jaquette, "Revolution by Fiat: The Context of Policy-making in Peru," *Western Political Quarterly* 25 (December 1972) for confirmation of this assertion.

7. The Peruvian authorities believed price controls did not distort market forces because they had taken real costs into account. John Sheahan takes exception, claiming that the Velasco government should have controlled only essential goods, allowing the market to take over in other areas, thus reducing the fiscal burden and alleviating distortions in relative prices. See Lowenthal and McClintock, eds., *The Peruvian Experiment Reconsidered*, pp. 387–414.

8. *El Peruano*, November 2, 1974, p. 2.

9. The point that Velasco could not galvanize popular support for his

program is made in Cynthia McClintock, "Velasco, Officers, and Citizens: The Politics of Stealth," in Lowenthal and McClintock, eds., *The Peruvian Experiment Reconsidered*, p. 276.

10. Wage data from Ministerio de Trabajo, "Dirección General del Empleo: Sueldos y Salarios," December 1979–February 1980, p. 7; deficit data from Rosemary Thorp and Geoffrey Bertram, *Peru 1890–1977: Growth and Policy in an Open Economy* (New York: Columbia University Press, 1978).

11. See McClintock, "Velasco, Officers, and Citizens," p. 281.

12. The Velasco regime, aided by the military's institutional unity and the disarray of the industrial bourgeoisie, displayed a relatively high degree of autonomy from social groups. This allowed for and in turn was reinforced by a closed policymaking style during the first four years. Thereafter, the Velasco government fell prey to private sector influence as the dominant classes regrouped. For more on this, see Peter S. Cleaves and Henry Pease García, "State Autonomy and Military Policy Making," in Lowenthal and McClintock, eds., *The Peruvian Experiment Reconsidered*, pp. 209–244.

13. General analyses of the Morales Bermúdez period are found in Lowenthal and McClintock, eds., *The Peruvian Experiment Reconsidered.* An important chronology of events for this period is Henry Pease García and Alfredo Filomeno, *Perú: Cronología Política: 1975–1980*, vols. 4–9 (Lima: Centro de Estudios y Promocion del Desarrollo, 1975–1982); more specific discussions on economic policymaking and performance are found in Rosemary Thorp and Alan Angell, "Inflation, Stabilization and Attempted Redemocratization in Peru, 1975–79," *World Development* 8 (1980): 865–886; Daniel M. Schydlowsky and Juan J. Wicht, "The Anatomy of an Economic Failure," in Lowenthal and McClintock, eds., *The Peruvian Experiment Reconsidered*, pp. 94–143; Carlos Amat y Leon, *La Economía de la Crisis Peruana*, Serie Materiales de Trabajo, no. 16 (Lima: Fundación Friedrich Ebert y Instituto Latinoamericano de Investigaciones Sociales, 1978); Humberto César Cabrera, *Perú: La Crisis y la Política de Estabilización*, Serie Materiales de Trabajo, no. 17 (Lima: Fundación Friedrich Ebert, ILDIS, 1978). To this day, much less has been written on the 1975–1980 period of military rule than on the period preceding it.

14. I examined several presidential speeches obtained from various issues of *La Prensa*, 1975–1978. Francisco Morales Bermúdez's June 30, 1975 speech as first minister was found in *Perú: Cronología Política*, vol. 4 (1975), p. 147.

15. Changing economic preferences were analyzed by examining public speeches by heads of state between November 1974 and August 1978. Among the most important sources used were: Minister of Economy and Finance General Amilcar Vargas Gavilano, speech of October 31, 1974, in *El Peruano*, November 2, 1974; Minister of Economy and Finance Luís Barúa Castañeda, speech of January 12, 1976, in *Ministerio de Economía y Finanzas, Obierna de Relaciones Públicas* (Lima, 1976); Minister of Economy and Finance Barúa Castañeda, speech of June 30, 1976 in *El Peruano*, July 1, 1976; Minister of Economy and Finance Walter Piazza Tanguis, speech of June 10, 1977, "El Programa de Emergencia," *Ministerio de Economía y Finanzas*; see also *Andean Report* 3 (June 1977); Minister of Economy and Finance Javier Silva Ruete, speech of June 14, 1977, in *La Crónica*, June 15, 1978; see also *La Crónica*, August 18, 1978; and IMF *Memorandum: Request for Standby Arrangement*, for further information on Silva Ruete.

16. *The Andean Report* 2 (August 1976): 146.

17. *Latin American Economic Report* 5 (June 1977): 91.

18. Ibid. 11 (May 20, 1977): 145.

19. *Institutional Investor* (October, 1977):187.

20. *Latin American Economic Review* 5 (July 15, 1977): 105.

21. Ibid. (September 30, 1977): 153.

22. The reserve figure is quoted in Nicholas Asheshov, "Peru's Flirtation with Disaster," *Institutional Investor* (October 1977):187.

23. Similar points are made by Peter S. Cleaves and Henry Pease García, "State Autonomy and Military Policy Making," pp. 209–244; and Luís Pasara, "When the Military Dreams," pp. 309–343, both in Lowenthal and McClintock, eds., *The Peruvian Experiment Reconsidered.*

24. For instance, the July 1976 nationwide state of emergency was declared in a period of relative tranquility. Labor strikes were localized, infrequent, and of small magnitude. Without the backing of the more conciliatory CGTP—the largest union confederation, representing an estimated 152,000 workers with 642 unions—the combined force of smaller and more defiant labor organizations posed no serious threat to the military regime.

25. In an interview with *Le Monde*, President Morales Bermúdez admitted that his crackdown on civil liberties in July 1976 was economically, not politically motivated. His intention was to demonstrate how urgent economic recovery was not only to the material well being of the population but to the nation's security as well. See *Peru: Cronología Política* 5 (1976): 2161–2167.

26. Thorp and Betram, *Peru 1890–1977*, pp. 238–241.

27. Ibid.

28. Becker, *New Bourgeoisie*, p. 301.

29. On mining losses, see Janet Campbell Ballantyne, "The Political Economy of Peruvian Gran Minería," Ph.D. dissertation, Cornell University, 1976, p. 184. For total export value, see Banco Central de Reserva del Perú, 1985.

30. Ballantyne, "Political Economy," p. 185.

31. Ibid.

32. For example, see Dirk Kruijt and Menno Vellinga, *Labor Relations and Multinational Corporations: The Cerro de Pasco Corporation in Peru (1902–1974)* (Assen, The Netherlands: Van Gorcum, 1979), p. 174.

33. This analysis can be found in Augusto Zimmerman Zavala, *El Plan Inca, Objectivo: Revolución Peruana* (Lima: El Peruano, 1977), pp. 106–107.

34. Ibid., p. 111.

35. Becker, *New Bourgeoisie*, p. 355.

36. Kruijt and Vellinga, *Labor Relations*, p. 170.

37. Details of the strike can be found in Kruijt and Vellinga, *Labor Relations*, pp. 167–180; *Perú: Cronología Política* 1 (1968–1973): 328, 331–333.

38. Kruijt and Vellinga, *Labor Relations*, p. 174.

39. See Thorp and Bertram, Peru 1890–1977, pp. 314–317.

40. Presidente de la República, General Francisco Morales Bermúdez, "Consideraciones Políticas y Económicas del Momento Actual," speech delivered March 31, 1976, reprinted in *La Revolución Peruana* (Lima: La República del Perú, 1976), p. 28.

41. Presidente de la República, General Francisco Morales Bermúdez, "Discurso," speech delivered April 30, 1976, reprinted in *La Revolución Peruana* (Lima: La República del Perú, 1976).

42. Labor Security Law, in *International Labour Organization*, "Legislative Series," November–December, 1971.

43. *Perú: Cronología Política* 5 (1976): 1964.

44. IMF, *Standby Agreement* (August 17, 1978), p. 6.
45. *Perú: Cronología Política* 7 (1978): 3188.
46. Ibid., p. 3185.
47. IMF, *Standby Agreement* (August 17, 1978), pp. 12, 28, 30.
48. *Perú: Cronología Política* 9 (1979): 3405.
49. The full interview is found in *Marka*, September 7, 1978, and September 14, 1978.
50. Deficit data from Banco Central de Reserva del Perú, *Memoria*, 1984.
51. Velasco's financing scheme was also a subject of controversy. Rather than support education through current expenditures, the military proposed that state enterprises and industrial cooperatives contribute money to the education of their workers. These contributions would help ease the central government's fiscal burden and would train more skilled workers through shared concern for human capital development between management and labor. SUTEP alleged that teachers' standards of living would fall as a consequence of the reform.
52. César Pezo del Pino, Eduardo Ballan Echegaray, and Luís Peirano Falconi, *El Magisterio y sus Luchas 1885–1978* (Lima: Centro de Estudios y Promoción del Desarrollo, 1981), pp. 191–199.
53. Barbara Stallings, "Peru and the U.S. Banks," in Richard R. Fagen, ed., *Capitalism and the State in U.S.–Latin American Relations* (Stanford: Stanford University Press, 1979), p. 246.
54. *Latin America Economic Report* 6 (June 23, 1978):185.
55. Facts about military repression from *Latin America Economic Report* 7 (June 15, 1979): 184.
56. These points are also made by Julio Cotler in "Military Interventions and 'Transfer of Power to Civilians' in Peru," in *Transitions from Authoritarian Rule: Latin America*, ed. Guillermo O'Donnell, Philippe C. Schmitter, and Laurence Whitehead (Baltimore: Johns Hopkins University Press, 1986), pp. 164–165.
57. *Latin America Political Report* 12 (July 21, 1978): 221.
58. *Latin America Economic Report* 6 (August 4, 1978): 233.
59. Ibid., 6 (August 11, 1978): 241. Later, it became apparent that the Carter administration, hoping to solidify the chances for a smooth transition to democracy in Peru, had asked the Fund to be lenient.
60. *Latin America Economic Report* 6 (August 18, 1978): 249.
61. *Latin America Political Report* 13 (January 19, 1979): 20.
62. *Amnesty International Report on Peru*, December 4, 1979, p. 2.
63. *Andean Report* 5 (June 1979): 81.
64. *Amnesty International Report on Peru*, p. 2.
65. *Latin America Economic Report* 7 (September 7, 1979): 273.
66. *Amnesty International Report on Peru*, p. 2.
67. Negotiation details given in *Andean Report* 5 (October 1979): 163–165.
68. Ibid.
69. Pedro-Pablo Kuczynski, *Peruvian Democracy Under Economic Stress: An Account of the Belaúnde Administration 1963–1968* (Princeton: Princeton University Press, 1977), p. 157.
70. Julio Cotler makes a similar point, claiming that the military wanted to place the economy on sound footing so that they could withdraw "with the satisfaction of a mission accomplished." See Cotler, "Military Interventions and the 'Transfer of Power to Civilians' in Peru," in O'Donnell et al., eds., *Transitions from Authoritarian Rule*, p. 160.

# PART FOUR
# COMPARISONS AND CONCLUSIONS

# 8
# Repression and Social Opposition in Comparative Perspective

## THE PRELUDE TO REPRESSION

When one compares the Argentine and Peruvian cases, differences abound. The Peruvian military regime, at least at its inception and throughout most of the first phase (under Velasco), was heralded as an ambitious experiment in "top-down" economic, social, and political reconstruction. The architects of the Peruvian "revolution from above" rejected the totalitarian aspects of communist rule yet strove for equality and collective well-being. Theirs was a middle-of-the-road development strategy designed to straddle the central planning of socialist states and the market reliance of Western capitalist states. They also wanted a more uniform polity, free from class polarization and partisan politics. Toward this end, workers, peasants, and other beneficiaries would be integrated into state-sanctioned, vertically organized associations. By contrast, the Argentine Proceso government was a classic representation of conservative, institutionalized military dictatorship, committed to reconstruction (or in its terms, reorganization) of a different variety. With a vision of a fully competitive economy, the junta set out to weaken or destroy all those popular organizations which could have interfered with its free-market plans.

At these points of origin, the situations are indeed different. If, however, we take as our starting point the waning years of the Perón (1974–1975) and Velasco (1974–1975) governments, then some interesting similarities emerge. These were governments in decline, and their decline set the stage for the economic and political shifts that occurred thereafter. The Argentine and Peruvian transitions from progressive to conservative government resembled each other in two ways, the first being economic in nature. The Arab oil embargo of 1973 and subsequent increases in the price of all oil-related imports jarred the world economy, and Argentina and Peru were not left unaffected. Unfortunately, policy inertia left them vulnerable to the exogenous shocks and contributed to their economic decline. The second and more important convergence was political: neither government was equipped to minimize the political damage the economic downturns caused. Weak, isolated, and conflict-ridden, the regimes succumbed fully to the crisis, in large measure because they could not either salvage (in the Argentine case) or generate (in the Peruvian case) social and political bases of support.

By 1974, the oil embargo sent the developed world reeling. For an underdeveloped country such as Peru, the steep rise in the price of oil and oil-dependent commodities was a mixed blessing. On the one hand, the evaporation of primary financial markets in the recessionary economies of the

First World sent the banks in search of creditors in the Third World on whom to unload their recycled petro-dollars. With a diversified stock of exportable commodities, Peru was considered by international lenders to be a good risk because of its capacity to generate foreign exchange to repay its debt. As a consequence, Peru received ample sums of bank credit. On the other hand, Peru's dreams of becoming a major oil exporter and profiting from the supplier's market were dashed when petroleum deposits turned out to be far smaller than had been projected. The country continued to import petroleum. Moreover, the price of Peru's imported capital and intermediate goods went up sharply while the price of some of its exports (especially sugar and copper) declined, producing a trade deficit of $1.1 billion in 1975.[1]

In Argentina, the embargo sent the oil bill skyward from U.S. $58 million in 1972 to U.S.$586 million in 1974.[2] Normally, the country could sell a sufficient amount of grain, beef, and mutton abroad to cover its import bill. However, Europe's 1974 ban on imported beef eliminated one of Argentina's principal markets. Furthermore, Argentina's populist government did not have Peru's reputation with international banks, nor was it particularly anxious to place itself in arrears with capitalist lenders. Without enough new foreign exchange from exports and lenders to cover the trade deficit, the Peronists dipped deeper into their already-limited current reserves.

Initially, both governments were lulled into inertia and a dismissal of the potentially lethal effects the international oil crisis could have on their vulnerable economies. At the time, the Peruvian government was exceedingly optimistic about its future export earnings potential and confident that these earnings could not only cover the import bill but contribute to debt repayment as well.[3] A devaluation of the sol to provide added incentive to export producers was not contemplated. Government planners were willing, and in fact anxious, to raise the nation's level of indebtedness as a means of financing the state's ambitious current and capital expenditure programs. So strong had the public sector economy (which included the general government and public enterprises) become that by 1975, it controlled 31 percent of corporate production, compared to just 16 percent in 1968, and accounted for nearly 50 percent of all fixed investment.[4] In some sense, public spending was born of necessity owing to the reluctance of private firms to invest. Regardless, state accumulation had its rewards, as the economy grew steadily between 1969 and 1975. With the government's price control and subsidy programs temporarily holding the inflation rate in check, and with the availability of foreign financing, no limits were placed on the state's continued expansion.

Argentine planners were equally optimistic. The nation was profiting from a continued boom in world commodities, as prices for its exports exceeded those for imports by 20 percent, and as overall earnings improved by 65 percent between 1972 and 1973.[5] Internally, the agreement signed among labor, management, and government in August 1973 to cooperate in the setting of wage and price limitations appeared to be working: inflationary pressures subsided, and economic growth resumed. Unashamedly, the central government spent lavishly on public sector wages, food subsidies, transfers to state enterprises, low-cost housing construction, and numerous other public works projects.

By 1975, it was evident that state expansion was no longer cost-free. Export shortfalls, dramatic increases in the price of imported capital goods, and the tremendous buildup of high-interest, short-term loans placed new burdens on Peru's debt-servicing capacity.[6] Faced with high debt servicing costs and a narrowing tax base as a result of the nationalization of barely solvent firms, Peru turned to the treasury to finance its budget deficit. Budget cutbacks or public sector service increases were considered politically too costly. Improvements were made in tax collection, but no substantial tax reform was undertaken, either because the military feared antagonizing the business sector any further, or because they anticipated such enormous growth in export-related tax revenues as to make tax reform unnecessary.[7] In Argentina, tax reform helped somewhat on the revenue side, but rapid inflation reduced the real value of governmental receipts between the time of assessment and payment.[8] Public expenditures grew (though at a declining rate), and the deficit increased from 7.5 percent of GDP in 1973 to 15.2 percent in 1975. Naturally, the unbalanced growth of expenditures in each case contributed to the inflationary spiral.

Despite the deterioration in their terms of trade and the erosion of currency value, both countries resisted devaluing their currencies until the eleventh hour. By then it was too late and even counterproductive. For example, the sudden adjustments in currency rates and in public goods and service charges made during "El Rodrigazo" (marking the term of economics minister Celestino Rodrigo) in June and July 1975, raised Argentine prices some 100–200 percent, whereas only 40 percent increases were conceded to wage earners. As Guido Di Tella puts it: "The direction of the changes was expected, but not their intensity."[9] Workers were taken aback by these measures, and retaliated against them by pressing their claims through tough union-by-union negotiations that resulted in an explosion of wage gains and the thorough repudiation of the government's latest conservative strategy. Competition for income shares had become a fiercely contested zero-sum game, with gains for one side representing losses for the other. By August, the wage-price spirals and the climate of uncertainty they had generated completely disrupted industrial activity and threw the Argentine economy into a steep recession.

Economists have concluded that the damaging effects of the international economic crisis upon the Peruvian and Argentine economies could have been dampened if policymakers had not rigidly held onto misguided expansionary programs.[10] The economic crisis that contributed to the erosion of political authority was, in their view, a consequence of unfortunate environmental changes combined with economic mismanagement. It would be hard to argue with the point that Perón and Velasco showed poor economic judgment. On the other hand, this view ignores an important question: to what extent could either government have weathered the economic storms more easily if it had shown better political judgment? The evidence suggests that political problems—especially government's isolation, the failure of executive leadership, and the sharpening of internecine conflicts—contributed decisively to the decline in political authority of one set of elites and its replacement by another.

### Government Isolation

Isolation was a characteristic trait of the Argentine Peronist government of 1974–1976. Isabel Perón found herself sealed off from the movement bearing her husband's name. Her trusted adviser, José López Rega, served as gatekeeper, controlling and limiting access to the president. Top Peronist party and labor officials complained repeatedly that they were unable to see the president but seemed powerless to do anything about it. As her contacts with these officers became less frequent, her policy positions also diverged more markedly from theirs. Isolation was more than a problem of limited contact, however. Isabel Perón's cabinet had no deep roots in the Peronist movement: José López Rega had been a former Argentine police officer; José Gelbard, the minister of economics, had affiliations with the Radical party and the small business confederation, the CGE; Benito Llambi, Isabel Perón's first interior minister, had served as an ambassador for Perón in the 1950s, but was quick to pledge allegiance to the 1955 coup that deposed Perón. And, of course, Isabel herself had been a former ballet dancer with no party experience.[11] The cabinet could claim few legitimate heirs to the Peronist tradition. That fact, coupled with the president's solitude, caused animosity and resentment within the movement and lost her government its legitimacy. The political cost of isolation was symbolized in October 1974 at a government-held rally to celebrate the signing of a labor contracts law. Despite the fact that the CGT had ordered an 8-hour work stoppage to generate participation, only 40,000 people attended—a small rally by Argentine standards.

For Peru, isolation was a double-edged sword. At first, the government's cloistered style helped to shield it from the complaints of the dominant class. Since nearly all its social and economic reform measures were incongruent with the interests of groups associated with the oligarchy, political and social distancing had its advantages.[12] Eventually, however, it proved to be a liability. The regime was equally distrustful of the popular classes who were to benefit from the "revolution." In keeping its distance from workers, peasants, trade unionists, and political parties of the Left, it was unable to properly anchor itself with any one class (or classes), and thereby make political capital out of the structural transformations it had induced.

Velasco could surely have benefited from civilian support, particularly as his regime found itself isolated regionally as well as domestically. With the fall of Chile's socialist president, Salvador Allende, and the rightwards drift in Uruguay and Argentina in 1974, Peru lost some valuable South American allies and was quickly emerging as the region's pariah. The Chilean state-controlled press launched acrimonious attacks against its "Marxian" neighbor, which were then picked up by the Peruvian mass media as well. In fact, the Peruvian press, in connivance with members of the business community, mounted a concerted propaganda offensive against the "totalitarian" features of the Peruvian revolution and in defense of economic and political pluralism; this offensive was not to quiet until Velasco's overthrow in August 1975. Such pronouncements were effective insofar as they placed the government on the defensive. Many officers went out of their way to proclaim publicly their aversion for communist solutions.[13] With a strong constituency, General Velasco could have turned the press in his favor by evoking emotional, nationalistic reactions to Chilean "intervention." As it turned out, he and the *Progresistas* lost the ideological war because they could not elicit appropriate sentiments from a public whom they had kept at arm's length.

### Failure of Leadership

Governmental decline was also attributable to the loss of presidential authority. Isabel Perón hardly capitalized upon the store of moral and political capital betrothed to her by her husband. Inexperienced, she was easily surrounded and manipulated by clever and ruthless politicians such as López Rega. She had neither the will nor conviction to defend the Social Pact, nor did she strongly believe in the conservative course upon which she was about to embark. She found herself pulled in two or more directions at once: under López Rega's guidance, she moved to the political and economic right, but for every three steps forward, she took one step backward under pressure from her angry labor constituency. Her erratic style caused profound consternation within the Peronist hierarchy and considerable distrust within the rank and file. Unable to withstand the pressures of the office, Isabel Perón suffered an emotional breakdown in August 1975 and was temporarily forced to leave office. Although she recuperated, Italo Luder's stay as interim president in the fall of 1975 indicated the extent to which the Peronist government had fallen on hard times. Luder kept the government in a holding pattern until her return on October 17, 1975. Soon thereafter, she was prepared to accept nearly all of the IMF's conditions for economic adjustment in a desperate attempt to stave off financial ruin. Her weakened position and her abandonment of populist goals is illustrated by the fact that her final appeal for trade union support took the form of a threat: either accept strict orthodox economic solutions or face military takeover.

By contrast, Peruvian President Juan Alvarado Velasco was a consummate politician who, for the first five years, skillfully held together an ideologically diverse corp of officers. As a member of the *Progresista* wing of the government, Velasco was able to maintain the cooperation of more moderate and even conservative factions. However, his influence appeared to wane once he took ill in the first part of 1973, slipping further with the amputation of his leg in March 1973.[14] From then on, he gave fewer addresses and was less publicly visible. By 1974, the economic crisis had gripped most of the Peruvian economy; it was strongly felt by the blue-collar worker, whose real wages fell for the first time since 1970. This was a time when presidential assurances were needed that revolutionary gains would be protected and reasonable economic adjustments would be made. Velasco gave no such assurances. More importantly, he neither acknowledged the gravity of the crisis nor made any social alliances to advance the struggle in concert with organizations of popular classes. Velasco had always wanted the revolutionary process to succeed for the popular classes but without their explicit participation in it. Now, he was reluctant to admit that the "revolution" itself was in jeopardy.

### Internecine Conflicts

Without strong social pillars of support, and with declining presidential leadership, disputes within the state and between state and civil society widened and took on more serious dimensions. In Argentina, the presence of a number of extremely conservative Peronists, such as Ricardo Otero as labor minister and Oscar Ivanisevich as education minister, placed the administration at loggerheads with the strong progressive wing of the movement. In cooperation with the Interior Ministry and the police, these officials conducted campaigns of intimidation against "combative unions" and campus "militants" designed to segregate workers and students from the guerrillas.[15] Their use of excessive force caused a profound rupture between the government and its popular base. With López Rega in charge, the authorities managed to alienate nearly everyone: the agricultural sector was displeased with government prices for grain purchases and with a devaluation they claimed was too mild; the leadership of the Central Confederation of Labor, already suffering from a credibility gap with the rank and file, was angered that the government would not support wage gains consonant with inflation; and the Frente Justicialista de Liberación (Frejuli), the electoral and congressional alliance that constituted the civilian front for Perón, was disintegrating. In short, horizontal and vertical cleavages were now threatening to undermine the Peronist government.

Latent ideological divisions became more pronounced in Peru in 1974. A nationalistic and conservative *Mision* faction emerged within the armed forces to challenge the hegemonic position of the *Progresistas* for the first time.[16] *La Mision* was largely the creation of one man, General Javier Tantaleán, an ambitious and charismatic figure who headed up the Ministry of Fishing. Tantaleán, whose support derived from fellow officers and from officials within state enterprises, wanted to mobilize the working class in defense of revolutionary closure. Convinced that the "revolution" had run its course, the *Mision* movement called for the repair of the economy through short-term remedial measures. To solicit labor's cooperation in this venture, *La Mision* established the Confederation of Revolutionary Peruvian Workers (CTRP) and the Movement of Revolutionary Workers (MLR). Neither organization could win many admirers, but, from their inception, these groups practiced a form of gangsterism and thuggery against rival labor-based organizations that caused enormous anxiety for the armed forces.

The progressives seemed unable to articulate a strong economic or political rebuttal to *La Mision.* Even more disturbing was the fact that President Velasco appeared to swing back and forth between criticism of *La Mision* and benign neglect. His inability or unwillingness to suppress this violence-prone faction cast a dark and lingering shadow over his administration and left a vacuum to be filled by yet a third group of officers devoted to institutional preservation. Led by Prime Minister Francisco Morales Bermúdez, the "Institutionalists" feared that continued dominance by *La Mision* would seriously tarnish the reputation of the armed forces. With this in mind, Morales Bermúdez and his cohorts overturned the Velasco government on August 29, 1975, officially bringing to a close the radical first phase of the "revolution" and inaugurating a second phase, which would be marked by economic adjustment and selective repression.

Likewise in Argentina, uncontrolled conflict, political violence, and executive weakness contributed to the empowerment of a third group. The widening gulf between the Peronist Left and Right, the retaliatory assassinations of Peronist militants and state security officers, and Isabel Perón's failed presidential leadership brought the armed forces to center stage. From the moment it was *officially* invited to participate in the war against the guerrillas under Isabel Perón's state of siege, the military assumed powers of state that it would not relinquish for eight years. Isabel Perón's dismissal of López Rega and Economics Minister Celestino Rodrigo in July 1975 was undertaken at the strong advice of the armed forces.[17] By September 1975, Argentina was effectively ruled by a tripartite coalition of the commanding officers of each service branch, union officials, and government ministers. The armed forces' complete occupation of the Argentine presidential palace (La Casa Rosada) was just a matter of time.

These periods of declining reform were complex and dynamic. Economic crisis and mismanagement, governmental isolation, intra-elite conflicts, social antagonisms, and the decline of executive authority combined to produce changes in personnel and political strategy. In Argentina, the military coup of March 24, 1976, resolved the contradiction of a government that was too weak to administer its own moderate reforms, by establishing a new and determined authoritarian regime. In Peru, the change in government—but not regime—on August 29, 1975, never produced a firm consensus about the choice of economic and political strategies. A deteriorating economic situation, however, prompted the military to give authoritarian free market formulas a reluctant try. In all, there was a certain sense of inevitability about the drift toward the political and economic Right. Pressures to extricate these systems from crisis conditions made longer-term structural remedies seem less feasible—even utopian—and short-term adjustments favored by the "liberal" technocrats (such as Celestino Rodrigo and then Martínez de Hoz) appear to be more attractive. Of course, if it were a simple matter of the quickest way out of an economic morass, then monetarism would have been easily chosen. In fact, choices were also political in character and made difficult by the constellation of complex and interrelated forces we have discussed.

These preludes help to define the initial positions of the new governments. The unfortunate demise of their predecessors provided generals Videla and Morales Bermúdez with a political "space" of broader dimensions than would have been otherwise imaginable. That space permitted both governments to explore new policy terrain. Unquestionably, the Argentine junta had greater leeway, having thoroughly deposed the Peronist government and having satisfied the public's yearning for a change. The Peruvian Institutionalists, on the other hand, had no popular mandate to speak of, and still had to contend with remnants of the first administration and a "revolutionary" legacy that they could not completely disavow. It is not surprising, therefore, to discover that the Argentine junta made more radical departures from the immediate past than did their Peruvian counterparts; in particular, the Argentines resorted to a form of political repression that was more extensive, more severe, and more debilitating. Consequently, while each government was motivated out of a similar set of economic objectives, the Argentine government, by virtue of its complete and unrivaled repudiation of Peronist populism, had a greater capacity to act than did the Peruvian government.

## Comparative Repression

Briefly, there were two general forms of repression: the first was organizational and included the state's infiltrating and intervening in unions, seizing party headquarters, and prohibiting union- or party-related activities; the second was individual and included arrests and executions of trade union officials, delegates, and members as a proportion of the population, and general denials of constitutional rights and freedoms.[18] In all categories except that of per-capita rank-and-file arrests, Argentine state terror was greater.

Organizationally, the Argentine Proceso first disallowed the unions their legal rights to collectively strike or to negotiate contracts. Next, they stripped unions of their autonomy, replacing elected labor officials with military appointees, prohibiting internal elections, and placing the union's operational, pension, and social welfare funds under state jurisdiction.

Finally, they attempted to "flatten" labor's organizational pyramid by outlawing third-tier confederations. Argentine repression was surgical in design: its objective was to permanently dismember the trade union movement by robbing it of its essential organizational assets. By contrast, Peruvian organizational repression was temporarily disruptive in nature. There were numerous reports of break-ins at union and party headquarters, and attacks on collective protests of one form or another. These measures had a momentarily chilling effect on trade union life, but no long-term consequence.

At an individual level, too, Peruvian repression was extensive but less severe. There was a higher per capita rate of imprisonment in Peru from 1975–1979 than there was in Argentina from 1976–1980,[19] but most of those detained in Peru were held for shorter periods of time. Of the 2,000 Peruvians arrested during the July 1977 national strike, only 300 were held six months or more; of the 6,000 detained between May 18 and May 23, 1978, most were released within days. Argentine political prisoners suffered longer-term imprisonment: by the end of 1977, it was reported that only 200 of an estimated 6,000 prisoners held since 1976 had been released: between 3,000 and 4,000 prisoners were detained under an executive edict permitting the junta summarily to prosecute political prisoners without trial—on average, these prisoners were held two to three years before being released.

An even sharper contrast at the individual level is exhibited with respect to treatment, executions, and disappearances. In Argentina, torture was completely routine. Virtually all political prisoners who passed through the secret detention centers were subjected to electric shocks and other forms of physical degradation.[20] In Peru, there were only sporadic reports of torture. Executions and disappearances were widespread in Argentina; in Peru, executions were committed on a much lower scale, and, at least through 1979, there were no reports of disappearances of which the author is aware. Insofar as the scope of terror was concerned, the Argentine variety was less discriminate. Casting their coercive net more broadly, the security forces lashed out at a sizable cross-section of the trade union population. Literally hundreds of unions were affected at one time or another, and we estimate that approximately sixteen to twenty unions and federations were systematically and repeatedly terrorized by the state over a four-year period.[21] Peruvian repression was much more selective, having centered on what were perceived to be a handful of strategic labor organizations such as those of the mine workers and teachers.

The terror option was not simply a function of initial position or economic bias. A third factor to consider is the structural difference between the two countries' labor movements. Presumably, repression could vary with the size and effectiveness of the respective trade union organizations. The Argentine labor movement has, for economic, organizational, and political reasons, been the more formidable one. Even if economic preferences establish motives, and initial positions establish the capacity for state terror, the actual conduct of terror could be intensified in strong labor societies and diluted in weak ones.

## THE SOCIAL OPPOSITION

The first ally of the Argentine trade union movement is the labor market. Argentina shares two traits with more highly developed societies: it has a low population growth rate and a small surplus labor pool.[22] The nation's comparatively low level of unemployment (it has rarely exceeded 4 percent, compared to rates of 10–20 percent elsewhere on the continent) and scarce supply of labor in relation to demand has been a source of leverage at the collective bargaining table. Moreover, the large proportion of the population that is economically active has provided a wide field for trade union recruitment, brining 36–40 percent of the work force into the organized sector.

While making impressive gains in the last twenty years, Peru's trade unions have not kept pace with the urgent demands of its impoverished constituencies. They have contended with a persistent jobless rate that undercuts their power in collective bargaining sessions; only 18 percent of the work force is organized. Undoubtedly, laws of supply and demand have worked in favor of the Argentine laborer and against the Peruvian worker.

The second union ally is organizational: power in the Argentine trade union movement is concentrated at the top; in Peru, it is dispersed among local units. In practice, this has meant greater financial and legal discretion for second- and third-tier Argentine syndicates whose jurisdictions are national in scope. Argentine law dating back to Juan Perón's first presidency grants official trade union status, or *personería gremial,* to only one association—usually a federation—for each occupational sector. This exclusive status has permitted federations legally to represent all workers within an industrial sector and to engage in collective bargaining on their behalf. It also entitles them to receive a proportion of the negotiated wage increase, equivalent to about 2 percent of each worker's monthly wage. Federations have other privileges: they may limit the range of issues that union affiliates can debate by obliging them to respect resolutions adopted by the national secretariats; they may also levy contributions from union and nonunion workers alike. Employers are required to withhold a portion of monthly salaries and deposit it directly in the federations' bank accounts. Those funds may then be disbursed downward to individual unions. Although there are unofficial guidelines for disbursement, it is widely recognized that labor bosses have used and abused those accounts to extend their own influence.

Historically, Peruvian federations have enjoyed considerably less power. They have had no representative status, which meant that more than one federation could compete for union loyalties in each occupational sector. The unions, not the federations, represented workers at collective bargaining sessions, thus shifting an important function to the lowest organizational level. Moreover, the Peruvian federations have been financially strapped. If monetary check-off systems exist at all, they are usually voluntary. Historically, union dues have composed about 0.5 percent of a worker's monthly salary. Of this amount, no more than 3–4 percent has been sent to the federations. By the time funds work their way up to the confederational level, there is little left. Confederations can not afford to hire many full-time employees, print newsletters, or contribute to strike funds.

The third and perhaps most important element favoring labor organization is the link between social and political power: Argentina's trade union movement has been integrally involved with party politics for years. Since the birth of the Peronist party in 1949, the alliance between it and the General Confederation of Labor has remained intact; the keystone to this alliance was Perón himself, who single-handedly lifted the trade union movement to a position of prominence while fashioning the party in his own image. But the relationship between party and union survived Perón's long exile (1955–1973) and became more institutionalized. Workers shifted their allegiances from the person (Perón) to the movement (Peronismo).[23] Although never displacing him as *El Caudillo* (the leader), many trade union officials acquired considerable influence, which extended downward through the union ranks and upward through the political party apparatus. This dual power was recently displayed by Lorenzo Miguel, the head of the powerful Metalworkers Federation, who almost single-handedly selected Italo Luder to head the Peronist ticket in the 1983 presidential elections. Traditionally, labor bosses could deliver the massive working-class vote to the Peronist candidate and insure electoral victory. It has been precisely that fear of a Peronist victory that has led repeated antilabor administrations coercively to proscribe Peronist participation in the democratic process.

Table 8.1 indicates that where the Peronist party (also known as the Justicialist party) ran its own candidate, it consistently outpolled rival parties. Where the Peronists could not run their own candidates, their constituents were urged to cast blank ballots, which, matched against the votes for opposition parties, show the Justicialists emerging victorious in 1957 and 1960, and second in the 1963 presidential vote with a 21.2 percent plurality. In 1963, the call for blank ballots was put out only two days before elections, accounting for the poorer showing. In the 1958 elections, Perón asked the workers to vote for the Radical party candidate Arturo Frondizi: Frondizi's 41.8 percent plurality was attributable to Peronist backing. The Peronists' first-place showings in the gubernatorial and legislative contests of 1962 and 1965 served notice on the nation that despite Perón's exile, the Peronists had not lost their popular appeal. For that reason, both election results were annulled, and soon thereafter the military intervened.

Prohibitions against party activities sealed one fissure while rupturing

**Table 8.1 Peronist Party Performance in National Elections**

| Year | Type of Election | Plurality[a] | Victory |
|---|---|---|---|
| 1957 | constitutional convention | (26.9) | |
| 1958 | presidential | | |
| 1960 | congressional | (27.3) | |
| 1962 | gubernatorial and legislative | 34.6 | yes |
| 1962 | military coup[b] | | |
| 1963 | presidential | (21.2) | |
| 1965 | gubernatorial and legislative | 38.8 | yes |
| 1966 | military coup[b] | | |
| 1973 | presidential | 49 | yes |
| 1976 | military coup[b] | | |

*Sources*: David R. Decker, *The Political, Economic and Labor Climate in Argentina*, Multinational Industrial Relations Series (Philadelphia: The Wharton School, 1983) p. 12. Data for 1963 is from Guillermo O'Donnell, *Modernization and Bureaucratic Authoritarianism: Studies in South American Politics* (Berkeley: Institute of International Studies, 1979), p. 191.
[a]Figures in parentheses indicate blank ballots cast.
[b]Indicates that the Peronist Party was outlawed.

another: when electoral doors were closed, Peronist leaders fell back on the militancy of their working-class constituents. For instance, the Peronists' resentments about their exclusion from the democratic process fueled the massive work stoppages of 1963–1964, known as the *Plan de Lucha*, that helped destabilize the Arturo Illia government. The multiple threat of Peronism—to win with either legal or extra-legal tactics in either political or social settings—posed a most formidable challenge to antilabor elites. The state's use of force must be understood in some sense as a reaction to both the political and social arms of the Peronist movement, and not to either one alone.

The Peruvian labor movement has posed less of a social or political challenge to the state, at least since the mid-1960s. Before then, labor operated collectively under the single roof of the CTP (Confederation of Peruvian Workers), itself dominated by APRA. Nearly all delegates to confederational assemblies and officers of the organization were APRA members. Important decisions were often made within the labor affairs bureaus (*buros sindicales*) of the party itself, then ratified at national assemblies. These bureaus, composed of trade union delegates from individual syndicates, drew up slates of APRA loyalists to run in union elections.

From 1963 to 1968, APRA's congressional alliance with the conservative UNO (Unión Nacional Odriísta—the party of former dictator Manuel Odría) alienated progressives, who soon deserted the party. What emerged was a new Peruvian leftist movement, which, under the influence of the Cuban revolution, joined a guerrilla struggle to seize land for poor peasants. APRA's appeal in rural areas declined, though it managed to retain most of its strength in the urban industrial sectors. However, the CTP's endorsement of a wage freeze during the economic crisis of 1967 cost it support among blue-collar workers as well. The decline of APRA-CTP influence was most pronounced after the military coup of 1968. The military's official recognition of the Communist party-backed CGTP (General Confederation of Peruvian Workers) and the Christian Democratic CNT (National Confederation of Workers) in 1971, and its creation of the government-sponsored CTRP (Confederation of Revolutionary Peruvian Workers) in 1972, undermined support for APRA by forcing its confederation to compete for union loyalties. The military took advantage of these divisions within the labor movement by playing one confederation off another with promises of favorable arbitration, legal recognition for union affiliates, or financial assistance. This strategy met with partial success.

The bankers, miners, and teachers, themselves alienated by APRA's conservative leadership, withdrew from the CTP and reaffiliated with the CGTP. This left the CTP with control over only two powerful unions: the textile and sugar workers' federations. Within a short time, the CGTP became Peru's largest confederation, with 950,000 members, compared to 600,000 for the CTP.[24] The rate of union and federation withdrawals from the CTP after 1968 was quite dramatic. One study of a sample of trade unions showed that 42 percent had changed affiliation between 1968 and 1975, and over 50 percent of these had left the CTP for the CGTP, the CTRP or had become independent. Of those that had changed, none had gone over to the CTP.[25] Between 1973 and 1975, only 15 (2 percent) of the newly recognized unions affiliated with the CTP, compared with 177 (23 percent) with the CGTP, and 188 (25 percent) with the CTRP.[26] The CTP's inability to get workers to respond to its strike calls in April and May 1973 and again in February 1976 was further evidence of its decline.

Trade union reaffiliation had some important effects. First, it reduced opposition to military rule. The CGTP, under the leadership of the pro-Moscow Communist party, applauded the military's anti-imperialism and its efforts to dethrone the oligarchy. It therefore counseled its affiliates to avoid political strikes that could embarrass the "revolution." While the Peruvian working class successfully mounted large national strikes in 1977 and 1978, labor solidarity should not be overemphasized. Equally important were the aborted national strikes in September 1977, June 1978, and January 1979. Plans fell through in each case when one major sector of the labor movement (usually the CGTP) refused to go along.[27]

Second, the military's divide and rule plan helped to split the political loyalties of labor. As APRA's influence declined, numerous leftist parties filled the political vacuum, each incapable of providing the organizational expertise to capture the widespread popular support that APRA had achieved. The Communist party took control of the CGTP but could not maintain the loyalty of all its members; few were Communist party members or sympathizers, and many were disenchanted with the party's support for the military government once the economic crisis sent real wages falling precipitously. Some unions reaffiliated with the CCUSC—the Committee for the Coordination and Unification of Classist Unions—formed in 1974 under the direction of the Maoist Communist party. Other unions, such as the mine workers and the teachers, refused to join the confederations but did collaborate with Marxist-Leninist parties. None of these marriages between labor and the Left proved to be enduring or particularly advantageous.

For the most part, the radical leftist parties were sectarian in their practices and ideologically dogmatic in their thinking. They could neither translate grievances into concrete political objectives nor formulate political slogans that held meaning for the average worker. They tended to confuse the parochial interests of their organizations with the broader objectives of the working-class movement. As a result, they failed to align strategically with other leftist parties in a coalition that could have seriously challenged the military regime. So where need be, the armed forces could rely on the self-defeating behavior of the Left rather than on the use of force to dilute their opposition.

These divisions were serious, leaving no single prolabor party sufficiently representative to make any valid claim for political leadership. This is borne out by the results of the 1978 Constituent Assembly elections shown in Table 8.2. Those leftist parties that drew the most votes had the

**Table 8.2 Trade Union Affiliations with Political Parties: 1978 Constituent Assembly Elections in Peru**

| Party | Vote (%) | Confederation | Membership |
|---|---|---|---|
| APRA | 35.3 | CTP | 600,000 |
| FOCEP | 12.3 | — | — |
| PSR[a] | 6.6 | CTRP | 80,000 |
| PC | 5.9 | CGTP | 950,000 |
| PDC | 2.4 | CNT | 85,000 |

*Sources*: Electoral results from Sandra Woy Hazleton and Stephen M. Gorman, "The Peruvian Left Since 1977: Ideology, Programs and Behavior," paper delivered at the 1982 annual meeting of the American Political Science Association, September 2–5, 1982, p. 26. Union membership data from Denis Sulmont, *El Movimiento Obrero Peruano 1890–1980: Reseña Historia*, p. 147.

[a]PSR stands for Revolutionary Socialist Party, which was formed in 1977 by groups sympathetic to Velasco's reforms.

weakest ties to organized labor. This was the case with FOCEP (the Front of Peruvian Workers, Farmers, and Students), a coalition of Trotskyist parties that had influence in a few industrial and rural unions, but not with any confederation. The party with the largest labor affiliation, the Communist party (PC), drew the fewest votes (not including the Christian Democratic party (PDC), which is reformist and not radical). Although the APRA-led CTP had the second largest membership, it was down from previous years, representing a loss of support to the CGTP.

In brief, there was no positive correlation between social and political power in Peru as there was in Argentina. As unions proliferated under military rule, the political direction of the trade union movement foundered. This only played into the hands of the Morales Bermúdez government, which was anxious to minimize the political costs of complying with the monetarist anti-inflationary program. It did so with a mix of strategies, never having to rely primarily on the use of political repression.

## NOTES

1. Thomas Scheetz, *Peru and the International Monetary Fund*, p. 162.

2. David Rock, *Argentina 1516–1987: From Spanish Colonization to Alfonsín* (Berkeley: University of California Press, 1987), p. 364.

3. Rosemary Thorp, "The Evolution of Peru's Economy," in Lowenthal and McClintock, eds., *The Peruvian Experiment Reconsidered*, p. 51.

4. E. V. K. Fitzgerald, "State Capitalism in Peru: A Model of Economic Development and its Limitations," in Lowenthal and McClintocks, eds., *The Peruvian Experiment Reconsidered*, pp. 70–71.

5. Guido Di Tella, "The Economic Policies of Argentina's Labour-based Government (1973–76)," in *Inflation and Stabilisation in Latin America*, ed. Rosemary Thorp and Laurence Whitehead (London: MacMillan Press, 1979), p. 187.

6. The United States was dismayed with Velasco's left-leaning foreign policies, and made unavailable to Peru concessionary funds from international development banks. See Thomas Sheetz, *Peru and the International Monetary Fund*, p. 128.

7. Fitzgerald, "State Capitalism in Peru," p. 78.

8. Guido Di Tella, *Argentina Under Perón, 1973–76: The Nation's Experience with a Labour-based Government* (London: MacMillan Press, 1983), p. 127.

9. Di Tella, "The Economic Policies of Argentina's Labour-based Government," p. 199.

10. This assessment has been made in the case of Peru by Daniel M. Schydlowsky and Juan J. Wicht, "The Anatomy of an Economic Failure," in McClintock and Lowenthal, eds. *The Peruvian Experiment*, pp. 94–143; Guido Di Tella has made similar observations with respect to Argentina.

11. This biographical data found in the *Latin America Political Report*, July 5, 1974, p. 201.

12. A point well-argued by Peter S. Cleaves and Henry Pease García; see their "State Autonomy and Military Policy Making," in *The Peruvian Experiment*, pp. 209–244.

13. See Henry Pease García, *El Ocaso del Poder Oligárquico* (Lima: Centro de Estudios y Promoción del Desarrollo, 1980), pp. 146–147.

14. This argument also made by Pease Garcia, *El Ocaso del Poder*, pp. 105–107.

15. *Latin America Political Report*, October 18, 1974, p. 327.

16. This dispute is detailed in Pease García, *El Ocaso del Poder*, p. 148–188.

17. *Latin America Political Report*, July 11, 1975, p. 209.

18. Organizational scores were derived by counting, weighting, and then aggregating individual acts of coercion. Weights were assigned depending upon whether a union (1), federation (2), confederation (5), or all labor organizations (10) were affected. In the example of legal restrictions on union activities, secondary weights were assigned according to the duration of the restriction. For individual repression, separate events were tallied for each year and then scored as a proportion of the population. Constitutional infringements were counted but then weighted according to the latitude of coverage (city, 1; region, 2; nation, 4) and the duration of coverage (less than a month, 1; one to three months, 2; four to six months, 3; or seven to twelve months, 4). The step-by-step procedures for deriving repression scores are explained in the appendix.

19. This and all subsequent data in this section was compiled by the author. For details on data retrieval, aggregation, and interpretation, consult the Appendix.

20. See Argentine National Commission on the Disappeared, *Nunca Más*, p. 20.

21. This estimate is the result of a statistical examination of data obtained from the Argentine Permanent Assembly for Human Rights, "Lista de los Detenidos Desaparecidos Registrados en la Asamblea Permanente por los Derechos Humanos" (Buenos Aires: APDH, 1985).

22. These more modern characteristics of Argentina are discussed in Carlos Waisman, *Reversal of Development in Argentina* (Princeton: Princeton University Press, 1987).

23. David Butler, "Charisma, Migration and Elite Coalescence: An Interpretation of Peronism," *Comparative Politics* 3 (April 1969): 423–439.

24. Denis Sulmont, *El Movimiento Obrero Peruano 1890–1980: Reseña Historia* (Lima: Tarea, 1980), p. 147.

25. Evelyne Huber Stephens, *The Politics of Worker's Participation: The Peruvian Approach in Comparative Perspective* (New York: Academic Press, 1980), p. 206.

26. Ibid., pp. 177–178.

27. There is evidence to suggest that popular organizations—based in the barrios of Peru's major cities and comprising students, workers, and the unemployed—were largely responsible for mobilizing the participants in the national work stoppages, and not the confederations. But, these groups were ad hoc, poorly financed, and unable to provide long-term leadership necessary to sustain a militant struggle.

# 9
# Economic "Experts" Against Dominant Classes

## IDEAS AND INTERESTS

On the face of it, the choice between acting on conceptual preferences or special interests is not easy, nor is it cost-free. Governments that exempt themselves from societal obligations will often be held accountable. In democratic systems, important constituents can withhold pledges of political allegiance in exchange for favorable policy adjustments. In nondemocratic systems, dissatisfied groups hold fewer bargaining chips but may undermine authority through violent and illegal means. Either way, conventional wisdom says governments are likely to find tradeoffs between conceptual consistency and political expediency. However, it may not always be so, as Eric Nordlinger writes:

> Even when societal sanctions are likely or expected, public officials sometimes act on their own preferences, because sanctions are not thought to have an especially telling impact upon them, the official preferences are more salient than are the consequences of societal sanctions, or the Burkean model of the modern public official is alive and well among some significant proportion of public actors.[1]

In some sense, the strongest defense of the proposition that ideas can share co-equal importance with interests has yet to be made. Political repression of labor is an easier choice for an authoritarian regime such as the one that ruled Argentina. After all, a conservative and privileged elite would not, in all likelihood, draw support from working-class sectors that are historically progressive and more economically disadvantaged. It would hardly take seriously the complaints of a class to which it owed no political debts or allegiance. Since it was not accountable to labor groups, it would perceive no political costs to the application of state violence against them.

A stronger defense of the ideas versus interests thesis could be made if it could be shown that elites chose and maintained theory-driven policies *despite* objections from a public to which they were initially accountable. In that instance, a conflict between interests and ideas could provoke a crisis for a regime that must worry about its authority as well as its ideals. On the other hand, elites could remain intransigent if they had sufficient autonomy from social classes *and* alternate support structures. With this in mind, we will briefly examine relations between economic decisionmakers and dominant classes in Argentina and Chile.

There is little doubt that the agricultural, industrial, and financial elites of Argentina awaited the policies of the military PRN government that came to power in 1976 with eager anticipation. The predecessor regime (that of General Juan Carlos Onganía, 1966–1970) had achieved 4 percent real growth, kept inflation at a moderate 28 percent, and increased the propertied sector's share of national income from 54.6 percent in 1967 to 57.9 percent in 1970. Unfortunately, Onganía did not anticipate the politically volcanic eruption of student-worker demonstrations in Córdoba in 1969 and was swept from power before he could solidify these gains. The capitalist classes watched in dismay as income shares shifted back toward labor under Isabel Perón's administration (1974–1976). With the coming to power of the PRN's General Jorge Videla, the bourgeoisie was confident that things would be different. Confronted at the outset by a formidable guerrilla movement and a mobilized working class, the military promised they would be ready. The higher level of "threat" would invite the necessary amount of force to secure a stable economic environment.

In the first year and a half there was reason for the propertied sectors to be optimistic, as inflation rates declined from 347.5 percent to 160.4 percent, the economy grew by 6.4 percent in 1977, and working-class income shares plummeted from 45.7 percent in 1975 to 31.2 percent in 1976. Unfortunately, this "progress" turned out to be ephemeral: recession was just around the corner; by 1979, wage earners would recoup some of their losses and corporate profits would decline. A sequence of policy decisions jarred first one faction and then another of the capitalist class. Perhaps the most serious upset was the revision of exchange rate policy in December 1978. To what extent did the exchange rate decision jeopardize private interests, and how accommodating was the regime to the concerns of its alleged class allies?

## The Tablita

The exchange rate decision (called the *tablita*) marked the third phase of an anti-inflationary program that had not as yet borne fruit. To rescue his program, the economics minister, José Martínez de Hoz, decided to trail the rate of devaluation of the peso behind the domestic rate of inflation, in effect revaluing the currency. Periodic devaluations in the past, he reasoned, had increased the money supply when the bulk of export surpluses were deposited in domestic peso accounts. The new policy would reduce export earnings and, more importantly, attract cheaper imports. As foreign commodities begin to flood the Argentine market, domestic prices would converge with international ones, and inflation would reach manageable levels. The exchange policy would in effect intensify the economy's exposure to the international market, suppressing prices along the way.

The plan yielded no benefits in the first year (1979) and mildly positive results in the second (1980). It had ruinous effects upon domestic firms that could not compete with products from abroad; industrial production fell 19 percent in real terms from 1979 to 1981. This merely steepened the descent begun in 1977 after free interest rates made borrowing investment prohibitive, and depressed wage earnings shrank domestic markets by as much as 50 percent. The result was a wave of bankruptcies that decimated the manufacturing sector.

Much more surprising were the negative consequences for the agricultural sector. During the first three years under military rule, the landed elite had prospered from the decontrol of exchange rates, the elimination of slaughtering quotas for meat producers, and export taxes for wheat and cereal growers. Exports grew on average by 22 percent a year. These trends were predictable, since the regime had promised to return to the laws of comparative advantage, which in Argentine terms traditionally dictated a preference for primary exports. By 1980, however, the year when the effects of the new exchange rate policy were felt most strongly, agricultural growth was –6.5 percent. The country's export sector, dominated by agricultural and fish products, contracted in real terms by 2.3 percent in 1979 and 3.9 percent in 1980. In 1980, the volume of Argentina's grain exports declined 28 percent from the previous year, while all meat and fish exports fell 35 percent over the same period.[2] CAPECO, an association of seventeen leading fish-export companies in Argentina, reported losses of over 20 percent in 1979 and 1980, and profit margins that plummeted from an average of 7 percent in 1976–1978 to 0 percent by 1980.[3]

Martínez de Hoz had never consulted with industrial or agricultural representatives about his exchange rate reversal; this was to be expected from a regime that practiced interest-group exclusion. At first, the landed elites had no complaints, since they believed their interests would be protected anyway. When things turned out differently, they were surprised to learn how little recourse they had. Despite the chorus of protest that sounded about the *tablita*, Martínez de Hoz refused to yield. The regime denied access to the most powerful interests groups in Argentine society, permitting the minister to proceed with his policies uninterruptedly. The following examples serve to make the point.

Since 1866, Argentina's landed aristocracy of large wheat growers and cattle ranchers was well represented by the Sociedad Rural Argentina (SRA). Formerly Argentina's most powerful economic interest group, the Sociedad has championed the cause of free trade, price decontrol, and low taxes. The SRA was thought to be in good standing with the economic minister, whose landowning family had helped found the organization. In an unexpected announcement on the fifth anniversary of the PRN coup, the SRA criticized the regime by citing the exchange rate policy of December 1978 as a "great error" that contributed directly to declining export sales and higher internal costs. It added that "urgent" corrective measures were needed to forestall further economic decline. (The SRA favored freely floating exchange rates.)[4] Other rural spokesmen joined in: Ardelio Balario, an original supporter of the military and head of the Confederaciones Rurales Argentinas (CRA), which represented medium-sized farms, said in October 1979 that "if this type of exchange rate control is prolonged to March of 1981, the little that remains of the national economy will be destroyed."[5] The minister's rebuttal to these groups was simple. Trade deficits were tolerable since (1) the surplus generated on the capital account more than compensated for the deficit on the current account, and (2) the benefits in the way of reduced inflationary pressures more than made up for the temporary loss to farmers of export revenue.

The difficulties went beyond exchange rates. The CRA explained to the economics minister the fact that interest rates, which were 98 percent in nominal terms and 26 percent in real terms in 1980, were making it prohibitive for farmers to finance the purchase of new equipment to raise yields. Many had already gone into serious debt; others were selling out as the cost of inputs rose faster than the domestic price of their commodities. The minister refused to provide credit on more lenient terms and responded with a ghastly logic: if there were those who were selling out, then others must be buying. The high cost of borrowing will challenge the new owners to avoid the inefficiencies of the past, raise levels of productivity, and contribute to the economy's growth.

The *tablita* had managed to alienate even the upper stratum of the bourgeoisie. The Consejo Empresario Argentino (CEA) is a leading association of entrepreneurs from giant national and transnational conglomerates in petrochemicals, banking, mining, commerce, construction, textiles, and agriculture. It was founded in 1967 with the assistance of then-economics minister Krieger Vasena, to serve as a channel of communication between government and the business community. The CEA does not normally voice opinions as a group but was compelled to do so in a report issued on the third anniversary of the coup. It took the government to task for failing to "apply the principles outlined in March of 1976 in a permanent and coherent form," and specifically criticized the minister's policies on public spending, inflation, salaries, and exchange rates.[6] The minister was never ruffled by these complaints and kept the *tablita* intact until just weeks before his scheduled departure from office in March 1981. His callous disregard for these comments was significant, since he himself was a past president of the organization and chair of the board of Acindar Corporation, the nation's largest private steel company and a member of the CEA.

If there is any direct evidence that the state is the guardian of the interests of capitalists, then it should be found in the social bonds between state officials and ruling class elites.[7] Argentina should have been an ideal test case for class dominance, given the personal links between the agricultural and industrial capitalists and a public official of such stature as Martínez de Hoz. Yet, it does not provide evidence for such a case. The state demonstrated considerable autonomy from all classes, and state leaders persisted with a consistent set of policies despite the strenuous objections of the private sector.[8]

**A Community of Peers**

The economics minister's intransigence raises an important question. How could he have withstood pressures that should have bothered any politician? The most obvious answer is that the military built a fortress-like environment around him. There, deep within the recesses of the well-guarded Economics Ministry, he was entirely insulated from demands of the most significant interest groups. He could surround himself with his loyal technical staff and engage in discussions about the refinement or application of his economic model without having to question its validity. Still, the vast erosion of public support for a policy is unnerving, even to an authoritarian leader; few governing officials desire to be unpopular. When they are, they must somehow vindicate themselves, if for no other reason than to shore up their own confidence. How did Martínez de Hoz vindicate himself?

Through the years he had cultivated very close professional ties to New York bankers, and chief among them was the president of Chase Manhattan Bank, David Rockefeller. Martínez de Hoz had worked for Chase Manhattan and had served on the Trilateral Commission—a policy group formed in 1973 to promote multinational investment. Rockefeller was for a time North American chair of the commission. After the 1976 coup, he used his personal prestige to convince the IMF and private lenders of Argentina's credit worthiness, paving the way for billions of dollars in loans to the military regime.

In November 1980, the economics minister invited Rockefeller to Buenos Aires to shore up his teetering stabilization plan. Upon his arrival, the prominent banker wasted no words in offering glowing praise for the minister's accomplishments and implored the military to continue with the program. He added that he would do his best to secure larger amounts of international investment in Argentina.[9]

Thomas Kuhn has told us that in the scientific world, researchers are organized into communities, sharing a common paradigm. In addition to their conceptual linkages, practitioners are bound by similar educational and professional experiences and united in pursuit of the same goals. Kuhn adds:

> To the extent, of course that individuals belong to the same group and thus share education, language, experience, and culture, we have good reason to suppose that their sensations are the same. How else are we to understand the fullness of their communication and the communality of their behavioral responses to the environment?[10]

Political leaders may themselves be part of communities of peers that cut across nation-state boundaries and share similar convictions and knowledge bases. Group members have a sense of solidarity by virtue of sharing common ideas rather than, or in addition to, sharing social or economic position. The groups provide positive reinforcement for the views of their members and, in doing so, sharpen opposition to outsiders.[11]

David Rockefeller wore two hats: first, that of a powerful representative of international financial interests who was invited to Argentina to insure the country's continued access to foreign capital; second, that of an important member of a peer group to which Martínez de Hoz also belonged. His trip is revealing because it underscored the importance of a social support mechanism in sustaining a program that could claim few domestic admirers. Martínez de Hoz was compelled to legitimate his own strategies through close association with his international financial peers. The stronger the assurances from fellow experts that his ideas were valid, the less incentive the minister had to modify his perceptions on the basis of evidence and public disapproval.

Was the Argentine case unique? Was the regime's rebuff of powerful classes and stubborn commitment to a particular model a function of its minister's personality, will, and intellect? The figure of Martínez de Hoz looms large in the military regime; he had turned his office into a super-ministry that had unrivaled autonomy. The minister managed to capture the attention and respect of military officers. In an interview with this author, ex-President General Roberto Viola admitted that he and many other officers were impressed by the minister's style, the apparent logic of his arguments, and his command of the facts.[12] This led them conditionally to approve the economic plan, despite their misgivings. Of course, we will never know how committed the regime would have been if someone else were in charge of economic planning, or if a president like General Jorge Videla were not there to provide unconditional, personal support for the economic program. What we do know is that a similar phenomenon occurred in Chile at about the same time, involving different individuals and circumstances.

### Chile's Monetarists and the Dominant Class

Some argue that the purest application of the monetarist model anywhere could be found in Chile from 1975 to 1983.[13] Under the direction first of businessman Jorge Cauas, and then of University of Chicago graduate Sergio de Castro and his team of technocrats, the Chilean state was unrelenting in its enforcement of austerity measures. Preferring "shock" treatment to gradualism, the Chilean economic team, in 1975, cut government spending by 27 percent in real terms, halved the state's investment expenditures, allowed interest rates to rise to 178.4 percent in real terms in the third quarter of the year, and sent real wages falling to 63 percent of their value in 1970.[14] These measures predictably led the economy into a deep recession. The government took steps to reactivate the economy in 1977 but never departed from its liberal blueprint.

The evaluation of the program's success in macroeconomic terms depends on the figures and time frame one chooses. Between 1977 and 1981, the economy grew on average by 8 percent a year, inflation declined to 9.5 percent, and the fiscal deficit disappeared. These results are impressive, particularly if one compares them to the Argentine experience. However, if one looks at investment, production, and employment figures for the same period, a different picture emerges—one with significant declines registered in all these categories.[15] Post-1981 figures show dismal performance all around.

Of course, the macroeconomic facts tell us nothing about who the principal winners and losers were. At least until 1981, Chile's economic clans appeared to have the upper hand. These clans were distinct from corporations because they had controlling interests in numerous firms across diverse sectors of the economy; and, as the name suggests, their principal social links were familial, though this was not true for all clans.[16] The largest clan, Cruzat-Larrain, had at its peak accumulated 25 percent of the assets of the 250 largest firms in Chile, with interests in manufacturing, construction, mining, commerce, and especially banking.[17] The clans were thought to have, by way of their extensive holdings throughout the economy, the dominant position within the capitalist class.

The Chilean junta of Augusto Pinochet had made the clans' ascent to the pinnacle of economic power possible in 1975 and 1976 by selling off state interests in ten major banks and auctioning off an additional 197 firms to the highest bidder. With control of the banks and with privileged access to foreign credit, aggressive entrepreneurs turned medium-sized firms into giants, quickly buying out their competitors who were struggling to keep afloat in the midst of the 1975 recession. The clans thrived on the misfortunes of others, loaning money out at exorbitant rates and profiting from the differential between the international and domestic cost of borrowing. Meanwhile, they themselves went into debt with U.S. and European creditors.

The steady growth of the domestic financial market provided the dominant groups with the illusion of economic security. In reality, all was not well in the Chilean economy. The clans' industrial establishments were losing business; many of these companies were forced out of production and into importation and, even then, only survived by borrowing from their parent clans. Many other companies were not so fortunate. In 1981, the nation's forty-eighth largest firm, CRAV (Compañía Refinería Azúcar Viña—Viña Sugar Refining Company), a member of the Cruzat-Larrain group, went bankrupt. Its demise was attributed to questionable lending practices by its principal creditor banks, themselves controlled by Cruzat-Larrain. In November of that year, the collapse of a major economic clan, Sahli-Tassara, forced the government to take control of its banks and finance companies and place its owners under arrest. The group had been dragged down through huge losses suffered by its major industrial and agricultural holdings.

The ferocious appetite for capital combined with irresponsible lending practices had finally led a clan and a giant agro-industrial conglomerate past the brink of insolvency. Clan instincts for survival told them to abandon their allegiance to the free market and press for greater state protection and production incentives, which they did.

Theoretically, the regime should have come to the clans' defense. These groups had an indisputably powerful position in the Chilean economy. More than that, they had placed top executives in key posts within the economic and finance ministries and the Central Bank, providing them with political clout as well.[18] The clans were particularly pleased with the appointment of Rolf Luders as finance minister in September 1982. As the second largest shareholder in the powerful BHC group (named after its flagship bank, Banco Hipotecario de Chile), Rolf Luders (himself a monetarist) was universally recognized as an important financial figure. With the economic groups in danger of crumbling under the weight of indebtedness and industrial stagnation, his appointment seemed like a rescue mission.

Luders's actions were completely unexpected: he drew himself closer to the monetarists and further away from the business establishment. His efforts to secure an $850 million loan from the IMF in the fall of 1982 to service the country's annual debt led him to back the Fund's call for tighter restrictions on money supply growth and ceilings on the fiscal deficit—even as the clans were demanding that government stimulate production and employment. Luders's final and dramatic break with the dominant class came in January 1983. Apparently acting on his own (though with the blessing of Pinochet), he intervened in eight major Chilean banks, four of which belonged to the country's two most powerful clans.[19] The state took over the administration of two financial institutions belonging to Cruzat-Larrain and liquidated the assets of the BHC bank, whose chief executive had been, ironically, Luders himself. In fact, of the five other banks affected, three had been run by past and present members of the monetarist team.[20] Together, these banks accounted for 34 percent of the nation's capital and reserves and U.S. $3.8 billion of its foreign debt. Without them, the clans, who had built their fortunes through indebtedness, could no longer finance their operations.

The state had dismantled the most powerful economic groups in the country. Moreover, it had done so with the approval of their former representatives. Faced with the choice of rescuing his own company or realigning with the monetarist school, Rolf Luders chose to realign. Although the personalities had changed in 1982 and 1983 (Sergio de Castro was replaced by Rolf Luders who was then replaced by Carlos Caceres), the monetarists remained in control before, during, and after the state's seizure of the clans' assets. True, the state had temporarily intervened in the marketplace, but, as the monetarists saw it, this was a small price to pay to see through to completion a program of fiscal and monetary austerity that would repair relations with international creditors—relations that had become damaged during the financial collapse.[21]

The junta's economic team enjoyed a special partnership with international financial and intellectual elites committed to the monetarist doctrine. They were members of an international monetarist community that reached beyond the confines of the University of Chicago and the IMF. This was not an amorphous collection of like-minded individuals, but rather a network of experts who had social contacts with one another. Those contacts were maintained in numerous ways. The Mount Pelerin Society, for example, brought Chileans into contact with free market disciples elsewhere. Founded in 1947 by Friedrich Von Hayek, a contemporary and critic of Sir John Maynard Keynes, the society combatted what it saw as the erosion of respect for free market principles. With over 600 members, the society spawned institutions worldwide, including the Center of Public Studies in Santiago, Chile. Milton Friedman—one of the original architects of the Chilean monetarist plan—was also one of Mount Pelerin's original members and served as its president in the 1960s. Von Hayek visited Chile on several occasions, and his views have had a lasting impact on the Pinochet regime.

The "Chicago Boys'" near-religious devotion to the tenets of the monetarist school made them prized members of this community. The Chilean economic experts, like Martínez de Hoz and his team, found alternative sources of legitimization for policies that had become unpopular at home with powerful business interests. Despite its narrow political base, the regime was reinforced by economic authorities who insisted that its assumptions and proposals for economic recovery were fundamentally correct. It was praised by Milton Friedman for pulling off an "economic miracle" and given hope by Arnold Harberger, who predicted that by 1991, Chile would have the same standard of living as Spain.[22] State officials who had personal commitments to the private sector overcame these by reinforcing their ties with intellectual peers. Thus, despite significant setbacks for important segments of the capitalist class, policymakers found sustenance within the monetarist school, rather than abandoning their principles to placate business elites.

## The Decline of Ideological Monetarism and Democratic Resurgence

At what point are regimes prepared to abandon ideas? In scientific inquiry, puzzles often remain persistently unsolvable, despite the application of trusted conceptual and methodological tools. This can result in a search for new tools when "awareness of anomaly [has] lasted so long and penetrated so deep that one can appropriately describe the fields affected by it as in a state of growing crisis."[23] Between the moment at which experimentation lays bare the inadequacies of old paradigms, and new paradigms are discovered, there is a period of confusion that gives birth to a sense of "pronounced professional insecurity." At this crossroad, scientists question their own convictions, quarrel with each other, and grope for new conceptual handles.

Likewise, in the political world, policy-relevant ideas decline in importance once their predictive powers are critically weakened—there lies a threshold beyond which the contradictions between theory and evidence become so glaring that policymakers must finally reckon with the inadequacies of their own views. The result is a crisis in leadership and a sharpening of intrastate conflict about the future.

For example, the rupture with monetarism in Argentina did not begin until mid-1980, when several of that country's major financial institutions went under.[24] The economic liberals had staked their success in large measure on the accumulation of finance capital to balance payment accounts and establish savings for future investment. According to the liberal plan, a financial market for investment would quickly develop after June 1977, when all ceilings on deposits and loans were lifted, and barriers to entry into the financial market were eliminated. Unfortunately, the financial institutions that had attracted credit from abroad were quickly saddled with insurmountable debts. Industries that were pushed to the wall by foreign competition borrowed funds but could not meet their repayment obligations, and their subsequent collapse left banks with an unacceptable proportion of bad debts to total capital. In a violation of free market principles, the government had to temporarily take over the operations of several banks and rescue others with rapid injections of credit. Investors became jittery, and, despite the Central Bank's best efforts, it could not stop the flight of capital, which began in May and continued through the fall of 1980—at the rate of $50 million a day. Capital flight also was quickened by the fact that many savers who were nervous about the Argentine economy had placed their funds in short-term deposits. By 1981, 70 percent of these accounts had maturities of thirty days or less.

The flight of capital was particularly irksome to a government whose economic strategy could count as one of its objectives—and indeed as one of its few successes—an early buildup of reserves. The military had been advised to ignore balance of trade deficits, since it was anticipated that a massive influx of capital from abroad would more than compensate for any loss in export earnings. Now, the export market was in a precarious position, and, for the first time in four years, the government could not confidently assure its foreign creditors that all loan obligations would be met. These events and the embarrassingly high levels of inflation (87.6 percent in 1981) placed the liberal model in jeopardy.

The crisis of economic liberalism brought to the surface disagreements within the regime that had for years remained dormant. As with all authoritarian regimes, it is difficult to get an insight on the internal squabbles between elites. Fortunately, some of these were publicly divulged. In an oblique reference to the economics minister, the commander-in-chief of the air force, Brigadier General Omar Rubens Graffigna, said; "We [the junta] do not remain indifferent to those responsible for the regime's problems."[25] Martínez de Hoz tried to distance his economic plan from the crisis by claiming that the problem was irresponsible management and lending policies on the part of a few firms, and that it was not symptomatic of the financial sector as a whole. However, by the fall of 1980, several more firms and banks went under, and foreign lenders signaled their worry by toughening the conditions for Argentina's receipt of new loans. The commander-in-chief of the navy, General Armando Lambruschini, painted a foreboding picture of the entire financial sector and then took the unprecedented step of disclosing to the press that the navy's "misgivings" about the financial situation had been brought to the attention of the junta.[26] This decision by a member of the junta to publicize internal displeasure over the economic policy, particularly in light of the navy's historical penchant for liberal orthodox programs of the kind the economics minister had advocated, was significant.

Several times during late April and May, Martínez de Hoz and his entire ministerial cabinet were called before high-ranking officials from all branches of the armed forces, who demanded an explanation and a guarantee against future calamities. In an interview with the author, the minister insisted these meetings had been planned months before and were routine.[27] But, the timing of the encounters, the presence of an unusually large number of top-ranking officers, and the intentional public disclosures of discontent that had preceded the meetings suggest otherwise. Furthermore, the financial crisis touched off the first serious debate within the Ministry of Economics itself. There were those such as the secretary of commerce, Alejandro Estrada, who, arguing along purely liberal lines, insisted that financial difficulties could be avoided in the future by freely floating the currency on the world market and by removing all guarantees on deposits. The minister disagreed and persisted with the *tablita*. But Estrada's dissent made it clear that the loss of faith signaled by the flight of capital was not limited to investors only; it had now crept into the government as well.

In March 1981, the installation of a new cabinet signaled the defeat of the economic strategy on which Martínez de Hoz had staked his reputation. General Roberto Viola assumed the presidency from his friend and classmate General Videla. Viola's cabinet included civilians who had either direct ties to or sympathies with specific economic sectors that had been injured by the liberal model. With the orthodox model thoroughly discredited, the government staggered, unable to devise an attractive alternative. This seemed to typify, in some sense, a paradigmatic interlude, as the authorities could neither completely abandon the discredited model nor discover a credible replacement. The government's reactions were ad hoc, as it lunged from crisis to crisis without any confident plan of action. The junta's use of repression became erratic, opening new opportunities for unchecked political protest from below. In short, the failure of the monetarist strategy to satisfy even the minimum requirements for success set in motion a process that ultimately ended in defeat for the junta's economic team and its military allies. The emergence of political liberty followed on the heels of the economic misfortune.

The familiar patterns of dictatorial rule throughout Latin America are disappearing, yielding to welcomed signs of democratic recovery. It is still too early to know whether these changes will be enduring, or just another pause between dictatorships. Still, the transition is a significant development in Latin American history. In part because of the failures of ideological monetarism, new democratic governments have invented (or reinvented) heterodox variations of the stabilization theme. Raúl Alfonsín's Plan Austral, for example, called for strict limits to be placed on public expenditures and on the treasury's financing of the deficit, as in the past. But, he combined this with a burden-sharing formula that imposed a simultaneous wage and price freeze, to be phased out once inflationary expectations were sufficiently reduced. Economic growth was to be stimulated by providing incentives for local investors *and* for manufacturing exporters.[28] Regardless of the relative success or failure of Plan Austral, it is clear that the intention of the program was to veer away from economic doctrine that was singularly devoted to demand suppression and to move toward a more balanced solution. What is certain is that the shortcomings of ideological monetarism and the subsequent foundering and discrediting of the authoritarian regime provided fresh opportunities not only for economic policy innovation, but for a strong renewal of political freedom and competition. Ironically, and by example of its terrible failure, the Proceso may have helped to inaugurate a more enduring democratic future for Argentina.

## NOTES

1. Eric A. Nordlinger, *On the Autonomy of the Democratic State* (Cambridge: Harvard University Press, 1981).
2. Fundación de Investigaciones para el Desarrollo, *Coyuntura y Desarrollo Anexo Estadístico XIV*, April 1983, p. 42.
3. *Latin America Weekly Report*, September 5, 1980, p. 5.
4. Sociedad Rural Argentina, *Boletín de la Sociedad Rural Argentina* 469 (April 15, 1981), pp. 2, 3.
5. *Latin America Economic Report*, October 26, 1979, p. 42.
6. Consejo Empresario Argentino, "A Tres Años del 24 de Marzo de 1976," Memorandum, March 24, 1979, p. 17 and entire document.
7. This is persuasively argued by Ralph Miliband in "The Capitalist State: Reply to Nicos Poulantzas," in *New Left Review* 59 (January–February 1970), p. 57. For the complete analysis, see Ralph Miliband, *The State in Capitalist Society: The Analysis of the Western System of Power* (London: Quartet Books, 1973).
8. This view is shared by Juan E. Corradi, *The Fitful Republic: Economy, Society, and Politics in Argentina* (Boulder, CO: Westview Press, 1985).
9. *Latin America Weekly Report* 46 (November 1980): 4.
10. Thomas S. Kuhn, *The Structure of Scientific Revolutions* (Chicago: University of Chicago Press, 1970), p. 197.
11. The treatment of community dynamics borrows from Robert K. Merton's concept of the collectivity. See his work entitled *Social Theory and Social Structure* (New York: Free Press, 1968), pp. 353–354.
12. General Roberto Viola, in a personal interview with the author, Buenos Aires, July 1984.

13. This section borrows from David Pion-Berlin, "The Defiant State: Chile in the Post-Coup Era," in *Armies and Politics in Latin America*, ed., Abraham Lowenthal and J. Samuel Fitch (New York: Holmes & Meier, 1986), pp. 317–334.

14. Alejandro Foxley, "The Neoconservative Economic Experiment in Chile," in *Military Rule in Chile: Dictatorship and Oppositions*, ed. J. Samuel Valenzuela and Arturo Valenzuela (Baltimore: Johns Hopkins University Press, 1986), pp. 21–25.

15. Ibid., p. 15.

16. Their structure bears out Maurice Zeitlin's study of Chilean corporate executives, which showed how industrialists and bankers were commonly related to large landowners through immediate and extended kinship ties. This suggests that significant portions of the industrial and agricultural bourgeoisie composed one unified social class. See Maurice Zeitlin and Richard Earl Ratcliffe, "Research Methods for the Analysis of the Internal Structure of Dominant Classes: The Case of Landlords and Capitalists in Chile," *Latin America Research Review* 10 (Fall 1975): 5–61.

17. The concentration of capital in the hands of these powerful economic groups is detailed in Fernando Dahse, *Mapa de la Extrema Riqueza: Los Grupos Económicos y el Proceso de Concentración de Capitales* (Santiago: Editorial Aconcagua, 1979).

18. For instance, Fernando Leniz, the junta's first minister of economics, later left government to run Cruzat-Larrain's forest industries. Jorge Cauas, the former minister of finance, later became head of Cruzat-Larrain's main bank, Banco de Santiago.

19. That this was Luders's personal choice was confirmed for me in an interview with a former top-ranking official of the Javier-Vial group. This same official was completely surprised by Luders's decision to break up his own company, having expected the economics and finance minister to take less drastic steps.

20. *Latin America Weekly Report* 21 (January 1983):1.

21. The view that the economic team remained true to principle is shared by Alejandro Foxley. He notes that notwithstanding the state's control of 50 percent of the credit in the financial system by virtue of takeovers, the basic postulates of the economic policy have not been abandoned. This is reflected in the very orthodox policy agreement signed with the IMF as well as the government's reluctance to initiate an economic reactivation program, trusting that reactivation will commence "automatically." See Alejadro Foxley, "The Neoconservative Economic Experiment in Chile," pp. 29–30.

22. *Fortune* 2 (November 1981):138, 140.

23. Kuhn, *The Structure of Scientific Revolutions*, p. 67.

24. This section on Argentina's financial crisis borrows from David Pion-Berlin, "The Fall of Military Rule in Argentina, 1976–1983," *Journal of Interamerican Studies and World Affairs* 27 (Summer 1985):55–76.

25. *El Economista*, April 1980, p. 1.

26. *La Nación*, April 28, 1980, p. 5.

27. Interview with Dr. José A. Martínez de Hoz, Buenos Aires, July, 1984.

28. A description of the Alfonsín plan can be found in Edward Epstein, "Recent Stabilization Programs in Argentina, 1973–86," *World Development* 15 (1987):991–1005.

# Appendix

The task of measurement poses a challenge to the researcher. Assuming that information is available, important choices must be made: which events and processes does one observe, which exclude; and should they be weighted equally or differently?

The field of appropriate phenomena for observation was narrowed by the author's concern with repression of labor, not with the population in general. Even within a single sector, repression will vary along many continua. For instance, was it carried out legally or arbitrarily? How many people were affected? Were they detained for long periods of time? Were they subjected to cruel and unusual forms of punishment? All of these questions are important, but because of the absence of detailed and reliable data on some of these factors, and for purposes of simplification, this study limited its focus to the scope or latitude of repression (i.e., how many were affected).

Coercion was measured at the level of the individual, organization, and activity. These categories are interdependent, yet mutually exclusive. Individual workers who belong to organizations may be deprived of their constitutional freedoms, even as their unions continue to function. Conversely, organizations can be outlawed or restricted while members carry out acts of defiance. The right to strike or to engage in political activity contributes to union effectiveness; but the union could survive if these rights were abridged. For that reason, prohibitions on union activities were distinguished from attacks on organizational structure itself. Also, because workers may express their grievances as individuals, interference in collective actions must be dissociated from a crackdown on civil liberties.

Repression was tallied by observing events. In any given year, all arrests and executions of trade unionists that were politically motivated were counted and taken as a percent of the nation's population for that year. Individual unionists matter, but not equally insofar as the condition of the labor movement is concerned. Certainly, the loss of a dozen top trade union leaders will impact labor's condition move severely than the loss of a dozen rank-and-file workers. Consequently, coercion against leadership and rank and file were treated as separate categories and weighted differently. On individual, organizational, and activity levels of analysis, there are different forms of coercion that correspond more or less to physical and legal attributes. Arrests and executions were counted as physical dimensions of repression at the individual level, and the suspension of constitutional guarantees or the declaration of a state of siege were counted as common legal strategies used by Peruvian and Argentine authorities to restrict individual rights and freedoms.

In Argentina, a state of siege may be passed (pursuant to Article 23 of the Constitution) during times of national emergency. Of course, it is always up to the discretion of the authorities to determine when an emergency has arisen. What is not open to interpretation are the stipulations that the state of siege can only be approved while Congress is in session, and that the executive branch is prohibited from rendering punishment or sentences. These limitations were violated by the military junta in its program of national reorganization.

A state of siege places restrictions on the freedoms and rights normally protected by the constitutional law. Because constitutional guarantees are automatically suspended with the passage of a state of siege, these measures were counted as one. The junta extended its grip under a state of martial law, which stripped prisoners of their rights of option (to choose voluntary exile in the face of indefinite detention). Consequently, the martial law decrees were counted separately.

In Peru, a state of emergency and the suspension of constitutional guarantees are very similar, the only difference being that under an emergency decree the military assumes control of all civil activities. Either way, five fundamental individual freedoms are abridged: individual liberties, right of domicile, right of assembly, travel, and freedom from arbitrary exile. A Peruvian state of siege, on the other hand, is more encompassing than a state of emergency, and was counted separately. In both Argentina and Peru, legal restrictions on individual freedoms were weighted according to the latitude of coverage (national, regional, or citywide), and each act was scaled according to its duration.

Organizational coercion was also segregated. Physical components included union intervention (where government appointees replace elected union officers, cancel internal elections, or freeze union funds) and seizing of union headquarters. Each report of such an action was counted as one. Intervention was weighted more heavily since it is more permanent and restrictive. Weighting was also done according to the size of the organization affected, with individual unions ranked lowest and confederations highest. Legal organizational restrictions were identified in the Argentine case and included the outlawing of unions and prolabor parties. Union organizations were ranked by their size, and political parties by their representativeness within the labor movement. As a rule, the Peruvian government did not declare union organizations to be illegally constituted, and so that country was not measured along this dimension.

Estimates of collective trade union activity were made. Within each year, strikes and demonstrations were ranked as small, medium, or large with respect to some mean value. The mean was derived by taking the average number of workers participating per strike as a proportion of the economically active population. Then weights were assigned to each collective action, depending on its proportion to the average strike/protest for that year.

In conclusion, we measured the repression of labor by taking into consideration legal and physical dimensions at individual, organizational, and activity levels. This procedure is summarized in Table A.1. It is clear that political repression is a multidimensional concept that defies narrow compartmentalization. If we were to rely on any single indicator (i.e., rank-and-file arrests) to serve as a valid measure of the concept, we would most certainly fail to reflect the phenomenon in its entirety or to capture the full range of its variation over time. For that reason, the indices were combined into a general index. To be sure that these indicators were sufficiently related to warrant their inclusion in a composite index, a correlation matrix was run. The matrix tells us the correspondence of each variable to every other and helps to assess the validity of each of the measures. Validity refers to the extent to which any indicator measures what it is intended to measure.[1] If two or more indicators correlate with one another, the chances that each is valid increase. This is known as convergent validity.[2]

A method known as factor analysis was used to assign standardized weights to each indicator score for a given year. Factor analysis is a "means by which the regularity and order in phenomena can be discerned."[3] It helps uncover hidden patterns within observable data. Complex concepts often give rise to data patterns that fall out much like overlapping rings. Indicators that group very strongly around a particular factor (or "load" on that factor) are more removed from the intersection of the rings; those that have weaker relations with a factor fall closer to the intersection. Loadings can be interpreted like correlation coefficients. As it turned out, the factor routine confirmed there were in fact physical and legal dimensions to the repression variable. However, there was sufficient commonality between these two dimensions to combine them into a single repression score.

The factor routine provided a method of scoring as well: the routine assigned weights to each indicator depending on the strength of their loadings; the higher the correlation, the higher the weight assigned. (Note: the weights affixed to the raw data prior to factor analysis were *intra*-variable in nature and separate from the factor weights, which were *inter*-variable.) Each of the eight variables (see Tables A.2 and A.3) that compose the repression indicators received a weight. Then the repression data on each variable for each year was multiplied by those weights, and the sum of those weight-data products yielded the final annual repression score. These are shown in Tables A.4 and A.5. Standardized scores always fall out on either side of the zero. To create the positive figures for repression (shown in the tables of Chapters 4 and 7), a numerical constant was added to each score.

**Table A.1 Dimensions and Levels of Labor Repression**

| | Individual | Organization | Activity |
|---|---|---|---|
| Physical | rank and file arrested, rank and file killed, leadership arrested, unionists injured | intervention, headquarters seized | strike disruption |
| Legal | constitutional guarantees suspended, state of siege | unions and political parties outlawed | strike banned |

**Table A.2 Political Repression Data for Argentina: 1956–1980[a]**

| YEAR | RFA | LEA | RFK | LOR | LIN | LAC | POR | PAC |
|---|---|---|---|---|---|---|---|---|
| 1956 | 8.8 | .8 | 2.5 | 5 | 0 | 1 | 0 | 0 |
| 1957 | 12.5 | 5.6 | 0 | 5 | 2 | 20 | 0 | 5 |
| 1958 | 22.5 | 1.5 | 0 | 0 | 8 | 31 | 20 | 10 |
| 1959 | 2.3 | 5.5 | 0 | 2 | 16 | 16 | 13 | 11 |
| 1960 | 1.9 | 6.3 | 0 | 2 | 16 | 0 | 20 | 0 |
| 1961 | 18.7 | 1.2 | 0 | 2 | 16 | 0 | 20 | 0 |
| 1962 | .7 | .1 | 0 | 7 | 16 | 0 | 20 | 0 |
| 1963 | 0 | 0 | 0 | 2 | 0 | 0 | 0 | 0 |
| 1964 | .1 | 0 | 0 | 7 | 0 | 0 | 0 | 50 |
| 1965 | 14.5 | .9 | 0 | 0 | 0 | 5 | 0 | 26 |
| 1966 | 3.3 | .2 | 0 | 10 | 0 | 30 | 0 | 10 |
| 1967 | .2 | .2 | 0 | 10 | 0 | 20 | 10 | 0 |
| 1968 | .8 | .1 | 0 | 10 | 0 | 20 | 10 | 5 |
| 1969 | 10.9 | .7 | .2 | 10 | 16 | 0 | 10 | 25 |
| 1970 | 0 | 0 | 0 | 10 | 16 | 0 | 10 | 12 |
| 1971 | 2.8 | .2 | 0 | 2 | 16 | 0 | 0 | 5 |
| 1972 | 2.6 | .2 | 0 | 2 | 16 | 0 | 10 | 0 |
| 1973 | 0 | 0 | 2 | 12 | 0 | 0 | 0 | 5 |
| 1974 | 1.2 | .1 | .2 | 0 | 0 | 0 | 0 | 0 |
| 1975 | 5.2 | .3 | 1.1 | 0 | 16 | 10 | 0 | 5 |
| 1976 | 13.4 | .8 | 5.2 | 10 | 32 | 40 | 78 | 3 |
| 1977 | 2.3 | .2 | 8.9 | 10 | 32 | 40 | 92 | 3 |
| 1978 | .7 | .1 | 2 | 10 | 32 | 40 | 182 | 0 |
| 1979 | .9 | .1 | 3.4 | 10 | 32 | 40 | 270 | 0 |
| 1980 | 0 | 0 | 2.3 | 15 | 32 | 40 | 342 | 0 |

[a]These are raw, not standardized scores.

RFA = Arrests of rank-and-file workers
LEA = Arrests of union leadership
RFK = Execution of rank-and-file workers
LOR = Legal organizational restrictions
LIN = Legal individual restrictions
LAC = Legal restrictions of activities
POR = Physical disruptions of organizations
PAC = Physical disruptions of activities

**Table A.3 Political Repression Data for Peru: 1956–1980[a]**

| YEAR | RFA | LEA | RFK | INJ | LIN | LAC | POR | PAC |
|---|---|---|---|---|---|---|---|---|
| 1956 | .7 | 3.4 | .2 | .6 | 4 | 0 | 0 | .2 |
| 1957 | 0 | 0 | .3 | .3 | 4 | 2 | 0 | .5 |
| 1958 | .8 | .6 | 0 | 3.1 | 3 | 2 | 0 | .6 |
| 1959 | 1.8 | 8.7 | 0 | 3.5 | 7 | 0 | 6 | .7 |
| 1960 | 0 | 0 | .5 | 0 | 0 | 0 | 0 | .6 |
| 1961 | 0 | 0 | .9 | 4.8 | 2 | 0 | 0 | 0 |
| 1962 | 0 | 0 | .3 | 8.5 | 3 | 1 | 0 | 2.3 |
| 1963 | 7.1 | 0 | .1 | .4 | 1 | 3 | 0 | 1.8 |
| 1964 | 3.6 | 2.1 | 0 | 0 | 3 | 0 | 1 | 1.5 |
| 1965 | 3.2 | 0 | .2 | 0 | 8 | 0 | 0 | .3 |
| 1966 | .3 | 2.1 | .3 | 4.1 | 2 | 2 | 0 | 0 |
| 1967 | .1 | 0 | 0 | 0 | 0 | 0 | 0 | .6 |
| 1968 | 0 | 0 | 0 | 0 | 12 | 0 | 0 | .3 |
| 1969 | .9 | 0 | 0 | 1.2 | 0 | 0 | 0 | .2 |
| 1970 | 0 | 0 | 0 | 0 | 0 | 0 | 0 | 0 |
| 1971 | 0 | .3 | .5 | 1.8 | 2 | 0 | 2 | .4 |
| 1972 | 2.3 | 0 | .4 | 3.0 | 0 | 1 | 0 | 1.2 |
| 1973 | 0 | .9 | .2 | 2.0 | 10 | 1 | 5 | 1.3 |
| 1974 | 1.1 | 1.4 | .1 | .3 | 0 | 1 | 0 | .9 |
| 1975 | .4 | 3.7 | 0 | .3 | 10 | 5 | 18 | 0 |
| 1976 | 4.5 | 11.5 | 0 | 2.5 | 12 | 11 | 16 | 2.1 |
| 1977 | 16.6 | 4.2 | .7 | 1.8 | 12 | 14 | 30 | 11.2 |
| 1978 | 36.3 | 8.1 | 4.1 | 3.5 | 6 | 4 | 1 | 35.6 |
| 1979 | 13.8 | 1.8 | 2.5 | 2.7 | 13 | 0 | 7 | 6.7 |
| 1980 | .3 | .3 | 1 | .2 | 0 | 0 | 1 | .7 |

[a]These are raw, not standardized scores.

RFA = Arrests of rank-and-file workers
LEA = Arrests of union leadership
RFK = Execution of rank-and-file workers
INJ = Injury of all workers
LIN = Legal individual restrictions
LAC = Legal restrictions of activities
POR = Physical disruptions of organizations
PAC = Physical disruptions of activities

**Table A.4 Single-Factor Scores For Repression in Argentina**

| Year | Factor Score |
|---|---|
| 1956 | –.466 |
| 1957 | –.508 |
| 1958 | –.294 |
| 1959 | –.318 |
| 1960 | –.500 |
| 1961 | –.510 |
| 1962 | –.276 |
| 1963 | –.724 |
| 1964 | –.678 |
| 1965 | –.834 |
| 1966 | –.154 |
| 1967 | –.212 |
| 1968 | –.224 |
| 1969 | –.331 |
| 1970 | –.261 |
| 1971 | –.507 |
| 1972 | –.454 |
| 1973 | –.550 |
| 1974 | –.762 |
| 1975 | –.331 |
| 1976 | 1.250 |
| 1977 | 1.725 |
| 1978 | 1.506 |
| 1979 | 2.032 |
| 1980 | 2.382 |

**Table A.5 Single-Factor Scores for Repression in Peru**

| Year | Factor Score |
|---|---|
| 1956 | –.353 |
| 1957 | –.829 |
| 1958 | –.296 |
| 1959 | .590 |
| 1960 | –1.012 |
| 1961 | –.762 |
| 1962 | –.193 |
| 1963 | .450 |
| 1964 | .134 |
| 1965 | .001 |
| 1966 | –.443 |
| 1967 | –.689 |
| 1968 | –.373 |
| 1969 | –.421 |
| 1970 | –.686 |
| 1971 | –.728 |
| 1972 | –.311 |
| 1973 | –.312 |
| 1974 | –.532 |
| 1975 | –.010 |
| 1976 | .905 |
| 1977 | 2.283 |
| 1978 | 3.174 |
| 1979 | 1.054 |
| 1980 | –.642 |

## NOTES

1. Edward G. Carmines and Richard A. Zeller, *Reliability and Validity Assessment*, Quantitative Applications in the Social Sciences, Sage University Paper no. 17 (Beverly Hills: Sage Publications, 1979).

2. Claire Selltiz, Lawrence S. Wrightsman, and Stuart W. Cook, *Research Methods in Social Relations* (New York: Holt, Rinehart and Winston, 1976).

3. R. J. Rummel, "Understanding Factor Analysis," *Journal of Conflict Resolution* 11 (1967):445.

# Bibliography

## BOOKS AND MONOGRAPHS


Abós, Alvaro. *Las Organizaciones Sindicales y el Poder Militar*. Buenos Aires: Centro Editor de América Latina, 1984.

Alexander, Robert J. *The Perón Era*. New York: Russell & Russell, 1965.

———. *APRISMO; The Ideas and Doctrines of Víctor Raúl Haya de la Torre*. Kent, OH: Kent State University, 1973.

Allardt, Eric, and Stein Rokkan, eds. *Mass Politics: Studies in Political Sociology*. New York: Free Press, 1970.

Almond, Gabriel, and James Coleman. *The Politics of the Developing Areas*. Princeton: Princeton University Press, 1960.

Amat y Leon, Carlos. *La Economía de la Crisis Peruana*. In Serie Materiales de Trabajo, no. 16. Lima: Fundación Friedrich Ebert and Instituto Latinoamericano de Investigaciones Sociales, April 1978.

Archdiocese of São Paulo. *Torture in Brazil*. Trans. Jaime Wright and ed. Joan Dassin. New York: Vintage Books, 1986.

Arendt, Hannah. *The Origins of Totalitarianism*. New York: Harcourt, Brace, 1951.

Argentine National Commission on the Disappeared. *Nunca Más*. New York: Farrar, Straus & Giroux, 1986.

Arriagada, Genaro Herrera. *El Pensamiento Político de los Militares*. Santiago, Chile: Centro de Investigaciones Socioeconómicas, 1981.

Ascher, William. *Scheming for the Poor: The Politics of Redistribution in Latin America*. Cambridge, MA: Harvard University Press, 1984.

Baily, Samuel. *Labor, Nationalism, and Politics in Argentina*. New Brunswick, NJ: Rutgers University Press, 1967.

Baran, Paul A., and Paul Sweezy. *Monopoly Capital: An Essay on the American Economic and Social Order*. New York: Monthly Review Press, 1966.

Barba Caballero, José. *Historia del Movimiento Obrero Peruano*. Lima: Ediciones Signo, 1981.

Becker, David. *The New Bourgeoisie and the Limits of Dependency: Mining, Class and Power in "Revolutionary" Peru*. Princeton: Princeton University Press, 1983.

Beltrán, Pedro G. *La Verdadera Realidad Peruana*. Lima: Editorial San Martin, 1976.

Blanksten, George I. *Perón's Argentina*. New York: Russell & Russell, 1953.

Blau, Peter M., and Robert K. Merton, eds. *Continuity in Structural Inquiry*. Beverly Hills: Sage Publications, 1981.

Bonilla, Heraclio. *El Minero de los Andes*. Lima: Instituto de Estudios Peruanos, 1974.

Bourricaud, Francois. *Power and Society in Contemporary Peru*. New York: Praeger Publishers, 1967.

Canitrot, Adolfo. *Orden Social y Monetarismo*. Estudios CEDES (4) no.7. Buenos Aires: Centro de Estudios de Estado y Sociedad.

Carmines, Edward G., and Richard A. Zeller. *Reliability and Validity Assessment*. Quantitative Applications in the Social Sciences, Sage University Paper no. 17. Beverly Hills: Sage Publications, 1979.

Carri, Roberto. *Sindicatos y Poder en la Argentina*. Buenos Aires: Editorial Sudestada, 1967.

Caves, Richard E., and Ronald W. Jones. *World Trade and Payments: An Introduction*. Boston: Little Brown, 1973.

Centro de Estudios Legales y Sociales. *692: Responsables del Terrorismo de Estado*. Buenos Aires: CELS, 1986.

Chaplin, David, ed. *Peruvian Nationalism: A Corporatist Revolution*. New Brunswick, NJ: Transaction Books, 1976.

Chomsky, Noam, and Edward S. Herman. *The Washington Connection and Third World Fascism: The Political Economy of Human Rights*. Volume 1. Boston: South End Press, 1979.

Cohen, Raymond. *Threat Perception in International Crisis*. Madison: University of Wisconsin Press, 1979.

Collier, David, ed. *The New Authoritarianism in Latin America*. Princeton: Princeton University Press, 1979.

Comblin, José. *Church and the National Security State*. Maryknoll: Orbis Books, 1979.

Cotler, Julio. *Democracia y Integración Nacional*. Lima: Instituto do Estudios Peruanos, 1980.

Dahl, Robert. *Political Oppositions in Western Democracies*. New Haven: Yale University Press, 1966.

Dallin, Alexander, and George Breslauer. *Political Terror in Communist Systems*. Stanford, CA: Stanford University Press, 1970.

Diaz-Alejandro, Carlos. *Essays on the Economic History of the Argentine Republic*. New Haven: Yale University Press, 1970.

Diesing, Paul. *Science and Ideology in the Policy Sciences*. New York: Aldine, 1982.

Dilthey, W. *Selected Writings*. Trans. and ed. H. P. Rickman. Cambridge: Cambridge University Press, 1976.

Di Tella, Guido. *Argentina Under Perón: 1973–1976*. London: Macmillan, 1983.

Di Tella, Guido, and Manuel Zymelman. *Las Etapas del Desarrollo Económico Argentino*. Buenos Aires: EUDEBA, 1967.

Dudeck, C. V. *Hegel's Phenomenology of Mind: Analysis and Commentary*. Washington, DC: University Press of America, 1981.

Duff, Ernest A., and John F. McCamant. *Violence and Repression in Latin America: A Quantitative and Historical Analysis*. New York: Free Press, 1976.

Eckstein, Harry, and Ted R. Gurr. *Patterns of Authority: A Structural Basis for Political Inquiry*. New York: John Wiley & Sons, 1975.

Edwards, Paul, ed. *The Encyclopedia of Philosophy*. Volume 4. New York: Macmillan, 1967.

Fagen, Richard R., ed. *Capitalism and the State in U.S.–Latin American Relations*. Stanford, CA: Stanford University Press, 1979.

Fein, Helen. *Accounting for Genocide*. New York: Free Press, 1979.

Fernandez, Arturo. *Las Prácticas Sociales del Sindicalismo (1976–1982)*. Buenos Aires: Centro Editor de América Latina, 1985.

Ferrer, Aldo, et al. *Los Planes de Estabilización en la Argentina*. Buenos Aires: Paidos, 1973.

Finlay, David J., Ole R. Holsti, and Richard R. Fagen. *Enemies in Politics*. Chicago: Rand McNally, 1967.

Fitzgerald, E. V. K. *The Political Economy of Peru: 1956–78*. London: Cambridge University Press, 1979.

Friedman, Milton. *Dollars and Deficits: Inflation, Monetary Policy and the Balance of Payments*. Englewood Cliffs, NJ: Prentice Hall, 1968.

Friedrich, Carl J., ed. *The Philosophy of Hegel*. New York: Modern Library, 1953.

Frontalini, Daniel, and Cristina Maria Caiati. *El Mito de la "Guerra Sucia."* Buenos Aires: Centro de Estudios Legales y Sociales, 1984.

Gadamer, Hans-Georg. *Philosophical Hermeneutics*. Trans. and ed. David E. Linge. Berkeley: University of California Press, 1976.

Gardner, Richard. *Sterling Dollar Diplomacy: The Origins and the Prospects of Our International Economic Order*. New York: McGraw Hill, 1969.

Geertz, Clifford. *The Interpretation of Cultures*. New York: Basic Books, 1973.

Gillespie, Richard. *Soldiers of Perón: Argentina's Montoneros*. Oxford: Clarendon Press, 1982.

Gilpin, Robert. *U.S. Power and the Multinational Corporation*. New York: Basic Books, 1975.

Gonzales, Santiago Senen. *Diez Años de Sindicalismo Argentino*. Buenos Aires: Corregidor, 1984.

Griffin, Keith. *Financing Development in Latin America*. London: Macmillan, 1971.

Grindle, Merilee. *Politics and Policy Implementation in the Third World*. Princeton: Princeton University Press, 1980.

———. *State and Countryside: Development Policy and Agrarian Politics in Latin America*. Baltimore: Johns Hopkins University Press, 1986.

Gurr, Ted R. *Why Men Rebel*. Princeton: Princeton University Press, 1970.

Hegel, G. W. Friedrich. *The Phenomenology of Mind*. Trans. J. B. Baillie. London: George Allen & Unwin, 1971.

Herman, Edward S. *The Real Terror Network: Terrorism in Fact and Propaganda*. Boston: South End Press, 1982.

Hirsch, Eric D., Jr. *Validity in Interpretation*. New Haven: Yale University Press, 1967.

Hirsch, Fred, and John H. Goldthorpe, eds. *The Political Economy of Inflation*. Cambridge, MA: Harvard University Press, 1979.

Hirschman, Albert O. *National Power and the Structure of Foreign Trade*. Berkeley: University of California Press, 1945.

———. *Journeys Toward Progress: Studies of Economic Policymaking in Latin America*. New York: Twentieth Century Fund, 1963.

———. *The Passions and the Interests: Political Arguments for Capitalism Before Its Triumph.* Princeton: Princeton University Press, 1977.

Hoare, Quinton, and Geoffrey Nowell Smith, eds. *Selections from Prison Notebooks of Antonio Gramsci.* New York: International Publishers, 1983.

Horsefield, Keith J. *The International Monetary Fund 1945–1965: Twenty Years of International Monetary Cooperation.* 3 vols. Washington, DC: IMF, 1969. Volume 1. *Chronicle.* Volume 2. *Analysis.* and Volume 3. *Documents.*

Hughes, Steven W., and Kenneth J. Mijeski. *Politics and Public Policy in Latin America.* Boulder, CO: Westview Press, 1984.

Humberto Cabrera, César. *Perú: La Crisis y La Política de Estabilizaci6n.* Serie Materiales de Trabajo, no. 17. Lima: Fundaci6n Freidrich Ebert and Instituto Latinoamericana de Investigaciones Sociales, April 1978.

International Monetary Fund. *The Monetary Approach to the Balance of Payments.* Washington, DC: IMF, 1979.

International Studies of Values in Politics. *Values in the Active Community.* New York: Free Press, 1971.

Jervis, Robert. *Perception and Misperception in International Politics.* Princeton: Princeton University Press, 1976.

Knorr, Klaus. *Historical Dimensions of National Security Problems.* Kansas City: University Press of Kansas, 1976.

Krasner, Stephen D. *Defending the National Interest: Raw Materials, U.S. Investments and U.S. Foreign Policy.* Princeton: Princeton University Press, 1978.

Kruijt, Dirk, and Menno Vellinga. *Labor Relations and Multinational Corporations.* Netherlands: Van Gorcum, 1979.

Kuczynski, Pedro-Pablo. *Peruvian Democracy Under Economic Stress: An Account of the Belaúnde Administration 1963–1968.* Princeton: Princeton University Press, 1977.

Kuhn, Thomas S. *The Structure of Scientific Revolutions.* Chicago: University of Chicago Press, 1970.

Laite, Julian. *Industrial Development and Migrant Labour.* Manchester: Manchester University Press, 1981.

Larrain, Jorge. *Marxism and Ideology.* London: Macmillan, 1983.

Lauer, Quentin. *Hegel's Idea of Philosophy.* New York: Fordham University Press, 1971.

Lernoux, Penny. *Cry of the People.* Garden City, NY: Doubleday, 1980.

Lowenthal, Abraham F., and J. Samuel Fitch, eds. *Armies and Politics in Latin America.* Revised ed. New York: Holmes & Meier, 1986.

Ludendorff, General Erich Von. *La Guerra Total.* La Paz, Bolivia: Editorial Renacimiento, 1941.

Luis Duhalde, Eduardo. *El Estado Terrorista Argentina.* Buenos Aires: El Cabollito, 1983.

McClintock, Cynthia, and Abraham Lowenthal, eds. *The Peruvian Experiment Reconsidered.* Princeton: Princeton University Press, 1983.

Machiavelli, Niccolo. *The Prince and the Discourses.* New York: Modern Library, 1950.

Magdoff, Harry. *The Age of Imperialism*. New York: Monthly Review Press, 1969.

Mallon, Richard D., and Juan V. Sourrouille. *Economic Policy Making in a Conflict Society: The Argentine Case*. Cambridge, MA: Harvard University Press, 1975.

Malloy, James, ed. *Authoritarianism and Corporatism in Latin America*. Pittsburgh, PA: University of Pittsburgh Press, 1977.

Mannheim, Karl. *Essays on the Sociology of Knowledge*. Ed. Paul Kecskemeti. London: Routledge & Kegan Paul, 1952.

———. *Ideology and Utopia: An Introduction to the Sociology of Knowledge*. New York: Harcourt, Brace & World, 1968.

Martínez de Hoz, José. *Bases Para Una Argentina Moderna: 1976–1980*. Buenos Aires: Compañía Impresora Argentina, 1981.

Merton, Robert K. *Social Theory and Social Structure*. New York: Free Press, 1968.

Miliband, Ralph. *The State in Capitalist Society: The Analysis of the Western System of Power*. London: Quartet Books, 1973.

Morales Bermúdez, Francisco. "Discurso," speech delivered April 30, 1976, reprinted in *La Revolución Peruana*. Lima: La República de Perú, 1976.

Morgenthau, Hans. *Politics Among Nations: The Struggle for Power and Peace*. New York: Alfred Knopf, 1967.

Mueller-Vollmer, Kurt, ed. *The Hermeneutics Reader: Texts of the German Tradition from the Enlightenment to the Present*. Oxford: Basil Blackwell, 1986.

Multipartidaria. *La Propuesta de la Multipartidaria*. Buenos Aires: El Cid Editor, 1982.

Nordlinger, Eric. *On the Autonomy of the State*. Cambridge, MA: Harvard University Press, 1981.

North American Congress on Latin America (NACLA). *Argentina: In the Hour of the Furnace*. New York: NACLA, 1975.

———. *Peru Today: The Roots of Labor Militancy*. No. 14. New York: NACLA, November–December, 1980.

North, Liisa, and Tanya Korovkin. *The Peruvian Revolution and the Officers in Power: 1967–1976*. Occasional Monograph Series no. 15. McGill University: Center for Developing Area Studies, 1981.

O'Dell, John. *U.S. International Monetary Policy: Market, Power and Ideas as Sources of Change*. Princeton: Princeton University Press, 1982.

O'Donnell, Guillermo. *Modernization and Bureaucratic-Authoritarianism: Studies in South American Politics*. Berkeley: Institute of International Studies, 1973.

———. *1966–1973: El Estado Burocrático Autoritario: Triunfos, Derrotas y Crisis*. Buenos Aires: Editorial de Belgrano, 1982.

O'Donnell, Guillermo, Philippe C. Schmitter, and Laurence Whitehead, eds. *Transitions from Authoritarian Rule*. 4 volumes. Baltimore: Johns Hopkins University Press, 1986.

Packenham, Robert. *Liberal America and the Third World: Political Development Ideas in Foreign Aid and Social Science*. Princeton: Princeton University Press, 1973.

Page, Joseph. *Perón: A Biography*. New York: Random House, 1983.

Parsons, Talcott. *The Social System*. Glencoe, IL: Free Press, 1951.

Payer, Cheryl. *The Debt Trap: The IMF and the Third World*. New York: Monthly Review Press, 1975.

Payne, James L. *Labor and Politics in Peru: The System of Political Bargaining*. New Haven: Yale University Press, 1965.

Perina, Ruben M. *Onganía, Levingston, Lanusse: Los Militares en la Política Argentina*. Buenos Aires: Editorial de Belgrano, 1983.

Peterson, Wallace C. *Income, Employment and Economic Growth*. New York: W. W. Norton, 1978.

Petras, James. *Class, State and Power in the Third World*. Montclair, NJ: Allanheld, Osmun, 1981.

Pezo del Pino, César, Eduardo Ballan Echegaray, and Luis Peirano Falconi. *El Magisterio y Sus Luchas 1885–1978*. Lima: Centro de Estudios y Promoción del Desarrollo, 1981.

Pike, Frederick. *The Modern History of Peru*. New York: Praeger, 1967.

Przeworski, Adam, and Henry Teune. *The Logic of Comparative Inquiry*. New York: Wiley-Interscience, 1970.

Ricouer, Paul. *The Conflict of Interpretations: Essays in Hermeneutics*. Evanston, IL: Northwestern University Press, 1974.

———. *Hermeneutics and the Human Sciences: Essays on Language, Action and Interpretation*. Ed. and trans. by John B. Thompson. Cambridge: Cambridge University Press, 1981.

Rotondaro, Ruben. *Realidad y Cambio en el Sindicalismo*. Buenos Aires: Editorial Pleamar, 1971.

Samuelson, Paul. *Economics*. New York: McGraw-Hill, 1976.

Santos Martínez, Pedro. *La Nueva Argentina:1946–1955*. Volume 2. Buenos Aires: Editorial Astrea, 1976.

Scammell, W. W. *International Monetary Policy: Bretton Woods and After*. New York: John Wiley and Sons, 1975.

Scheetz, Thomas. *Peru and the International Monetary Fund*. Pittsburgh, PA: University of Pittsburgh Press, 1986.

Schmidt, Steffen W., et al. *Friends, Followers, and Factions: A Reader in Political Clientelism*. Berkeley: University of California, 1977.

Schvarzer, Jorge. *Martínez de Hoz: La Lógica Política de la Política Económica*, Centro de Investigaciones Sociales Sobre el Estado y la Administración, Ensayos y Tesis 4. Buenos Aires: CISEA, 1983.

Selltiz, Clair, Lawrence S. Wrightsman, and Stuart W. Cook. *Research Methods in Social Relations*. New York: Holt, Rinehart and Winston, 1976.

Sheehan, John. *Patterns of Development in Latin America: Poverty, Repression and Economic Strategy*. Princeton: Princeton University Press, 1987.

Simpson, John, and John Bennett. *The Disappeared and the Mothers of the Plaza: The Story of the 11,000 Argentinians Who Vanished*. New York: St. Martin's Press, 1985.

Smith, Adam. *An Inquiry into the Nature and Causes of the Wealth of Nations*. Ed. Edwin Cannan. New York: Modern Library, 1965.

Sorbol, Lester A., ed. *Argentina and Perón: 1970–75*. New York: Facts on File, 1975.

Stein, Steve. *Populism in Peru: The Emergence of the Masses and the Politics of Social Control*. Madison: University of Wisconsin Press, 1980.

Stepan, Alfred. *The Military in Politics: Changing Patterns in Brazil*. Princeton: Princeton University Press, 1971.

———. *The State and Society: Peru in Comparative Perspective*. Princeton: Princeton University Press, 1979.

———. *Rethinking Military Politics: Brazil and the Southern Cone*. Princeton: Princeton University Press, 1988.

Stephens, Evelyne Huber. *The Politics of Worker's Participation: The Peruvian Approach in Comparative Perspective*. New York: Academic Press, 1980.

Stern, Fritz. *The Politics of Cultural Despair: A Study in the Rise of the German Ideology*. Berkeley: University of California Press, 1973.

Stohl, Michael, ed. *The Politics of Terrorism*. New York: Marcell Dekker, 1984.

Stohl, Michael, and George A. Lopez, eds. *Governmental Violence and Repression: An Agenda for Research*. Westport, CT: Greenwood Press, 1986.

Sulmont, Denis. *El Movimiento Obrero Peruano 1890–1980: Reseña Histórica*. Lima: Tarea, 1980.

Taccone, Juan José. *900 Días de Autogestión en SEGBA: Una Experiencia Argentina de Participación*. Buenos Aires: Fundación 2001, 1977.

Tamarin, David. *The Argentine Labor Movement, 1930–1945: A Study in the Origins of Peronism*. Albuquerque: University of New Mexico Press, 1985.

Taylor, Charles. *Philosophy and the Human Sciences: Philosophical Papers*. Volume 2. Cambridge: Cambridge University Press, 1985.

Taylor, Charles Lewis, and David A. Jodice. *World Handbook of Political and Social Indicators*. 3d ed., volume 2: *Political Protest and Government Change*. New Haven: Yale University Press, 1983.

Thorp, Rosemary, and Geoffrey Bertram. *Peru 1890–1977: Growth and Policy in an Open Economy*. New York: Columbia University Press, 1978.

Thorp, Rosemary, and Laurence Whitehead, eds. *Inflation and Stabilization in Latin America*. New York: Holmes & Meier, 1979.

Timmerman, Jacobo. *Prisoner Without a Name, Cell Without a Number*. New York: Alfred Knopf, 1981.

Treber, Salvador. *La Economía Argentina: Análisis, Diagnóstico y Alternativas*. Buenos Aires: Ediciones Macchi, 1977.

Trinquier, Roger. *Modern Warfare: A French View of Counterinsurgency*. New York: Praeger, 1964.

Tucker, Robert C., ed. *The Marx-Engels Reader*. New York: W. W. Norton, 1972.

Valenzuela, Arturo, and J. Samuel Valenzuela, eds. *Military Rule in Chile: Dictatorship and Oppositions*. Baltimore: Johns Hopkins University Press, 1986.

Vergara, Pilar. *Auge y Caida del Neoliberalismo en Chile*, Documento de Trabajo no. 216. Santiago, Chile: FLACSO, 1984.

Villanueva, Víctor. *El CAEM y la Revolución de la Fuerza Armada*. Lima: Campodónico Ediciones, 1972.

Villegas, Osiris. *Políticas y Estrategías para el Desarrollo y la Seguridad Nacional*. Buenos Aires: Pleamar, 1969.

Wachter, Susan M. *Latin American Inflations: The Structuralist-Monetarist Debate*. Lexington, MA: Lexington Books, 1976.

Waisman, Carlos. *Reversal of Development in Argentina*. Princeton: Princeton University Press, 1987.

Waldman, Peter, and Ernesto Garzón Váldez, eds. *El Poder Militar en la Argentina: 1976–1981*. Buenos Aires: Editorial Galerna, 1983.

Walker, Eugene V. *Terror and Resistance*. New York: Oxford University Press, 1969.

Walter, Ingo, *International Economics*. New York: Ronald Press, 1975.

Waltz, Kenneth. *Man, the State and War: A Theoretical Analysis*. New York: Columbia University Press, 1959.

———. *Economy and Society: An Outline of Interpretive Sociology*. Ed. Guenther Roth and Claus Wittich. Volume 1. New York: Bedminster Press, 1968.

Weber, Max. *The Methodology of the Social Sciences*. Trans. and ed. Edward A. Shils and Henry A. Finch. Glencoe, IL: Free Press of Glencoe, 1949.

———. *The Protestant Ethic and the Spirit of Capitalism*. Trans. Talcott Parsons. London: George Allen & Unwin, 1980.

Wright, David M. *The Impact of the Union*. New York: Kelley and Millman, 1956.

Wright, Winthrop R. *British-Owned Railways in Argentina: Their Effect on Economic Nationalism, 1854–1948*. Austin: University of Texas Press, 1974.

Wynia, Gary. *Argentina in the Post War Era: Politics and Economic Policy Making in a Divided Society*. Albuquerque: University of New Mexico Press, 1978.

Zavala, Augusto Zimmerman. *El Plan Inca, Objectivo: Revolución Peruana*. Lima: El Peruano, 1977.

## ARTICLES

Amat y Leon, Carlos. "La Experiencia Peruana y La Miopía del FMI." *Nueva Sociedad* (November–December 1979):5–21.

Ayres, Robert L. "The Social Pact as Anti-Inflationary Policy: The Argentine Experience Since 1973." *World Politics* 28 (July 1976):473–501.

Baer, Werner. "The Inflation Controversy in Latin America: A Survey." *Latin American Research Review* 2 (Spring 1967):3–25.

Block, Fred. "The Ruling Class Does Not Rule: Notes on the Marxist Theory of the State." *Socialist Revolution* 7 (May–June 1977):6–28.

Buchanan, Paul. "State Corporatism in Argentina: Labor Administration Under Perón and Onganía." *Latin American Research Review* 20 (1985):61–95.

Butler, David. "Charisma, Migration and Elite Coalescence: An Interpretation of Peronism." *Comparative Politics* 3 (April 1969):423–439.

Calvo, Roberto. "The Church and The Doctrine of National Security."

*Journal of Interamerican Studies and World Affairs* 21 (February 1979): 69–87.

Campos, Robert. "Two Views on Inflation in Latin America." In *Latin American Issues*, ed. Albert O. Hirschman. New York: Twentieth Century Fund, 1961.

Camps, Ramón C. Interview in *La Semana*, June 2, 1983, p. 8

Cardoso, Fernando Henrique. "On the Characterization of Authoritarian Regimes in Latin America." In *The New Authoritarianism in Latin America*, ed. David Collier. Princeton: Princeton University Press, 1979.

Carranza, Mario Esteban. "The Role of Military Expenditure in the Development Process: The Argentine Case 1946–1980." *Ibero-Americana* 12 (1983):115–166.

Cotler, Julio. "The New Mode of Political Domination in Peru." In *The Peruvian Experiment: Continuity and Change Under Military Rule*, ed. Abraham Lowenthal. Princeton: Princeton University Press, 1975.

Crockett, Andrew D. "Stabilization Policies in Developing Countries: Some Policy Considerations." *IMF Papers* 28 (March 1981):54–79.

Dimase, Leonardo E. "La Política Económico-Social Inaugurada en 1976 y sus Efectos en los Sindicales que Nuclean Trabajadores de Empresas Estatales." *Revista del Centro de Investigación y Acción Social* 30 (April 1981): 33–67.

Di Tella, Guido. "The Economic Policies of Argentina's Labor-Based Government (1973–76)." In *Inflation and Stabilization in Latin America*, ed. Rosemary Thorp and Laurence Whitehead. New York: Holmes & Meier, 1979.

Epstein, Edward. "Politicization and Income Redistribution in Argentina: The Case of the Peronist Worker." *Economic Development and Cultural Change* 23 (July 1975): 615-631.

———. "Anti-Inflationary Policies in Argentina and Chile or Who Pays the Cost." *Comparative Political Studies* 11 (July 1978):211–230.

———. "Recent Stabilization Programs in Argentina, 1973–86." *World Development* 15 (1987):991–1005.

Feierabend, Ivo K., and R. L. Feierabend. "Systemic Conditions of Political Aggression: An Application of Frustration-Aggression Theory." In *Anger, Violence and Politics: Theories and Research*, ed. Ivo K. Feierabend, R. L. Feierabend, and Ted R. Gurr. Englewood Cliffs, NJ: Prentice Hall, 1972.

Ferrer, Aldo. "El Retorno del Liberalismo: Reflexiones Sobre la Política Económica Vigente en la Argentina." *Desarrollo Económico* 18 (January–March 1979):485–510.

Ferrucci, Ricardo Jorge. "Doctrinas Económicas Filosofía del Liberalismo Argentino." *Realidad Económica* (July–September 1979):54–82.

Frenkel, Roberto, and Guillermo O'Donnell. "The 'Stabilization Programs' of the International Monetary Fund and Their Internal Impacts." In *Capitalism and the State in U.S.–Latin American Relations*, ed. Richard R. Fagen. Stanford: Stanford University Press, 1979.

Friedman, Milton. "The Role of Monetary Policy." *American Economic Review* 58 (March 1968):1–17.

Fundación de Investigaciones para el Desarrollo. "La Distribución del

Ingreso Entre 1974 y 1982." *Coyuntura y Desarrollo* 60 (August 1983): 33–40.

George, Alexander. "Case Studies and Theory Development: The Method of Structured, Focused Comparison." In *New Approaches in History, Theory and Policy*, ed. Lauren Paul Gordon. New York: Free Press, 1979.

Goldthorpe, John H. "The Current Inflation: Towards a Sociological Account." In *The Political Economy of Inflation*, ed. Fred Hirsch and John H. Goldthorpe. Cambridge, MA: Harvard University Press, 1979.

Gordon, Robert. "The Demand For and Supply of Inflation." *Journal of Law and Economics* 18 (1975):807–835.

Grindle, Merilee. "Policy Change in an Authoritarian Regime." *Journal of Interamerican Studies and World Affairs* 19 (November 1977): 523–555.

Guasti, Laura. "The Peruvian Military and International Corporations." In *The Peruvian Experiment Reconsidered*, ed. Cynthia McClintock and Abraham F. Lowenthal. Princeton: Princeton University Press, 1983.

Gunn, J. A. W. "Interest Will Not Lie: A Seventeenth Century Political Maxim." *Journal of the History of Ideas* 29 (December 1968): 551–564.

Heyderbrand, Wolf V. "Marxist Structuralism." In *Continuity in Structural Inquiry*, ed. Peter M. Blau and Robert K. Merton. Beverely Hills: Sage Publications, 1981.

Hirschman, Albert O. "The Turn to Authoritarianism in Latin America and the Search for Its Economic Determinants." In *The New Authoritarianism in Latin America*, ed. David Collier. Princeton: Princeton University Press, 1979.

James, Daniel. "Power and Politics in Peronist Trade Unions." *Journal of Interamerican Studies and World Affairs* 20 (February 1978): 3–36.

Jaquette, Jane S. "Revolution by Fiat: The Context of Policy-making in Peru." *Western Political Quarterly* 25 (December 1972): 648–666.

Jelin, Elizabeth. "Conflictos Laborales en la Argentina, 1973–1976." *Estudios Sociales* no. 9. Buenos Aires: Centro de Estudios de Estado y Sociedad, 1977.

Kaufman, Robert R. "Industrial Change and Authoritarian Rule in Latin America: A Concrete Review of the Bureaucratic-Authoritarian Model." In *The New Authoritarianism in Latin America*, ed. David Collier. Princeton: Princeton University Press, 1979.

Klare, Michael, and Cynthia Arnson. "Exporting Repression: U.S. Support for Authoritarianism in Latin America." In *Capitalism and the State in U.S.–Latin American Relations*, ed. Richard R. Fagen. Stanford: Stanford University Press, 1979.

Krasner, Stephen. "State Power and the Structure of International Trade." *World Politics* 28 (April 1976): 317–347.

Martel, Julian. "Domination by Debt: Finance Capital in Argentina." In *NACLA Report on the Americas* 12 (July–August 1978): 20–36.

Marx, Karl. "The Eighteenth Brumaire of Louis Bonaparte." In *The Marx-Engels Reader*, ed. Robert C. Tucker. New York: W. W. Norton, 1972.

Pion-Berlin, David. "Political Repression and Economic Doctrines: The Case of Argentina." *Comparative Political Studies* 16 (April 1983):37–66.

———. "The Fall of Military Rule in Argentina, 1976–1983." *Journal of Interamerican Studies and World Affairs* 27 (Summer 1985): 55–76.

———. "The National Security Doctrine, Military Threat Perception and the 'Dirty War' in Argentina." *Comparative Political Studies* 21 (October 1988):382–407

Polak, J. J. "Monetary Analysis of Income Formation and Payments Probelms." *IMF Staff Papers* 6 (1957):1–50.

Prebisch, Raúl. "Commercial Policy in the Underdeveloped Countries." *American Economic Review* 49 (May 1959): 251–273.

"The Problem of the Economic Development of Argentina." *Economic Bulletin for Latin America* 4 (March 1959): 13–24.

Purcell, Susan K. "Decision-Making in an Authoritarian Regime: Theoretical Implications from a Mexican Case Study." *World Politics* 26 (October 1973): 28–54.

Ruggie, John. "International Regimes, Transactions and Change: Embedded Liberalism in the Postwar Economic Order." *International Organization* 36 (Spring 1982): 379–415.

Rummel, R. J. "Understanding Factor Analysis." *Journal of Conflict Resolution* 11 (1967):444–480.

Schumpeter, Joseph A. "Science and Ideology." *American Economic Review* 39 (March 1949): 345–359.

Sears, Dudley. "A Theory of Inflation and Growth in Undeveloped Economies Based on the Experience of Latin America." *Oxford Economic Papers* 14 (1962):173–195.

Serra, José. "Three Mistaken Theses Regarding the Connection Between Industrialization and Authoritarian Regimes." In *The New Authoritarianism in Latin America*, ed. David Collier. Princeton: Princeton University Press, 1979.

Sheahan, John. "Economic Policies and Structural Change 1968–78." *Journal of Economic Studies* 7 (1980):3–27.

———. "Market-oriented Economic Policies and Political Repression in Latin America." *Economic Development and Cultural Change* 28 (January 1980):267–291.

Singer, J. D. "Threat Perception and the Armament Tension Dilemma." *Journal of Conflict Resolution* 2 (1958):90–105.

Stallings, Barbara. "Peru and the U.S. Banks: Privatization of Financial Relations." In *Capitalism and the State in U.S.–Latin American Relations*, ed. Richard R. Fagen. Stanford: Stanford University Press, 1979.

Stepan, Alfred. "The New Professionalism of Internal Warfare and Military Role Expansion." In *Armies and Politics in Latin America*, ed. Abraham F. Lowenthal. New York: Holmes & Meier, 1976.

Stohl, Michael, and Raymond D. Duvall. "Governance by Terror." In *The Politics of Terrorism*, ed. Michael Stohl. New York: Marcell Dekker, 1984.

Sunkel, Osvaldo. "Inflation in Chile: An Unorthodox Approach." *International Economic Papers*, no. 10 (1960).

Swedberg, Richard. "The Doctrine of Economic Neutrality of the IMF and the World Bank." *Journal of Peace Research* 23 (1986): 377–390.

Thompson, John. "Argentine Economic Policy Under the Onganía Regime." *Inter-American Economic Affairs* 24 (Summer 1970): 51–75.

Thorp, Rosemary. "Economic Policies in Argentina in the Post-War Years." *Oxford University Institute of Economics and Statistics Bulletin*, nos. 27–28 (1965–1966):3–44.

Thorp, Rosemary. "Inflation and the Financing of Economic Development." In *Financing Development in Latin America*, ed. Keith Griffin. London: Macmillan, 1971.

## GOVERNMENT AND OTHER DOCUMENTS

Amnesty International. *Visit Beautiful Argentina . . . But Remember Its Forgotten Prisoners.* New York: Amnesty International, 1978.

———. *Report for 1986.* London: Amnesty International, 1986.

Barúa Castañeda, Minister of Economy and Finance. Speech, January 12, 1976, in *Ministerio de Economía y Finanzas, Obierna de Relaciones Públicas,* 1976.

———, Minister of Economy and Finance. Speech, June 30, 1976, in *El Peruano,* July 1, 1976.

Centro de Estudios y Promoción del Desarrollo. *Cronología Política.* Volumes 1–12. Lima: DESCO, 1968–1980.

Frondizi, Arturo. *Mensajes Presidenciales: 1958–62.* Volume 1. Buenos Aires: Centro De Estudios Nacionales, 1962.

Inter-American Development Bank. *External Public Debt of the Latin American Countries.* Washington, DC: IABD, July 1982.

International Labour Office. *Legislative Series.* July–August 1974.

———. *Yearbook of Labour Statistics,* 1956–1981. Geneva: ILO.

International Monetary Fund. *International Finance Statistical Yearbook.* Washington, DC: IMF, 1981, 1982.

———. *Summary of Proceedings of the Annual Meetings of Board of Governors* (1948–1958). Washington, DC: IMF.

———. *Memorandum: Request for Standby Arrangement.* Peru, 1977, 1978.

Organization of American States. *Report on the Situation of Human Rights in Argentina.* Washington, DC: General Secretariat, OAS, 1980.

Piazza Tanguis, Walter, Minister of Economy and Finance. Speech, June 10, 1977, "El Programa de Emergencia," *Ministerio de Economía y Finanzas.*

República Argentina. Proyecto de Ley, Cámara de Diputados de la Nación, May 3, 1948.

———. *Memoria: Marzo 1976–Marzo 1981.* Volume 3. Buenos Aires: Ministerio de Economía, 1981.

Statistical Abstract of Latin America. Volumes 20–24, 1980–1985.

UNESCO. *Statistical Yearbooks.* 1972, 1979, 1980, 1982, 1983.

Vargas Gavilano, Amilcar, Minister of Economy and Finance. Speech, October 31, 1974, in *El Peruano,* November 2, 1974.

World Bank. *Economic Memorandum on Argentina,* June 22, 1984.

## UNPUBLISHED MATERIALS

Ballantyne, Janet Campbell. "The Political Economy of Peruvian Gran Minería." Ph.D. dissertation, Cornell University, 1976.

Dragisic, John. "Peruvian Stabilization Policies 1939–1968." Ph.D. dissertation, University of Wisconsin, 1972.

McCamant, John, Richard Bissell, Clara Haignere, and Mark Picklo. "Varieties of Political Repression." Unpublished manuscript, 1978.

Pion-Berlin, David. "Ideas as Predictors: a Comparative Study of Coercion in Peru and Argentina." Ph.D. dissertation, University of Denver, 1984.

Robichek, E. Walter. "Financial Programming–Stand-By Arrangements and Stabilization Programs." Unpublished lecture, January 16, 1981.

Sloan, John. "State Repression and Enforcement Terrorism in Latin America." Paper delivered at the Midwest Political Science Association Convention, Milwaukee, Wisconsin, April 28–May 1, 1982.

## NEWSPAPERS AND RELATED SOURCES

*Andean Regional Report* (London)
*Andean Report* (Peru)
*El Clarín* (Buenos Aires)
*El Comercio* (Lima)
*El Diario del Juicio* (Argentina)
*Institutional Investor* (New York)
*La Crónica* (Lima)
*La Nación* (Buenos Aires)
*La Prensa* (Buenos Aires)
*La Prensa* (Lima)
*Latin America Economic Report* (London)
*Latin America Political Report* (London)
*Latin America Weekly Report* (London)
*Peruvian Times* (Lima)
*Southern Cone Regional Report* (London)

## INTERVIEWS WITH AUTHOR

Roberto Alemann, Minister of Economics, Argentina (December 1981–June 1982), Buenos Aires, June 18, 1984.

Alejandro Estrada, Secretary of Commerce, Argentina (1977–1981), Buenos Aires, July 3, 1984.

Rosendo Fraga, adviser to the PRN government, Argentina (1976–1981), Buenos Aires, July 2, 1984.

Horacio Liendo, Minister of Labor, Argentina (1976–1980), Buenos Aires, July 2, 1984.

José A. Martínez de Hoz, Minister of Economics, Argentina (1976–1981), Buenos Aires, June 28, 1984.

J. J. Polak, IMF staff, Washington, DC, May 20, 1983.

Lorenzo Sigaut, Minister of Economics, Argentina (March 1981–December 1981), Buenos Aires, July 19, 1984.

Roberto Viola, President, Argentina (March 1981–December 1981), Buenos Aires, July 17, 1984.

Ricardo Yofre, Subsecretary-General to the Presidency, Argentina (1976–1978), Buenos Aires, October 6, 1986.

# Index